THE PENGUIN BOOK OF
MORE AUSTRALIAN JOKES

collected by *Phillip Adams*
and *Patrice Newell*

Phillip Adams is an odd assortment of people who write things, film things, say things on wireless and appear on television. All of whom share an anthropological fascination for jokes. The Adams's hobbies are levity and levitation.

Patrice Newell has been a model, a television researcher and a presenter of public affairs programs on both SBS and the Nine Network. She now raises politically correct beef on a large cattle property.

THE PENGUIN BOOK OF MORE AUSTRALIAN JOKES

collected by *Phillip Adams*
and *Patrice Newell*

Penguin Books

Penguin Books Australia Ltd
487 Maroondah Highway, PO Box 257
Ringwood, Victoria 3134, Australia
Penguin Books Ltd
Harmondsworth, Middlesex, England
Viking Penguin, A Division of Penguin Books USA Inc.
375 Hudson Street, New York, New York 10014, USA
Penguin Books Canada Limited
10 Alcorn Avenue, Toronto, Ontario, Canada M4V 3B2
Penguin Books (NZ) Ltd
182–190 Wairau Road, Auckland 10, New Zealand

First published by Penguin Books Australia Ltd 1996
10 9 8 7 6 5 4 3 2 1

Cover illustration by Ned Culic

Typeset in 12pt Weiss Regular by Post Typesetters
Made and printed in Australia by Australian Print Group

National Library of Australia
Cataloguing-in-Publication data:

The Penguin Book of More Australian Jokes.

Includes Index
ISBN 0 14 0253548.

I. Australian wit and humour. I. Adams, Phillip, 1939–
II. Newell, Patrice, 1956– . III. Title: Book of More Australian Jokes.

A828.02

To Rory, for all the laughs.

CONTENTS

Life Before Death

'A laugh is the hilarious declaration
made by man that life is worth living.'
Sean O'Casey

'It never cost me a stab nor squirm
to tread by chance upon a worm.
Aha, my little dear, I say
your clan will pay me back one day.'
Dorothy Parker

'It's not that I'm afraid to die. I just don't
want to be there when it happens.'
Woody Allen

'Dust thou art, and to dust shalt thou
return.'
God

1

You're going to die.

Sorry to be the bearer of sad tidings, but it's true. No matter how fast you run, how high you climb, no matter how rich or powerful you are, no matter if you're as encrusted with honours as a pier with mussels, no matter how much of the academic alphabet you can string behind your name, you're going to cark it. Kick the bucket. Shuffle off this mortal coil.

Before this preface borrows too heavily from the Dead Parrot sketch, you may want to know what your death, inevitable if not imminent, has to do with a collection of jokes. The answer is: absolutely everything. Laughter is a life-and-death issue.

These days, an average Australian life span amounts to around 650 000 hours. Well, in 650 000 billion years you'll still be dead. And those billions will be just the beginning of your death sentence, but a fleeting moment in great dollops of eternity.

If we didn't die, if we didn't have to face that endless vista of non-existence, we wouldn't have, wouldn't need, a sense of humour. The issues simply wouldn't arise.

Humans are dignified by doom, defined by an awareness of mortality. As far as we know, no other creature has this essentially tragic awareness. Even those who assuage anxieties by believing in God are confronted by the fact that He's the cosmic comic who, in the greatest of all practical jokes, has provided us with a slapstick fate. Where a handful are condemned to the chair, the gallows, the gas chamber, the garrotte or the fatal injection, God has condemned the entire six billion of us to the hospital, the hospice, the car accident, the plane crash, the stroke.

And not just us human beings, but every living creature. And not just living creatures, but everything that exists. In a catch that makes Catch 22 look reasonable, His Majesty has cursed the entire universe with the Second Law of Thermodynamics, which means that the whole shebang comes to a grinding halt. Shades of those lights are going out all over Europe; the suns, the countless billions of them, will go out all over space-time. And it's not just the solar systems and the galaxies that will be extinguished – it's ditto for the minuscule subatomic particles that cavort in the realms of quantum mechanics.

The end. Finito. Kaput. Facing this awesome and unpleasant fact, human beings, despite the optimism energetically marketed by a plethora of faiths, have every reason to feel just a little depressed. Either that, or an almost orgasmic terror that thrills and chills every atom of our being. So much so that we cry out in rage, in horror, in despair.

Or we laugh.

Laughter is the other way of reacting to the raw deal of our brief existence. Whilst closely related to screaming, it is less shrill and more congenial. And it seems to produce in humans some as-yet undiscovered enzyme that dulls pain and gives a feeling of pleasurable acquiescence. Scientists studying tears of sorrow have recently detected a chemical that cannot be found in tears of joy – it seems that simply by weeping we produce infinitesimal amounts of an internal narcotic that hits receptors in the brain and, in turn, dulls our pain.

The editors of this compilation are convinced that a similar narcotic is produced by laughter, that millions of years of evolution have provided this method of mollifying the melancholia that comes from the prospect of our individual and collective martyrdom – of our inescapable mortality. Until that neuronal narcotic is isolated, synthesised and sold at the supermarket, it's probably a good idea to laugh as often as possible.

Having done death to death, let's now concede that not all jokes directly concern it. Other aspects of our mortal coil come into play, a long list of topics dealing with pains, problems, perils. Nonetheless it is hard to find a joke that doesn't, in some way, focus on the fates.

Almost as much as the grave, we fear the bed where we suffer illness and, even worse, sex. Men fear female sexuality and signal other forms of sexual insecurity by telling homophobic jokes or laughing at the penis. We fear 'the other', what we deem to be foreign or alien, and so tell savage, uncivilised jokes about Aborigines, Jews, migrants. The professions that have power over us are regularly pilloried – politicians, lawyers, priests. Jokes that are bigoted, blasphemous or phobic outnumber all other categories.

If bottoms and genitalia are immensely amusing, then so is constipation, flatulence, premature ejaculation, impotence, pregnancy, defecation, micturition and erections (or the lack of them).

Nuns are funny, because nun jokes combine blasphemy with sexual obscenity, giving you two for the price of one.

The only jokes that seem comparatively free of fear and hatred involve the liberating nonsense of the shaggy dog or pun. All other jokes are, to some extent, tiny acts of exorcism – or at very least, verbal counterparts to the oyster's pearl, wherein an irritant is transformed into something less uncomfortable, more appealing.

Not all laughs are born equal. There are deep, dull laughs like clods of clay falling on coffin lids. There are little shuddering laughs evoking the noise of slipping ropes as the coffin descends. There are screeching laughs, like the sound of unoiled wheels on a hearse. There are last-gasp laughs, death-rattle laughs and laughs like the peals of church bells. There are laughs born in the throat, as guttural as growls, and deep, echoing laughs that come from the belly. There are laughs that barely escape the mouth, which sound wheezy and asthmatic. And laughs that are loud and self-advertising.

And not all laughter is infectious. We know that laughter can be cruel, threatening, intimidating, humourless. And we also know that what provokes laughter in one person may have no effect on another. Whenever people gather together to tell jokes, there's always someone whose response is a bewildered, 'I don't get it'.

Your editors have tried, assiduously, to gather together jokes in every current genre. We have travelled in taxis, hung about in pubs and indecently exposed ourselves to graffiti in public loos, examining it like archaeologists transcribing hieroglyphs. We have appealed for assistance in letters and newspaper columns, and have received and acknowledged over a thousand letters. Consequently, the book you're about to read has more authors than most volumes you're likely to open, and we would like to thank the taxidrivers, the dunny philosophers, the drunks, the accountants and the hosts of helpful correspondents for their generosity of spirit. In doing so we single out elderly ladies for special expressions of gratitude as, almost invariably, the bawdiest and most obscene jokes came from them. We cannot account for this phenomenon. We simply report it.

Having failed to find any jokes that are authentically, unequivocally Australian, we've also failed to find many jokes that are in good taste. They're as rare as rocking-horse manure, as unicorns in gardens, as generous insurance assessors. Like UFOs, good-taste jokes may exist, but there's little hard evidence of them. Perhaps they're being hidden in freezers in the White House, along with the corpses of crashed aliens.

Conversely, whenever we found a joke that might have been regarded as tasteful, it failed another important test – it wasn't funny. It seems that humour is to the disreputable what guilt is to sexual excitement.

At this point it has to be said that we were surprised, indeed shocked, by the community's reception of our previous volume. Conservative estimates suggest that at least a million Australians must have read the previous *Penguin Book of Australian Jokes*, and yet not one complaint was received by us, your intrepid hunter-gatherers, or by Penguin. Whilst advance copies were demanded from us by the Human Rights Commission, whilst notorious wowsers and supporters of anti-vilification legislation demanded review copies, whilst people identified with the pieties of political correctness are known to have looked for trouble, we were neither condemned nor pilloried.

What are we to make of this? Did we sell our book into a moral vacuum? Was our solemn exercise in scholarship deemed unworthy of serious attention? Or were we saved by *The Hand that Signed the Paper* winning the Miles Franklin on our publication date? Did Ms Demidenko/Darville deflect our wrath?

Or was it simply because our readers acknowledged a tendency to bigotry, blasphemy, homophobia and racism? Few of us can claim to be wholly free of such pollutants. And racism is clearly becoming increasingly popular in Australian society, as any analysis of the recent federal election attests.

This is probably a good time to say that we, your editors, find many if not most of the following jokes offensive. Our slim, implausible excuse for collecting them is that we wanted to identify the sorts of jokes that Australians are telling each other at the dawn of the Howard era. It is not the job of an anthropologist to pass judgement on the behaviour of the tribes under observation, but to simply and scientifically record what the hell is going on.

Thus we've decided to repress our sense of outrage at the prejudices your jokes reveal, hoping that the flow of royalties will ease our pain.

For a time we proposed indicating the acceptability of a given joke by employing visual symbols. We wanted something along the lines of the stamps proffered well-behaved students by their primary school teachers, like the little koalas indelibly pressed in one's exercise book, or on the back of one's hand. Many a long, thoughtful meeting was held at Penguin, wondering what icons could be employed. What about a scale of one, two and three plaster ducks for the least offensive jokes? Or tiny portraits of Caroline Jones? To vice the versa, as it were, was a simpler matter. Clearly bad-taste jokes could be identified with stylised images of penises or toilet bowls. In the end, however, we decided that you might prefer to do your own definitional doodles. Hence the provision of generous margins.

We offered a $1000 prize for a great Australian joke we hadn't heard before. No such joke was forthcoming. Rather than returning the money to consolidated revenue, we forwarded a $1000 donation to the literary quarterly *Overland*. Under

the motto 'Temper democratic, bias Australian'
Overland has been plugging away on behalf of
Australian culture for decades.

Whilst urging you to proceed with caution,
your editors wish to pay tribute to Sandra Blood,
who's been forced to type out countless thousands of
jokes for these Penguin volumes. This first dulled
and finally destroyed Sandra's sense of humour. She
has made it clear that she will never listen to another
joke as long as she lives, let alone type one. Sandra is
now urgently seeking more congenial employment,
perhaps as a Hansard reporter or typing up autopsy
reports for the City Coroner. People wishing to be
voluntarily euthanased need not go to the Northern
Territory. Simply say, 'Have you heard the one
about . . .?' to Sandra and she'll cheerfully re-enact
the famous scene from *Psycho*, stabbing you to death
in your shower.

The greatest oxymoron of all is 'life after death'.
This notion demonstrates how oxymoronic human
beings can be. Whilst a subject of humour, life after
death is, of course, beyond humour's power to
provide. Nor can it, finally, ward off death. But
laughter does provide a great deal of life before
death. Which is, after all, when you really need it.

When Dick Met Fanny

A couple of gladiators were in the Colosseum in Rome, waiting for their event to begin. They stood waiting in front of the thousands of grinning, salivating spectators.

'Hey, look over there. Is that the emperor?'

'Yep, that's him all right. That's Nero. And that sheila with him, the one with the big knockers, that's his girlfriend. And you'll never guess what happened last night.'

'No, what?'

'Well, she came to my cell downstairs.'

'Nero's girlfriend did?'

'Yep. And she moved towards me.'

'Nero's girlfriend did?'

'Yep, she stroked my hair.'

'Yeah!'

'And kissed me.'

'Yeah!'
'Yeah, with her tongue. And then started lifting up my toga.'
'Yeah!'
'And then she . . . Sorry, I'll tell you later. Here come the lions.'

What does Stevie Wonder's wife do after they've had a fight?
Shift the furniture.

A woman was looking into the window of Raymond Castles admiring a pair of silver shoes when a bloke sidled up beside her. 'Like those shoes? I'll buy them for you if you come to bed with me.'
'Okay. But be warned. I don't like sex very much.'
He bought the silver shoes and took her back to his hotel where, once again, she emphasised her lack of enthusiasm. And, indeed, she just lay there motionless giving him not the slightest encouragement. So much so that he was getting bored himself.
Whereupon she suddenly lifted her legs high in the air and shouted, 'Wow!'

'I thought you didn't like sex,' he said with mounting excitement.

'I don't. But I just love these new silver shoes.'

A little bloke goes into the chemist. 'I want a packet of tampons.'

'Are they for your mother?'

'No.'

'Your sister?'

'No, for me.'

'Why would you want a packet of tampons?'

'Well, on the telly it says if you've got a packet of tampons you can swim, dive, play tennis and ride horseback.'

'**A**re you the chemist?'

'Yes, I am.'

'But you're a woman.'

'Lots of women are chemists. In fact, this pharmacy is owned by two women, myself and my twin sister. We are devoted to this business. We live it day and night. In fact, we've sacrificed any chance of marriage, any opportunity for a social life.'

'Well, I need advice. I'm desperate.'

'What is it? How can we help?'

'I've got this insatiable urge to fuck, fuck, fuck. And I suffer from a constant, never-ending erection. I'm being driven mad by lust. What can you do for it?'

The chemist consulted her twin sister. 'The best we can offer is $300 a week, and free board.'

'Is it in?'

'Aah, yes.'

'Does it fit?'

'Aah, yes.'

'Does it hurt?'

'No, it feels wonderful.'

'Shall I wrap your old shoes?'

Sid arrived at the family butcher's and confessed that it was his birthday. His 57th. He decided to celebrate it by ordering a pound of steak rather than his usual lamb's fry and snaggers. With cries of 'Happy Birthday, Sid' echoing in his ears, he headed for the bus stop, where a little old sheila asked him why he was looking so pleased with himself. 'Well, it's me birthday. How old do you think I am?'

'Come to the back of the shelter and open yer fly,' she said. After Sid's grin, and another feature, had broadened, he obliged. 'You're 57,' said the old sheila.

'Jeez, howd'ya work that out?'

'Easy, love. I was standing behind yuz in the butcher's.'

'**M**y husband's like a sports car,' said the first woman. 'A fantastic performer.'

'My husband's like a Rolls Royce,' said the second. 'Smooth, powerful, silent.'

'My husband's like a vintage car,' said the third. 'Only rallies once a year and has to be started by hand.'

Bruce was really sophisticated. He knew how to smooth talk a sheila at a party. 'G'day,' he'd say, or, 'How ya goin'?'

And at this particular party, it worked. He got a very friendly smile. 'Wanna come back to my place?' he inquired suavely. 'For a root?'

'Oh, I'm very sorry but I can't,' she replied shyly. 'You see, I'm on my menstrual cycle.'

'No worries,' said Bruce, 'just follow me. I'm on a Yamaha 500.'

19

A lad from Woolloomooloo
took his girlfriend out to a do.
As he kissed her goodnight
she crossed her legs tight
and broke his glasses in two.

Two blokes and a sheila are marooned on a desert island. After two weeks, the girl is so ashamed with what she's doing with the guys that she kills herself. After another two weeks, the guys are so ashamed with what they're doing with her, they bury her. And after a further two weeks, the guys are so ashamed with what they are doing together, they dig her up again!

It's after hours in the Fitzroy Gardens and a young bloke is lying between the thighs of a girl. 'Christ,' he mumbles, 'I wish I had a torch.'

'So do I,' said the girl. 'You've been munching grass for the past ten minutes.'

'We have two test tubes here,' said the professor of IVF studies from Monash. 'They contain two carefully synthesised ingredients that we can now use to create human life. Solution A is a genetically engineered copy of all the ingredients in the female ovum, while Solution B replicates the active ingredients in male spermatozoa. 'If I mix them in this aseptic glass container a new human life will be conceived. Now, any questions?'

'Could you possibly give us a demonstration?' asked an awed member of the audience.

'I'm sorry, not tonight,' said the professor, 'Solution A has a headache.'

A dirty old man caught the same bus every day because it was packed with office girls. He'd organised to be jammed between the breasts of various attractive women. And there he was, on this particular day, almost wedged between the breasts of a tough feminist.

'Would you like a bust in the gob?' she snarled.

'Oh, you mind-reader, you!' he smiled.

'How can I improve my sex life?'

'Well, you'd better tell me about it for starters.'

'All I do is masturbate. And that gets very, very boring.'

'Okay, here's some advice. Sit on your hand until its numb. Then it will feel like a total stranger's.'

An old sailor, shipwrecked on a desert island, had been masturbating for years. But he was finding it harder and harder. He'd run out of fantasies.

Then, suddenly, he grabbed his old telescope and scanned the horizon. 'My God! A ship!' he said to himself. 'And there, on the deck, a naked blonde. Christ, she's gorgeous. And the ship is heading this way.'

By now he had a great erection. So he flung the telescope away and grabbed it. 'Tricked you, you bastard. There's no bloody ship.'

She arrived at the introduction agency to meet her latest computer-matched date. And was horrified. 'You have to be kidding,' she whispered. 'He's short, he's old, he's fat, he's bald, he is appallingly dressed and he clearly has a problem with personal hygiene.'

'There's no need for you to whisper,' said the agency receptionist, 'he's deaf as well.'

'Can I? Please?'
'No, I don't think we should.'
'Ah, come on, please let me.'
'Well, perhaps. If . . .'
'Anything! Anything!'
'You'll have to buy me a mink.'
'Okay, it's a deal! On one condition.'
'What's that?'
'You'll have to clean out the cage.'

A young couple were breakfasting in the nude in the honeymoon suite at the Sebel Town House. As the woman bent over the tray she tenderly murmured, 'You're so sexy! You make my nipples tingle!'

'Well, no wonder, darling,' he replied. 'You've got one in my tea and the other in the porridge.'

Two blokes down on their luck are boozing in a low-rent pub.

Fred says, 'What do you prefer, Harry, a good root or a wet dream?'

After a thoughtful pause, Harry said, 'I dunno, I'd just as soon a wet dream m'self.'

'Why's that, mate?'

'Well, with a wet dream a man's always inclined to get a better class of sheila.'

A shift worker arrived home to find his wife in bed with three of his mates.

'Hello, hello, hello!' he bellowed.

'What,' she replied, 'aren't you speaking to me?'

What is the best thing about a blow job?

Ten minutes silence.

An Englishman, a Frenchman and an Irishman are discussing lovemaking techniques. In a thick French accent, the Parisian describes taking his wife to a very expensive restaurant, giving her a delicious meal of snail, bouillabaisse and Bollinger, and taking her home to bed. 'She rises two metres from the bed,' he says.

The Englishman describes a delicious dinner at the Dorchester, with roast beef and a fine bottle of wine. 'And when I take her home, she rises ten feet from the bed.'

Not to be outdone, the Irishman talks about

going to the local pub, drinking a dozen pints of Guinness, followed by a visit to the local Indian restaurant for a beef vindaloo. 'And when I get home, she hits the roof!'

Who are the five most important men in a woman's life?

Her doctor, her dentist, her coalman, her interior decorator and her bank manager.

Why?

The doctor gets her to remove her clothes; the dentist tells her to open up; the coalman asks if she wants it in the front or the back; the interior decorator says, 'Now that it's up, do you like it?'; and her bank manager advises against withdrawal for fear of losing interest.

A woman's wedding was rapidly approaching and she was becoming increasingly curious about sex. Matters came to a head when her parents invited the boyfriend to stay and she blundered in on him in the bathroom. There he was, stark naked.

'Mummy,' she whispered later, 'what was that thing hanging down between his legs?'

'It's a penis, my dear. Nothing to worry about.'

'And the knob on the end? Like a fireman's helmet?'

'The glans,' said her mother.

'And what about the two round things about 13 inches back? What are they?'

'For your sake, my dear, I hope they're the cheeks of his arse.'

'**M**ate,' said Arthur, 'I've got a real problem. I'm on the horns of a dilemma. You see, I've got to choose between two women. One is young and beautiful and I love her very, very much. But she's stone, motherless broke. The other is a much older woman, a widow, with a crook head. But she's a multi-millionaire. What should I do?'

'Follow your heart. Marry the young girl you love. And give me the phone number of the widow.'

After an engine malfunction, a NASA space probe crashed on Venus and the Venusians hauled the survivors, a male and female astronaut, from the wreckage. They saw to their injuries and treated them very, very kindly. And they told them about Venusian biology and culture. For example, they demonstrated how they made baby Venusians –

through the mass production of clones. 'And how do you make humans?' they asked.

The astronauts, feeling 100 per cent after all the care they'd received, gave an energetic demonstration of bonking. When they finished, the Venusians asked, 'Where are the babies?'

'That takes nine months,' said the astronauts.

'Then why were you in such a hurry at the end?'

Three blokes and a woman were in the lift at Australia Square when the cable broke. The lift started plummeting down, down, down. Within a few minutes they'd all be dead. The woman looked at the three men and said, 'Is there one last chance of being a woman?'

Whereupon one dropped his trousers and said, 'Here, love. Iron these.'

A couple were lying in bed together after a bout of lovemaking when she murmured, 'Darling, if I'm pregnant and we have a baby, what will we call him?'

The bloke ripped off his condom, tied it in a knot and chucked it out the window. 'If he gets out of that, we'll call him Houdini.'

'G'day, gorgeous. How 'bout a root?'
'Piss off, ya smooth talkin' bastard.'

Sophie and Eddie were engaged in erotic pleasures of the 69th variety when, despite this particular form of eroticism generally precluding conversation, Eddie embarked on a theme concerning the fatalities caused by volcanoes throughout the ages. He mentioned the number of people killed in Vesuvius, Mt Etna, Gnung Agung and other sundry volcanic operations. Sophie said she was surprised at his depth of knowledge about the subject and asked where he had learned so much about eruptions.

Eddie took a brief respite from his erotic efforts and said, 'Oh, it's nothing, Sophie. I'm just reading it from the page of a *Reader's Digest* that's stuck in your arsehole.'

Two blokes were ambling along the footpath of King William Street in Adelaide when a stunning young woman walked towards them. She had a great figure and a magnificent head of bright-red hair. As she passed them, a delightful zephyr of intoxicating perfume assailed their nostrils. One bloke turned to the other and said, 'Hey, mate, have you ever slept in bed with a beaut bluey sheila like that one?'

'No, mate,' said the other, 'not a bloody wink!'

'You know, I went for 12 years without sex. I was totally celibate.'

'Bothered by it?'

'No, not a bit. Then I had my 13th birthday.'

A bloke was walking along St Kilda Beach one evening at twilight when he accidentally stepped on another bloke's naked bum. And a girl's voice said, 'Thank you!'

The stuttering, scrawny, shy, Woody Allen look-alike entered the Redfern Taxi Club in the wee hours of the morning. Getting himself a beer he sat at a table with one of his taxidriving mates. He had a tale to tell.

'Guess what, mate?' he began. 'Last night I picked up a fare outside the Theatre Royal. The fare was a fantastic-looking woman wearing a full-length mink coat. She just oozed charm and money. Her

29

perfume filled the cab. She even gave me a Darling Point address. She was a 'ten', mate.

'When we got to the address, she found that she had no cash with her, so she invited me to keep the meter running and to come upstairs with her to get the fare and a large tip.

'Well, guess what, mate? We went into the biggest, richest-looking penthouse you'll ever see.

'And guess what, mate? She offered me a drink. I said yes, and she went and brought back a bottle of Chivas Regal.

'Well, guess what, mate? She said that she was hot and slipped her coat and shoes off. She told me I could do the same.

'After a couple of Chivas, she said to me that it seemed to be getting even warmer and she stood up and unzipped her long black gown. She let it fall at her feet. I've never seen a body like it, mate. She was nearly six feet, had huge breasts, long legs and the most creamy skin I've seen. I said yes, it's getting hotter. And I took off my shirt. She had another drink and peeled off her bra and knickers. I took off my trousers and underpants.

'And guess what, mate? She asked me to follow her and we went into another room, her bedroom.

'And guess what, mate? She turned on some soft music and lay down on a huge round bed with black silk sheets.

'And guess what, mate? She had a bottle of

massage oil and she oiled herself all over while I stood there. It was just terrific.

'And guess what, mate? She lay back and stroked her crutch. She moaned and writhed right in front of me. It was fantastic.

'And guess what, mate? I reckon I could have fucked her!'

It was just after sunset and Harry and Bert were enjoying a quiet one in the bar of the local when Harry mentioned that he was starting a new job next week, going on to shift work, he was.

At the mention of shift work, Bert looked at his watch, put his half-finished pot down on the bar and bolted out the pub door.

Harry was very surprised at this unexpected behaviour of his old drinking mate, but drank on regardless.

Exactly an hour later, a stinking, wet, bleeding and very angry Bert staggered back into the bar and joined Harry. 'Jeez, I'm pissed off!' he rasped.

Harry just looked aside at him and said, 'Yairs, I'm not surprised. You left your beer half full. Anyway, why did you bolt?'

'It was partly your fault,' said Bert. 'When you mentioned shift work, I remembered an old girlfriend down the road who had told me her husband was on shift work this evening, and she gave me the nod that I could be in like Flynn.'

'Ah, so that's why you are pissed off, you found out he wasn't at work,' said Harry.

'No,' replied Bert. 'Why do you think I am so wet and stinking – and have a look at me flamin' knuckles! I went round to her place, she opened the door and in pretty short order we were tucked up in her bed. I no sooner thought of what to do next when there was this sound of a car pulling into her driveway and the slamming of a car door. She told me to hide, quick smart, as it must be her husband coming back for his 'lunch' box, which he had left on the kitchen table.'

'Ahah! That's why you are so pissed off – you dipped out and have a bad case of lover's nuts,' interjected Harry.

'No, wrong again,' said Bert. 'I was going to hide under the bed, then in the laundry, and finally I crawled out the bedroom window and hung by my fingertips while the old flame closed the window and dashed into the kitchen. Her husband, the bastard, must have seen the look in her eyes when he ran into the kitchen, or twigged to the way she was dressed for romance, because he galloped into the laundry first, then looked under the bed, and finally caught me hanging on like grim death to the windowsill. He laughed like mad, then ran to the laundry and came back with a bloody mallet which he used on my fingers like a bloody xylophone. I hung on real tight, though, and then the bastard went to the bed and pulled out the half-filled gazunder from underneath it. You know what happened next? He tipped it all over me.'

'So that's why you're pissed off so bad,' commented Harry. 'You got pissed on!'

'No – I'll tell you why I'm so pissed off,' said Bert, as he drained his pot. 'After dipping out on my naughtie, having my hands belted with a mallet and having a piss pot tipped all over me while hanging on for dear life at that bloody window, I looked down and saw that my feet were only three inches from the ground! That's what really pissed me off!'

A married pair of high-school maths teachers had served together all over Queensland, and always took their holidays at Noosa. Eventually they both retired, and the husband said, 'Look, we've always gone away together. Why don't we have a change and go our own ways for a couple of weeks. After all, we've been living in each other's pockets for 40 years.'

'Good idea,' replied his wife. 'We could both do with a real break.'

So, he went up to Cairns and she went to the Gold Coast. After they'd been apart for a week, the husband phoned his wife. 'How's it going, then?' he asked.

'Real good,' she replied. 'What about you?'

'I'm having a great time,' her husband said. 'I've met this girl. She's only 20, lovely figure, blonde hair. We go down to the beach every day. How about you? Getting a bit lonely?'

'No,' answered the wife. 'I'm having a lovely time. I've met this young surfie. Only 19, but tall, bronzed, muscles everywhere and very charming. And he takes me out in his panel van.'

'I see,' her husband said gruffly. 'Well, I'm glad you're enjoying yourself.'

'Yes, I am,' said the wife. 'And I'll tell you something else – 19 goes into 60 more often than 65 goes into 20.'

A millionaire has four girlfriends and can't decide which one to marry. He gives them $250 000 each.

The first one flies off to Paris and spends hers on a Gucci shopping spree.

The second pays off her mother's mortgage and sets up an annuity for her.

The third donates it all to charity.

And the fourth invests it, doubles the money and pays back the millionaire.

Which one does he marry? The one with big tits.

A couple were making love in a 5 Series BMW when the bloke's back seized up. The ambulance men were afraid to move him in case of serious damage to his spine. So the police decided to use the 'jaws of life'. They simply cut the entire top of the car off so the patient could be safely lifted out without bending.

When the ambulance departed the girl sat weeping beside the abbreviated 5 Series BMW.

Feeling sorry for her, a cop patted her on the shoulder. 'He'll be all right,' he reassured her. The girl rounded on him savagely. 'Oh, sod him,' she exclaimed. 'How am I going to explain to my husband what happened to his BMW?'

The newlyweds travelled to a Surfers Paradise hotel and moved into the honeymoon suite. As they were about to undress, the groom remembered that he didn't have any condoms. Excusing himself, he rushed down the steps to the hotel chemist and, in his haste, tripped and hurt his penis. He consulted the hotel doctor who confirmed that the penis was, indeed, broken. He'd have to put a splint on it. The doctor fashioned the splint from a couple of wooden tongue depressers and a bandage.

Returning to the honeymoon suite the groom found his bride was already undressed and lying on the bed. How would he tell her that he couldn't have sex for at least a fortnight? She started to stroke her legs, saying, 'Look at my long smooth, slender legs. They have never been touched by the hand of man.' The she shifted her attention to her breasts. 'Oh, what lovely round breasts I have. And they've never been touched by the hand of man.'

Then she placed both her hands between her legs and said, 'Right here, under my hands, is something else that's never been touched by the hand of man.'

At this moment, the groom decided he had the perfect opportunity to reveal the problem of his broken penis. 'What are you skiting about? Look at my dick! It's still in its packing case.'

Because of a car breakdown after a late reception, a honeymoon couple were forced to spend their first night in an isolated motel that was entirely booked out. The best the proprietor could offer was a single camp stretcher in a small storage room.

Undismayed and with the bloke on top, the couple began to consummate their marriage. Trouble is, camp beds are somewhat unstable. Under the influence of their motion, the bed began to rock, and then to gradually move forward, a couple of inches at a time. A few bumps against the storage room door proved sufficient to open it, and the stretcher began to inch its way down the length of the corridor.

Finally it finished up against the door of Room 17, and began a gentle, rhythmic tapping. A few seconds later, the door was opened by a clergyman in his dressing-gown who, gazing down in shocked disbelief, said, 'Young fellow, that's disgraceful. I forbid you to do that here.'

The young bloke looked up in surprise. 'I'm sorry, mate,' he said. 'I didn't realise where we were. Turn the bed around and I'll fuck off back again . . .'

The girl from the city was fully experienced in carnal matters and had become totally bored with what was available round town. Then she heard there were still some real he-men left in the bush and so set off in search of them. And she came upon a bloke who'd just finished ploughing a huge paddock with a horse team. He was a big, muscular bloke and obviously very, very angry. He unhitched each horse and chucked it bodily over the fence. Then he lifted the six-furrow plough and chucked it over too. The girl had never seen anything so masculine and sexy. She called out to him, 'I need rooting!'

He said, 'So do I. I've just ploughed the wrong bloody paddock!'

The old farmer was on his deathbed. He beckoned his faithful wife to move closer. 'Dearest, you were with me through the Great Depression.'

She dabbed at a tear.

'You were with me through all those droughts.'

She sobbed silently.

'You were with me when we lost the place in the bushfires. And here you are again, by my side when I'm about to kick the bucket.'

Her shoulders were heaving.

'You know, I'm beginnin' to reckon that you brought me a lot of bad luck.'

A cocky drives the 350 km to the nearest town one morning and buys a new pair of riding boots. The best that R. M. Williams can make. They cost him two arms and a leg. He wears them home and clumps up and down the verandah, but no one notices his pride and joys. He puts the feet on the table at tea time. Still no one notices. He polishes them six times whilst playing cards that night. No one says a damned thing.

Feeling very disappointed, he goes to bed early. In any case, he has sheep to crutch in the morning. But he's still determined that somebody will notice his boots. So he clumps into the bedroom where his wife is lying on the bed. Her hair's in curlers and she's got a mud pack on her face because while he's crutching sheep she'll be off to church. She's lying there reading a *Women's Weekly* that can't be more than a month old.

The farmer strips off entirely except for his new boots. He stands at the end of the bed, feet astride, hands on hips. 'Do you notice anything?' he demands.

His wife peeks over the top of her glasses and the *Women's Weekly* and scans the awesome sight.

After what seems an eternity, she replies, 'Your dick is hanging down . . . as per bloody usual.'

The cocky is speechless, lost for words. Not to be outdone, he finally says, 'Too bloody right, woman! It's pointing at me bloody new boots!'

With a twist of the lips and a condescending roll of the eyes, she admires her hubby's new acquisition. Then, very slowly, she looks upwards again and observes with an insight that only 35 years in the bush can provide, 'Pity you didn't get a new Akubra!'

It's a country wedding in Queensland. The MC grabs the microphone and makes the following announcement. 'Sorry, we've had to cancel the reception. The beer hasn't arrived and the bride's been raped.'

The bad news causes considerable distress to those assembled. And just as they're filing out in disappointment, the MC grabs the mike again. 'It's okay! The beer's arrived, the bloke's apologised.'

A truckie is driving along a country highway. Despite signs warning that kangaroos and wombats cross the road for the 'next 5 km' he sees any number of dead bodies on the road. So he slows down. Which is just as well because, suddenly, he spots something moving, right smack bang in the middle of the highway. He slams on the anchors, bringing the truck to a halt a few feet away from a young couple furiously bonking. He winds down the window and starts yelling obscenities at them. The young bloke stands up and apologises. 'Sorry, mate. I was coming, she was coming, and you were coming. But you were the only one that had brakes.'

A travelling salesman finds himself stranded in the tiniest town in Australia. And he knocks on the door of the little pub.

'Sorry, we don't have a spare room,' says the publican, 'but you're welcome to share with a little red-headed schoolteacher if that's okay.'

'Oh, that'll be great,' says the bloke, grinning from ear to ear. 'That'll be bonzer. And don't worry, I'll be a real gentleman.'

'Just as well,' says the publican. 'So is the little red-headed schoolteacher.'

What is 12 inches long and white?
    Nothing. If it's 12 inches long, it's black.

How do you make an Australian woman give up sex?
    Marry her.

What do motorcycling and sex have in common?
    There comes a time when you don't do it any more.

What is the definition of a man?
    Life-support system for a penis.

Why is pubic hair curly?
    So it doesn't poke your eyes out.

What's the best thing about making love to your wife instead of your lover?
    The ten minutes of *absolute* silence!

What do an orgasm and a drum solo have in common?

    You know it's coming, but there's nothing you can do about it.

What's the difference between a male chauvinist and a sensitive new-age guy?

    Three beers.

What's the difference between a woman and a typhoon?

    No difference. It starts with a blow job and you finish up losing your house.

What's the difference between erotic and kinky?

    Erotic is when you use a feather. Kinky is when you use the whole chicken.

What's the difference between a condom and a meat pie?

    You get more meat in a condom.

Why is an anniversary like a toilet seat?
Men miss both.

How do you stop a woman giving you blow jobs?
Marry her.

What is pink and wrinkly and hangs out your pants?
Your grandma.

Why did the woman cross the road?
More the point, what was she doing out of the
kitchen?

What does a Double Bay widow wear to her
husband's funeral?
A black tennis dress.

What did the leper say to the prostitute?
Keep the tip.

A randy regular was denied admission to the Touch of Class because of previous bad behaviour. 'I want to come in,' he yelled.

'Okay, then slip $50 through the mail slot.'

He did. Nothing happened. 'Hey, I want to be screwed!'

'What?' said a woman's voice. 'Again?'

A bloke approached his mate at work. 'Look, I've got bad news for you. It's about your wife. I was at the Touch of Class at the weekend and there she was. Mate, I hate to be the bearer of bad news, but your wife is a prostitute.'

'No she's not,' he said. 'She's a substitute. She only fills in at weekends.'

A virgin goes to a knock shop in Elwood for a trial run. He was very, very polite and made a nice impression on the Madam. So she introduced him to one of the nicest of her girls.

A few minutes later he was leaving with a big smile on his face. 'What about some money?' asked the Madam.

'Oh, no thanks. You've been so nice to me already.'

A sailor gets into Sydney after month at sea, desperate for a bonk. He heads straight for the Touch of Class only to discover that there's a Rotary convention in town and all the girls are taken. 'Look, $5000 for one of your girls,' he says to the Madam.

'I'm sorry, sir, but the situation is hopeless. I can't squeeze you in anywhere.'

'Well, how about you?'

'Oh, I'm afraid I couldn't. Really, I haven't done it for ages.'

'Look, I'm really desperate.'

'Sorry, sir, you really wouldn't enjoy it. I'm so out of practice.'

'Look, $5000 plus a pair of Reeboks I bought in Honolulu.'

'Reeboks, eh! All right, but don't blame me if you're disappointed.'

He starts going hammer and tong and is a little bit disappointed because she just lies there. Then, suddenly, she puts an arm around him. And then another!

Encouraged, he renews his efforts and soon she throws a leg around him. And then the other.

When they're finished the sailor smiles with his approval. 'That really wasn't too bad, considering you're out of practice. You really got into it there at the end, arms, legs, the whole bit.'

'Oh, that. No, I was just trying my Reeboks on.'

It was a very expensive brothel but the women all looked like his auntie. There they were, sitting in a row, hair in curlers, fluffy slippers and chenille dressing-gowns. The Madam explained, 'We specialise in clients who suffer from premature ejaculation.'

The bloke went to an S&M parlour and asked the mistress for a woman he could whip. 'You want to do the whipping? We don't usually go in for that sort of thing here. That'll cost you extra. A thousand dollars.'

Insisting on payment in advance, the Madam introduced him to an expert in bondage who copped a few minutes of flagellation before protesting.

'Christ, I've had enough of this. When are you going to stop?'

'When?' screamed the client. 'When you give me my money back.'

A bloke went to a brothel at Kings Cross and it was really busy. So he finished up with an old bird who'd been on the game for decades. Deciding to make the best of it, he went hammer and tong.

'Why the hurry, love?' she asked.

'Sorry, but I haven't had a fuck for months,' he said.

'A sailor, are you?'

'No. I've just got out of the VD clinic.'

'What's the tucker like, love?' said the woman. 'I'm going in tomorrow.'

A bloke goes to a brothel in Kings Cross and is led to a tiny bedroom where a prostitute awaits him. He is about to engage in an act of congress when he notices a cut in the side of her stomach. 'Christ, shouldn't you have that appendix sewn up?'

'No. It's so I can make a bit on the side.'

'You are charged that on the third of June you battered your wife to death with a hammer,' said the clerk of courts.

From the back of the court, a voice yelled, 'You rotten bastard.'

'You are further charged that on the same day you battered your mother-in-law to death with a hammer.'

The voice from the back shouted, 'You filthy rotten bastard!'

The judge had the bloke hauled before him. 'I'm

sorry, your Honour, but I'm his next-door neighbour,'
he explained. 'And when I asked him for a loan of
the hammer, the rotten filthy bastard said he didn't
have one.'

The cops raided a brothel in Kings Cross. In one of
the booths they found an Asian bloke bonking like
crazy. 'What's your name?'

'My name is Ting.'

In the next room they found another Asian
bloke sitting quietly in a shabby armchair. 'And
what's your name?'

'My name is Ting.'

'Oh yeah,' said the sergeant suspiciously. 'How
come we've just arrested Ting in the room next
door?'

'He is Ru Ting. I am Wah Ting.'

A woman decided she wanted a divorce and
consulted a solicitor.

'Have you any grounds?'

'Yes, about four acres.'

'Do you have a grudge?'

'No, but we've a lovely carport.'

'Does he beat you up?'

'No, I'm up first every morning.'

'Then why do you want a divorce?'

'Because he cannot carry on an intelligent conversation.'

'**Q**uick! I can hear my husband coming. He's a policeman and he's twice as big as you.'

'Where's the back door?'

'We haven't got one.'

'Okay, where would you like one?'

RULES

1. **The Female Always Makes the Rules**
   a. The rules are subject to change at any time without notice.
   b. No man can possibly know all the rules. Nearly all females are born with this knowledge.
   c. If the female suspects the males know any of the rules, she may immediately change any or all of the rules.
2. **The Female Is Never Wrong**
   a. If the female is wrong, it is because of a misunderstanding which was the direct result of something the male did or said wrong.
   b. If rule 2a applies, the male must apologise immediately for causing the misunderstanding.

3. **The Female Can Change Her Mind at Any Given Point in Time.**
   a. The male must never change his mind without written consent from the female.
4. **The Female Has Every Right to Be Upset or Angry at Any Time.**
   a. The male must remain calm at all times, unless the female wants him to be upset or angry.
   b. The female must under no circumstances let the male know whether or not she wants him to be upset or angry.
5. **Any Attempt by the Male to Change Any of the Rules Will Not Be Tolerated.**

A motorist was cruising along the Hume Highway at the normal speed when he suddenly noticed a police car right behind him. He accelerated to 100 km/h and then to 115 km/h, and so on, ever increasingly with the police close behind. Soon the squad car overtook and signalled him to stop. A very irate constable demanded an explanation for his erratic and illegal behaviour. The motorist was most anxious to explain. 'It's like this, Sergeant. Last week one of your officers ran away with my wife, and I was afraid he was bringing her back!'

She was worried about her breasts. 'Do you think I should try silicon implants?'

'Too expensive,' grunted her husband. 'Just get a roll of Sorbent and rub it along your cleavage.'

'Will that make them bigger?'

'Well, it did a great job on your arse.'

After years of marriage they were still hopelessly in love and had a marvellous sex life. But after a mild heart attack his doctor told him that he had to give up sex.

'In your delicate state, intercourse would almost certainly be fatal,' said the doctor.

So husband and wife agreed that they'd sleep apart. She upstairs, he downstairs.

For a week they endured this, tossing and turning and feeling increasingly randy.

Then, next night, they met on the stairs. 'Darling, I was just on my way down to kill you,' said the wife.

'Funny you should say that, dearest. I was just coming up to commit suicide.'

She was looking younger than she'd looked for years. Quite radiant. 'Darling, can you see anything different about me?' she inquired of her husband.

'Yes, dear, you're not wearing a bra.'
'However did you know that?'
'Well, all the wrinkles have gone from your face.'

She: 'Just one more word out of you and I'm going home to Mother.'
He: 'Taxi!'

It was a warm Sunday afternoon, the wife was browsing through a magazine, he was just dozing.
Looking up from her magazine, she said, 'Bruce, do we have sex relations?'
'Of course we do, woman.'
'Then how come they never send us any Christmas cards?'

'I found my wife in bed with my best friend.'
'You bitter?'
'Yeah, and I bit him, too.'

A bloke came home and caught his wife in bed with the next-door neighbour. He shoved him against the wall and aimed his shotgun at his testicles. 'I'm going to blow your balls off.'

'Come on, mate. I'm a sitting duck. How about giving me a sporting chance?'

'Okay, swing 'em!'

'I'm into wife swapping. I'll accept anything in exchange.'

Two blokes were talking about Freudian slips.

'Don't talk to me about them,' said one. 'I made the worst Freudian slip of my life this morning.'

'What happened?' asked the other.

'Well, I was at breakfast and I meant to say to the wife, "Darling, please pass the Corn Flakes". But by mistake, it just slipped out. I said, "YOU'RE RUINING MY FUCKING LIFE, YOU BITCH!!!!".'

A big bloke was working on a construction project in Africa, and while he was there he fell in love with a small, beautifully formed pygmy

woman. They married and he brought her
back to Australia, proudly introducing her to his boss.

'Good grief, John,' he whispered. 'She's not
much bigger than your hand.'

'I know,' he whispered back, 'but she's a bloody
sight better.'

It's late, late, late on a foggy, foggy night. And
there's a knock at the front door.

The wife said, 'Don't sit there like a beached
whale. Go and see who it is.'

The grumbling husband opened the door and
there, in the shadows, surrounded by swirling mists,
was a terrifying figure in a black cloak.

'Who are you?' the husband whispered.

'Jack the Ripper.'

The husband turned his head and shouted,
'Darling, it's for you!'

Do you remember, dear,' said the old woman to her
husband on their 60th anniversary, 'how, 60 years
ago tonight, in this very room, you didn't even give
me time to take off my shawl before you started
making wild, passionate love to me?'

'Yes, dear, I remember,' the old bloke replied in

a quavery, wavery voice. 'But the way I feel now, you'd have time to knit one.'

She was suing her husband for divorce. The reason: his insatiable appetite for sex. He was at it day and night and night and day. Finally she'd had enough and threw herself on the mercy of the court. 'Very well,' said the judge, 'I'll hear your case, but first you must go over to the clerk and file your petition.'

'File my petition, your Honour? I couldn't even touch it with a powder puff.'

The wife was furious when she arrived home unexpectedly and found her husband bonking a lady midget. 'You promised me weeks ago that you'd never cheat on me again,' she raged.

'Take it easy, darl,' said the husband. 'Can't you see I'm tapering off?'

Sarah is dying. Sam at her bedside looks thoughtful. With a final effort, Sarah lifts her head off the pillow and says, 'Sam, before I go, grant me my dying wish.'

'What is it?' asks Sam.

'Promise me that you'll never marry again.'

'I have to remain alone for the rest of my life?' cries Sam, raising his arms.

'Perhaps that is a bit much to ask,' says Sarah, 'but promise me that if you remarry you won't let her wear my dresses.'

'Sure, my dear. I promise you that,' says Sam. 'They don't even fit her.'

A knight of the realm awoke in his Toorak mansion and was astonished to see that he had a sizeable erection. He called for his butler. 'Yes, a magnificent weapon,' said the loyal serf. 'Shall I inform her ladyship?'

'Christ, no. Bring me my baggy golf trousers and I'll try to smuggle it down to my mistress.'

A bloke was telling his mate that he'd just got a letter from an irate husband. 'He says he'll shoot my balls off if I don't stop screwing his wife.'

'Well, stop screwing her and you'll be okay,' said the mate.

'It's not that simple,' said the bloke. 'The letter was anonymous.'

Staring up at the ceiling during sexual intercourse, the wife yawned and said, 'This room needs decorating.'

The husband snarled in response, 'The bloke who invented decorating needs fucking.'

To which his wife replied, 'How times have changed. On our wedding night you said the bloke who invented fucking needs decorating.'

I had a funny dream last night,' said the wife at breakfast. 'I dreamt I went to an auction where they were selling willies. There was one there which was fabulous – nine inches and thick, with a fine-skinned head surrounded by a foreskin like a frill-necked lizard.' She sighed, 'Liz Taylor bought it for two and a half million dollars.'

Her husband said, 'Love, did you see any of my size there?'

'Yes,' she said, 'they were selling at a dollar a bundle.'

Next morning the husband came down from bed and said, 'Funny thing, after your dream last night I dreamt I was at an auction where they were selling vaginas.' He smiled dreamily. 'There was one there that was obviously a double-rose, surrounded by the fluffiest pubic hair, and the silkiest clitoris imaginable. Kerry Packer paid five million for it.'

'Did you see anything like mine there, darl?' the wife asked.

'Yeah,' said the husband, 'but I didn't wait to see it sold – the auctioneer was standing in it!'

'I was just thinking, darling, we've had such a marvellous marriage, we've enjoyed a great life together, but one of these days one of us will pass on.'

'True, but don't worry about that now.'

'Well, I was just thinking, when it does happen, I'd like to go and live in Queensland.'

'What the hell do you think you're doing?' yelled the husband when he found his wife in bed with a total stranger.

'There you are,' said the wife to her lover. 'I told you he was thick.'

'Why are you taking so long?' demanded the wife during a protracted bout of intercourse.

'I'm trying, I'm trying,' said her puffing spouse, 'but I just can't think of anyone.'

'How come your marriage has lasted 50 years?'

'Simple. We decided from the beginning that she'd make all the little decisions and I'd decide the major issues.'

'Such as?'

'Well, she decided where I'd work, where we'd live, what school the kids would go to. And I made the major decisions. Like what to do about the ozone hole, the Balkans and sanctions in South Africa.'

'Let's try it a different way tonight.'

'Ooo, let's. What do you have in mind?'

'Back to back.'

'How do we do that?'

'I've invited another couple.'

Though still regarding herself as attractive, the young wife noticed that her husband was becoming less and less interested in their sex lives. So she bought a copy of *Cosmopolitan* and opened the sealed section. It told her to try a few novelty turns, like greeting her husband at the front door wearing nothing but Glad wrap, or high-heeled boots. And there was also a mail-order catalogue that allowed you to order kinky things. But none of it worked. Her husband still seemed bored and listless.

So she persuaded him to visit a psychiatrist and, after a few visits, he was as good as new. And she was enjoying multiple orgasms. But there was a mysterious aspect to his behaviour. Often, during the middle of making love, he'd leap out of bed and rush into the bathroom. She could hear him mumbling something for a minute or two and then he'd return rearing to go.

Finally, she could not contain her curiosity. So when he ran into the bathroom and shut the door, she peeped through the keyhole. And there he was, staring into the mirror, muttering to himself, 'She's not my wife . . . she's not my wife . . . she's not my wife.'

A bloke who was very, very good at Australian history won a pile of prizes on *Sale of the Century*. There were all sorts of things – a new house, a new car, a new boat, a holiday home at Surfers.

Driving up to Queensland, he was stopped by a policeman. 'Did you know you were driving without tail-lights?'

The bloke leapt out of his brand new Lexus looking highly agitated. The policeman recognised him. 'Ah, you're the bloke off *Sale of the Century*. Look,

mate, don't worry, it's not a major offence. Nothing
to get too upset about.'

'It mightn't mean much to you,' said the bloke,
'but to me I've lost the missus, two kids and my
brand new caravan.'

A bloke and his wife went to a family planning clinic.

'We've been married for ten years and we've got
no kids,' said the husband. 'And the next-door
neighbours say it's because we're stupid.'

'Nonsense,' smiled the doctor. 'It's probably to
do with your diet. Or it might be a question of
timing. How many times a week do you do it?'

'Do what?' asked the wife.

A Colonel in the Australian Army, stationed in
Melbourne, would tell his wife that he had to go
away on military manoeuvres every weekend. In fact,
he was off bonking a girlfriend in Bendigo. She was
really pretty, early thirties, affectionate and
energetic. And after their rapturous weekends he'd
always offer her a present. 'Would you like a watch?
A bangle? A necklace?'

'No, darling,' she'd reply, 'I don't want anything.
Just you. Just our weekends together.' But he'd insist

that he wanted to buy her something. Whereupon she'd say, 'Well, I would like one of those Swiss Army knives. You know, with the red handle, the little blade, the big blade, the corkscrew, the magnifying glass, the scissors and the thing for taking stones out of horses' hooves.'

Next weekend he was back again for 48 hours of rapturous lovemaking. And, on his departure, he'd ask her what present she'd like. He promised to bring it the very next time they met.

'A little watercolour? A lovely piece of porcelain?'

'No, just the pocketknife.'

The next time he came, he had bad news. 'I'm afraid the Army has posted me to Perth. So I won't be able to see you again, perhaps for years. But I have brought you the memento you asked for.'

Though weeping at the thought of losing him, she smiled bravely as she unwrapped the tissue paper. And there, lo and behold, was the Swiss Army knife, with the red handle, the little blade, the big blade, the nail file, the magnifying glass, the little scissors, the miniature pliers and the thing for taking stones out of horses' hooves. Wiping away her tears, she crossed the room and opened a drawer, which turned out to be full of . . . Swiss Army knives.

'My darling,' said the Colonel, somewhat confused, 'why all the pocketknives?'

'My dear, at the moment I'm an attractive woman. Men desire me. But let's face it, I won't

always keep my looks. Time will exact its toll, take
its ravages upon me. But when it does, my dearest,
there isn't much that a boy scout wouldn't do for a
good pocketknife.'

In a pub toilet a couple of blokes are standing side
by side having a pee. One spits and says, 'Shit, she
could drive.'

The other said, 'Who?'

'This sheila. I was travelling from Geelong to
Melbourne when my car broke down and I had to
hitchhike. Excuse me, shit she could drive. Now,
where was I? Yeah, hitchhiking. Suddenly this
souped-up Fairlane 500 pulls up and there's a blonde
driving. She leans over and unlocks the door. I climb
in and she floors it. I look across at the speedometer
and see that, even allowing for parallax, we're doing
about 160 km/h. "You're a quick driver, lady", I sez. I
see a slight smile on her face. Well, it's not long
before we get into traffic on the outskirts of
Melbourne. She weaves in and out – doing
120 km/h. I'm a bit concerned at this stage. (He
spits.) Shit, she could drive! Somehow we made it to
Footscray. She's still doing 100 km/h through thick
traffic. Then she pulls on to the wrong side of the
road, makes a squeeze between a tram and a semi-
trailer coming towards us. By now I'm crouching

under the dash with fear. (Spits again.) I said to her, "Lady, if you make it through the gap I'll suck your box dry". Shit she could drive!'

After months at sea, a sailor checked into a waterfront pub and asked reception to 'send up a whore'. Unfortunately he was talking to the new owner, a formidable Catholic lady in her sixties who abhorred adultery and licentiousness. She went upstairs to get her husband to throw the sailor out. He reminded her that he was a regular guest. And as well, he was a pretty big bloke. 'You're too frightened to throw him out? Then I'll do it myself.'

So she marched up the stairs and, pretty soon, there was the sound of breaking furniture, thumps and curses. Finally the sailor came down, shirt torn and exhausted. 'That was quite a whore you sent up,' he said to the publican, 'but it was more like a wrestle than a screw.'

A bloke came into the pub with a huge bruise on his head. 'What happened to you?' asked the barman.

'Well, me and the sheila next door were doing it doggy-style in the back yard. She heard her husband coming and ran under the house.'

A bloke goes into a country pub. Says to the bar lady, 'How about a quickie?' She tells him to behave himself. He says it's worth $100. And, as things are a bit tight, she agrees. This goes on for five nights. She doesn't see him the next week. 'Where have you been?' she asks him when he finally returns.

'Oh, I went back to Brisbane.'

'Oh,' she said, 'I've got a brother in Brisbane.'

'Yeah, I know,' he said. 'He gave me $500 to give you.'

'Quick, barman, give me a drink.'

'Okay, what would you like?'

'Ten whiskies.'

'Ten?'

'Yeah, I've just had my first blow job.'

'And you're celebrating?'

'No. I'm trying to get the taste out of my mouth.'

For months they'd sat side by side on the verandah of the twilight home. Little by little they'd moved their rocking chairs closer together. After this tentative, shy foreplay he said, 'Fuck you.'

And she said, 'Fuck you, too.'

There was a long silence. Finally he said, 'So much for oral sex.'

'**I** may be 87, but I make love nearly every night of the week.'

'Bullshit.'

'No, I'm dinky-di. I nearly made it on Monday, I nearly made it on Tuesday . . .'

Three old blokes from the twilight home were given, as a treat, a day at the beach. And it turned out to be a nudist beach. They were watching the various young women agog.

When the prettiest of them all walked by, one of the old blokes said, 'I'd like to give her a hug.'

'I'd like to give her a kiss,' said the second.

And the third old bloke said, 'What was that other thing we used to do?'

Bigamy: One wife too many.

Monogamy: Same idea.

'Sir, this is the reception desk. Are you entertaining a woman in your room?'
'Just a minute, I'll ask her.'

Always be sincere even if you don't mean it.

If it floats, flies or fucks, rent it, don't buy it!

If it has tits or wheels you are bound to have trouble with it!

A bachelor is a man who hasn't made the same mistake once!

There were two queues at the Pearly Gates. One, quite long, was ranged behind a sign saying MEN DOMINATED BY THEIR WIVES.
Another read MEN NOT DOMINATED BY THEIR WIVES. There was just one bloke in the queue, and he

looked extremely timid. St Peter asked him, 'Are you sure you should be standing here?'

'Yes,' came the reply, 'my wife told me to.'

Two queens got into a heated argument at a party so they went outside and exchanged blows.

This isn't a beer gut – it's a solar panel for a sex machine.

A bloke bought himself a new Schick blade and, after some days of shaving, replaced it. His wife retrieved the discarded blade and used it to shave her armpits. Then his daughter used it to shave her legs. And his mother-in-law, most inadvisably, used the blade to cut some dental floss caught between her teeth.

Unfortunately she swallowed the blade, but that's not the end of the story. Far from it. On its way down, it performed a tonsillectomy, an appendectomy and a hysterectomy. It subsequently circumcised her husband, castrated her lover, gave the bishop a hare lip, amputated the fingers of several close friends – and still had five good shaves left in it.

Two ladies were reclining in deckchairs as the ocean liner crossed the Atlantic. 'I can't believe that I'm here,' said one.

'My husband had to scrimp and scrape to get the money together.'

'Your first trip?' the other asked snootily. 'This is my 30th crossing. You see, my husband works for Cunard.'

'Well, so does mine,' said the first woman. 'I told you that. But there's no reason to swear about it.'

An American tourist pulls over the Hertz car in the middle of nowhere for a pee. Suddenly a bloke jumps out from behind a tree, pointing a shotgun at him. 'Pull yourself off,' he orders.

'What?'

'Masturbate. Right now.'

Nervously, the tourist obliges.

'Now, do it again.'

'I can't do it again.'

'*Do it again!*'

So the tourist masturbates for a second time.

69

'Okay, once more.'

'I couldn't do it once more, no matter what. You may as well shoot me.'

'No, that's fine. Now you can give my sister a lift to the next town.'

The captain of a Boeing discovered a very serious fault in the aircraft at 35 000 feet. After breaking the news to the crew he announced to the passengers that the plane would crash in about 15 minutes. He told them that the stewardesses would be available for nooky at the back of the aircraft if anyone was interested. Whereas he, himself, was wondering whether the very beautiful African American woman in 2B would be willing to join him in the cockpit.

Why not? she thought, asking the pilot, 'But why me?'

'Well, when a plane goes down, they always find the black box, and I want to be in it.'

A tourist arrived in a very small town and stopped for petrol. The place seemed deserted. Finally he spotted a funeral procession with a big bloke and a big dog walking behind the hearse. And behind them, in single file, about a dozen blokes trudged in respectful silence.

'Somebody important died?' the tourist asked.

'Yeah, the wife,' answered the bloke with the dog.

'What happened?'

'The dog savaged her.'

Whereupon the traveller asked, 'Do you want to sell the dog?'

'Yeah,' said the big bloke, 'but join the queue.'

The Methodist missionary had been living with the tribe on the Sepik River for a couple of years when the chief took him aside. 'We might be halfway up the Sepik, but you're up shit creek.'

'Why? What have I done?'

'Yesterday a white baby was born to my daughter and you're the only white man for hundreds and hundreds of miles.' The chief started fondling his axe.

'But, Chief, I know it looks bad. But see your pigs wallowing in the mud?'

'Of course I can see them.'

'Well, all of them are white. But there's one black pig and . . .'

'Okay,' said the chief. 'I'll keep quiet if you keep quiet.'

Bill, a blacktracker, never got along with his constable. He resented being called Abo, blackie or nigger. One day, while they were tracking a couple of drunks who'd escaped from the local lock-up, Bill spotted the legendary yellow-belly goanna. Legendary, because traditional belief holds that whoever catches this rare creature is granted three wishes. At the same time, twice as much of the same wish is granted to whomever you hate the most.

So Bill caught the goanna and, twirling it round by the tail, wished aloud, 'I want a big house.' Lo and behold, a big house appeared from nowhere along with two big houses for the constable.

'Shit,' said the constable. 'Girls, Billy, girls. Wish for some sheilas.'

'Okay, okay,' said Bill. 'I want a hundred beautiful girls.' Instantly, 100 pulchritudinous women appeared by Bill's house and 200 beside the constable's houses. Just as the constable was about to go rushing in the front door with some of his girls, Bill gave the goanna another twirl and whispered his third wish.

'I want my sex urge reduced by 50 per cent.'

Family Ties

It's still very, very hard for kids to get jobs. So when one woman met another in the supermarket, she said, 'Tell me, how's your son Basil?'

'Basil's getting along fine. He's a scientist, as you know, and just got first-class honours in quantum mechanics at Sydney University.'

'And your daughter?'

'She's smart too. She graduated from the University of New South Wales with degrees in arts, economics and the law.'

'You must be very proud of them. What a talented family. And little Fred? What's he doing?'

'Well, Fred's a drug dealer. If it wasn't for him, we'd all be starving.'

Around lunchtime Fiona left school and headed for home, crying because her first period had started and she had no idea what it was. The teacher, reluctant to get involved, had suggested she talk to her mum.

Between the school and home was a bridge, and as she was halfway across it, a little boy who was wagging school came out from beneath it and said, 'Why are you crying?'

She said, 'Billy, I'm bleeding.'

He said, 'Give us a look.'

She cheerfully obliged.

'Christ,' he said. 'No wonder you're bleedin'. Your cock's been cut off.'

A kid missed the school bus and turned up hours late on his pony. The teacher demanded an explanation.

'Dad went to bed with no pyjamas.'

'And what's that got to do with anything?'

'Well, Dad went to bed with no pyjamas and at 2.30 this morning we heard a noise in the chook shed, so Dad got the shotgun and we went to look. Dad had the gun and no pyjamas and Mum, me and the dog walked behind him. We got outside the chook shed and Dad cocked the gun, pushed the door open and said, 'Who's there?' Just then, my dog put his cold nose on Dad's bum, and I've been cleaning up fuckin' chooks all morning.'

A kid walked out of the toilet into the kitchen where his mum was mixing a cake.

'Can I lick the bowl, Mum?'

'No, you little bugger. Flush it like anyone else.'

What's the difference between street kids and elephants?

Street kids try to forget.

What's the difference between a black baby and a white baby?

Five minutes in a microwave oven.

A little boy woke up crying and ran to see his mother.

'Mummy, Mummy. A voice came to me in my dreams. It said that my grandmother would die today.'

The mother comforted him and told him not to worry, that it was only a dream.

But when he returned from school he found his mother sobbing in the kitchen. She told him that her mother had died just a few hours ago.

That night the voice returned. This time it said that the house on the corner would burn down on Friday night. The mother comforted him, telling him not to worry. But on Saturday morning the whole family was awoken by the sound of the fire engines.

A few days later the voice returned saying, 'Your dog Spot is going to die today.'

His mother tried to comfort and soothe him, but as he returned from school he saw the dog skittled by a car.

A few weeks passed and the voice in his dreams returned. This time it said, 'Your father is going to die at exactly 12 noon today.'

The poor little boy was horrified. So Dad said he'd stay home and help soothe the little lad. He did his best. As they sat at the table for lunch, the hands on the face of the clock reached 12 noon and nothing happened. The child relaxed and became cheerful as the minutes ticked by. But after five minutes there was a great banging at the door. The mother opened it to find the woman from over the road who blurted out, 'Come quick, or let me use your telephone. The milkman dropped dead in the middle of the street about five minutes ago.'

'How did you break your arm?'
'I swerved to avoid a child and fell out of bed.'

The butcher could still remember the day it happened. That young woman, babe in arms, coming into the shop and announcing that the little boy was his. What was he going to do about it?

He tried to hush her up as best he could by promising to supply her with free meat until the kid was 16. And he'd been ticking off the years ever since.

Finally the kid came in to collect the week's supply and announced, 'Guess what? I'll be 16 tomorrow.'

'Yes,' said the butcher with a grin. 'So tell your mum this'll be the last free steak, chops and sausages she'll get. And watch the expression on her face.'

'Mister, she told me to tell you that she's been getting free bread, milk and groceries for the past 16 years. And to watch the expression on your face.'

What's the difference between broccoli and snot?
    You can't get kids to eat broccoli.

Grandfather was becoming a pain in the neck. He lived with his grandson and granddaughter-in-law, both very successful professional people who often entertained influential friends and colleagues at dinner parties in their beautiful home. On these occasions, Grandfather was not left out. He attended the dinner parties and, fancying himself as the star turn of the evening, often dominated the occasions with loud and garrulous pronouncements on irrelevant subjects, non-stop from the first martini to the passing of the port, embarrassing everybody in the process.

At last his grandson realised that something had to be done about Grandfather, so he took him aside one day and asked him, kindly and tactfully, if he would tone things down and take more of a back seat in future. Grandfather seemed surprised at this request, to which, however, he finally agreed. His grandson was very relieved, assured his wife that the problem was solved and that Grandfather would turn out to be a paragon of social virtue.

And so Grandfather proved to be. On the next occasion, he sat at the table, quietly eating and drinking, listening attentively to the scintillating table-talk and nodding agreement from time to time – well-mannered, civil and circumspect. His family were delighted.

Towards the end of dinner, Grandfather rose slowly to his feet, put down his napkin, and gave a little bow. 'Turning in?' his grandson enquired, a little hopefully. Grandfather pushed back his chair and walked slowly to the door of the dining room. He opened the door and turned to face the company. He nodded.

'Yes,' he said, 'I think I'll have a quick shit and hit the sack!'

Hire teenagers while they still know everything.

A father-to-be was waiting anxiously outside the labour ward where his wife was hard at it. A nurse popped her head around the door. 'You have a little boy. But it might be an idea to go and have a cup of coffee because we think there might be another.'

Turning pale, he left. An hour later he returned to be told that he was the father of twins. 'But we think there's another one on the way. Come back in a little while.'

This time he went to the pub next door, phoning in to hear that there was a third baby, with a fourth imminent.

After a few stiff whiskies he called the hospital again but was so pissed that he dialled a wrong number – and got the recorded cricket score. Emitting an agonised cry, he collapsed on the floor. As the barman picked him up he heard the voice from the phone, 'The score is 96 all out. And the last one was a duck.'

'My dad's so fast,' said one boy, 'that he can fire an arrow at a tree, run like buggery and catch the arrow before it hits it.'

'My dad's faster than that,' said the second kid. 'He can drop a brick from the tenth floor of a building and run down the stairs and catch it before it hits the ground.'

'My dad's faster than your dads,' said the third kid. 'He works for the Brunswick Council. He knocks off at five and he's always home by two thirty.'

'Mum, where did I come from?'
'From under a cabbage, dear.'
'And where did you come from, Mum?'
'The stork brought me.'
'Grandpa?'
'The stork brought him too.'
'Mum, doesn't it worry you to think that there've been no natural births in our family for three generations?'

The young mum was having coffee with her friends when her three-year-old raced into the room saying, 'I wanna piss. I wanna piss.' Embarrassed, she took him to the toilet and told him, 'Next time you want to do wee-wees, don't use that word. Come in and whisper.'

Shortly thereafter, the child interrupted again by rushing in, hopping from one foot to the other. 'I gotta whisper. I gotta whisper.'

Well, it was something of an improvement, so his mother gave him a slice of tart.

That night he climbed out of his cot and ran into his parents' bedroom. Mum wasn't there but his dad was just dozing off. 'What is it, little fella?'

'I wanna whisper, Daddy, I wanna whisper.'

'Fine, son, fine. Come and whisper in Dad's ear.'

There are two sisters who are Siamese twins, one of whom is a major Tom Jones fan. She sees a poster saying, *Tom Jones. One Night Only in Chicago.*

'We've got to go!' she cries.

'Do we have to?' says the other sister, who's much more into jazz.

'Oh, please, please, please! It'd mean a lot.'

'Oh, okay,' says the other sister, and off they go.

On the night of the concert the sisters have a front-row seat. Tom does a great gig. The joint is jumping. Everyone has a wonderful time. When it's all over, the sisters wait till everyone else has left the auditorium because they hate all the pointing-and-staring-at-the-Siamese-twins routine. Once outside, the sister who's the fan says, 'Wasn't that great! Did you enjoy it?'

'Yeah, as a matter of fact, I did,' replies the other sister.

'Great! Then you won't mind if we hang around the backstage door to see if we can get a glimpse of Tom.'

'Ohhh, do we have to?' says the other sister.

'Yeah, come on, it'll be great!'

'Oh, okay . . .'

So they're hanging around the backstage door and out comes Tom. He can't help but notice the Siamese twins standing there, so he goes over to talk to them.

'Hi,' says Tom. 'I saw you there in the front row. Did you have a good time?'

'Yeah, it was *great!*' the sisters chorus.

Feeling a little uncomfortable with the whole situation, Tom says, 'Look . . . um . . . why don't you two come backstage, have a drink?'

'Great! Love to!' says the sister who's the fan, and off they all go.

So, they drink a few champagnes and, after a while – lo and behold – a bit of a rapport is building between Tom and the sister who's the fan. She says, 'Tom, pardon me for being forward, only, when you're a Siamese twin, you learn not to stand on courtesy. But, have we got a bit of a vibe happening here?'

Tom thinks about this and says, 'Yes . . . yes we have.'

To which she replies, 'Well, Tom. Pardon me for being forward again, but I think you'd like to make love to me, wouldn't you?'

Tom thinks about this even longer, then says, 'Yes, but . . .'

'It's my sister, isn't it, Tom?' says the sister who's the fan.

'No, it's . . .'

'Tom, my sister and I have *grown up* as Siamese twins. We're used to these situations. We have mechanisms for dealing with these sorts of things. If you'd like to make love to me, Tom, and I would dearly like to make love to you, then my sister will do what she always does in such situations. In order to tune herself out, she will play the trombone.'

'She'll *what?*'

'Play the trombone.'

And, sure enough, for the next hour and a half – as Tom and the sister who's the fan make glorious, passionate love – the other sister plays a very commendable selection of jazz, Dixie and some blues trombone.

And at the end of an hour and a half, as the other sister packs away her trombone, Tom and the sister who's the fan kiss each other a starry-eyed goodbye. It's been a wonderful experience. No questions asked. No commitment expected. Once-in-a-lifetime. Goodbye.

Two years later, up go the posters, *Tom Jones. One Night Only in Chicago*.

'Tom's back!' says the sister who's the fan. 'He's on! We've gotta go!'

'Oh, come on,' says the other sister. 'We've done that.'

'Yeah, but we had a great time, didn't we?'

'Yeah . . .'

'Well, let's go!'

'Oh, all right then.'

'*And,*' says the sister who's the fan, 'if we hang around backstage, maybe Tom'll see us. Maybe he'll invite us back for a few drinks. *Maybe* something more could happen!'

'Oh, *come* on!' says the other sister. 'What makes you think he'll remember us?'

W hat's the definition of confusion?
Father's Day in the western suburbs.

W hat does *pas de deux* mean?
You're the father of twins.

School of Hard Knocks

Two naked professors are sitting on a verandah at the local college talking about life, death, God and general theories of existence.

One turns to the other and says, 'By the way, have you read Marx?' To which the other replies, 'Yes, aren't these cane chairs murder!'

A university lecturer asked her students to describe in a page or less the difference between ignorance and apathy. She was forced to give an A-plus to the student who replied, 'I don't know and I don't care.'

A lecturer in sociology at La Trobe University was touring north-eastern Victoria and called into Glenrowan pub for a beer. He struck up a conversation in the bar with some of the locals and, naturally enough, the topic soon drifted around to that of Ned Kelly. Undeterred by the fact that most of the locals claimed to be related to Ned, even if somewhat remotely, the academic decided to provoke his audience by claiming that a number of psychologists and historians of his acquaintance had put forward the hypothesis that Ned was homosexual.

Springing to Kelly's defence, one of the locals straightened himself up and, with a defiant look at the lecturer, said scornfully, 'I don't know anything about that, mate, but if he was, he would have been a bloody good one!'

A modern fable: An owl hovering in the forest spotted a rabbit in a small clearing. The rabbit was wearing gold-rimmed glasses and was seated at a computer typing away earnestly. Bemused, the owl perched in a tree and watched.

A huge black bear lurched into the clearing and roared, 'I am going to eat you for lunch.'

'No, no!' said the rabbit. 'I'm writing my thesis

on the topic that bears don't eat rabbits – rabbits devour bears.'

The bear guffawed, whereupon the rabbit said, 'Come into this cave and I'll show you.'

Into the cave they went. The owl heard screams and thuds.

After five minutes, the rabbit emerged, brushing a few specks of black fur from his pelt, sat down and resumed his typing.

A large grey wolf appeared. 'I'm going to eat you for dinner.'

'No, no!' said the rabbit. 'I'm writing this thesis on the topic that wolves don't eat rabbits – rabbits consume wolves.'

The wolf sneered, whereupon the rabbit said, 'Come into this cave and I'll show you.'

Into the cave they went. The owl heard screams and thuds. After five minutes the rabbit emerged, brushing grey hair from his pelt, sat down and resumed his typing.

The owl was puzzled. 'May I go into the cave you entered?' he asked.

'By all means,' answered the rabbit.

In the depths of the cave it was very dark, and even the owl had to wait a few moments before he could make out the scene inside. Then he saw an enormous lion, sitting on his haunches, surrounded by cleanly picked bones and a few patches of black and grey fur. Thoughtfully, he flew out.

'What I have witnessed must have a moral,' he told the rabbit.

'Yes,' said the rabbit, 'and here it is. It doesn't matter what the topic of your thesis is – as long as you've got a strong supervisor.'

Three kids were having an experimental smoke behind the school shelter shed.

'My dad can blow smoke through his nose.'

'My dad can blow smoke through his ears.'

'My dad blows smoke through his arse. You can see the nicotine stains in his undies.'

On the first day of school, the children were asked by their teacher what they did in their holidays.

Jasmine said, 'We went to Cairns and saw the rainforest and went on a boat to see the Barrier Reef. We had a lovely time.'

Brittany said, 'We went whale watching at Stradbroke Island. We camped and saw whales and dolphins. We had a top time.'

Aaron said, 'We went to stay on Uncle John's farm and we rode horses and helped with the milking. It was terrific.'

Rhys said, 'We had a great time. We put sticks of dynamite up cane toads' arses . . .'

The teacher said, 'Rhys! The correct term is rectum.'

'That's right, miss. Wrecked 'em! Blew their fuckin' brains out!'

A female teacher stands at the blackboard and says, 'Okay, kids, we're going to have a quiz today. Now, if there were three crows sitting on a fence, and a farmer shoots one, how many will be left?'

A smartarse puts up his hand and says, 'Ooo, me, Miss. I know this one!'

'Not you, Jeff. You're always answering.'

'But I know this one.'

'Okay, okay.'

'There'd be no crows left. One would be dead and the other two would've flown off at the gunshot.'

'No, no, no,' says the teacher. 'This is a maths quiz. If there were three and the farmer shot one, there'd be two left.'

So the smartarse kid says, 'Okay, Miss. I've got a little quiz for you. There are three women eating iceblocks. One of them's sucking it, one of them's licking it and one of them's biting it. Which one of the women is married?'

The teacher doesn't know how to answer. She

thinks a bit. She looks around. She thinks some more. 'Well,' she says finally, 'perhaps the woman who is sucking the iceblock.'

'No,' says the kid. 'It's the one with the wedding ring on her finger. But boy, I *like* the way you're thinking.'

A proud mother prepared her little boy for his first day at school. 'Now, if you want to have a wee-wee, hold up your hand in the class and the teacher will ask you what you want. Tell her you want to go to the toilet and she'll give you permission to leave the room.'

During his first class, the little boy felt the urge and put his hand up. The teacher asked what he wanted. 'I have to go to the toilet,' he said.

'Okay, it's the door on the right at the end of the corridor.'

A moment later he was back at the classroom door looking agitated. 'I can't find it,' he said.

The teacher said, very slowly and carefully, 'Go out, turn left, go to the end of the corridor, and through the door on the right.'

No sooner had he disappeared than he was back again, choking back tears.

'I still can't find it.'

The teacher hailed an older boy walking along the corridor and asked him to show the little lad where the toilet was. They disappeared. When they came back the teacher asked if everything was all right. He said, 'Yes, teacher. He had his underpants on back to front.'

It was a little bush school back o' Bourke. It was the first day for a new teacher, a young woman from the city. She stood nervously at the blackboard.

'Give me a word beginning with A.'

'Arsehole,' said little Mick.

She blushed and said, 'And a word beginning with B?'

'Bastard,' said Freddie.

She decided to give C a miss and asked for a word beginning with D.

'Dwarf,' said Johnny.

Sighing with relief, she asked Johnny to explain what a dwarf was. 'A little cunt about this big,' Johnny said.

The teacher was giving a spelling lesson. She turned to the first boy. 'Now, Tommy, tell the class what your father is, and spell it.'

'My father's a carpenter. C-a-r-p-e-n-t-e-r.'

'Very good, Tommy. Now, Eddie.'

'My father's a butcher. B-u-t-c-h-e-r.'

'Very good, Eddie. This class's spelling is improving.' She turned to the next boy. 'Now, Willie.'

'My father's a shipwright, teacher. S-h-i-t-w-r-i-g-h-t.'

'No, Willie. Try again.'

'S-h-i-t-w-r-i-g-h-t.'

'You are wrong again, Willie. The correct spelling is s-h-i-P-w-r-i-g-h-t. Go and write it on the blackboard. Now, while Willie's doing that, you, Charlie, stand up and tell us what your father is and spell it.'

Charlie jumped to his feet. 'My father's a bookmaker. B-o-o-k-m-a-k-e-r. And six to four Willie writes s-h-i-t on the board!'

'Miss Paterson, as headmaster I must remind you that it's against the rules at this school for teachers to fraternise with students. There's a high level of concern in the community about paedophilia.'

'Yes, sir, headmaster, I know.'

'I'm told that you have a husky young 15-year-old at your home most nights. Ostensibly doing homework.'

'Yes, but it's platonic.'

'Platonic?'

'Yes, it's play for him and tonic for me.'

An art teacher was trying to encourage her young students to approach drawing and painting with freshness, originality. So she drew a circle on the blackboard and asked if anybody could think of a way to use it to represent the theme of poverty.

Little Mildred drew the skeleton of a fish inside the circle. 'You see, a family had only a little fish for dinner. And all that's left on the plate are the bones.'

'Very good, Mildred. But if the people were experiencing real poverty, wouldn't they have boiled the bones to make fish soup?'

She rubbed out the fish, redrew the circle and asked for another suggestion.

Little Fiona stepped up to the blackboard. She drew a series of dots in the circle.

'This family had only a loaf of bread to eat. Those dots are the crumbs left on the plate.'

'But if they were really hungry, wouldn't they have licked the plate completely clean of crumbs, Fiona? Now, that would be real poverty.'

The teacher rubbed out the dots and redrew the circle. 'Anyone else?'

Little Bruce stepped up. He drew a small ring in the centre of the circle and criss-crossed it with thin, spidery lines.

'And what does that represent?' asked the teacher.

'That is a bum covered with cobwebs. And if that isn't poverty, I don't know what is.'

The biology teacher at Ascham was making sure her young ladies had done their homework.

'Angela,' she asked, 'please name for me the organ of the body which, under the right conditions, expands to six times its normal size.'

'I'm sorry, Miss,' said Angela, 'but that's hardly a fit and proper question to ask a nice girl.'

'Denise?' said the teacher, 'can you answer the question?'

'Yes, Miss,' said Denise, 'the pupil of the eye, in dim light.'

'Perfectly correct,' said the teacher. 'And now, Angela, I have just three things to say to you. Number one, you haven't done your homework. Number two, you've a dirty mind. And number three, one of these days you're going to be very, very disappointed.'

A new teacher had taken over the class and she was very pretty.

'How old do you reckon she is?' said young Bruce.

'Dunno. But if we can get her knickers off, we'll know.'

'How come?'

'Well, on the back of mine it says eight to ten years.'

The little boy was having trouble with arithmetic, and whatever the teacher asked him he'd count on his fingers.

'Two plus two?'

'Four.'

'Three and three?'

'Six.'

'Now I want you to stop using your fingers. Put your hands in your pockets and tell me what is five plus five.'

The kid fumbled quietly before he gave the answer.

'Eleven,' he said.

Animal Magnetism

A lady had a very beautiful cat. She utterly adored it. As is the wont of ladies who live alone and adore their cats, she lavished tender care on the truly magnificent animal. One evening as she sat by the fireside stroking his wonderful coat, she dreamed of him turning into a handsome prince. In that instant there was a flash of light. The whole world seemed electrified. And lo and behold, before her stood the most handsome prince anyone could possibly imagine. She was dumbfounded. Whereupon this gorgeous hunk of masculine pulchritude said, 'Aren't you sorry now that you took me to the vet last week?'

A bloke was walking his kelpie along by the river when it slipped and fell in. And although it was a terrific cattle dog, the damn thing couldn't swim. Fortunately a German tourist was taking photos of gumtrees when he saw what happened. Quick as a flash, he dived in, dragged the dog out and gave it mouth-to-mouth.

'Are you a vet?' asked the grateful owner.

'Vet?' replied the German. 'I'm bloody soaking!'

Some drovers were arguing over the relative intelligence of their dogs. 'This mongrel of mine,' said one bloke, 'never, never gets it wrong. And I'm not talking simple commands like "Stay" and "Sit" and "Heel". I'm talking about five-word sentences and instant obedience.'

'Bullshit,' said the others, and collected $50 to back their scepticism. There was soon $100 on the bar so the bloke picked up his dog, threw it in the fire and roared, 'Digger, get out of that fire!'

David Stratton was at the pictures watching *Sense and Sensibility*. There was a blind bloke sitting beside him, and beside him, a labrador. And Stratton couldn't help but notice that the dog seemed to be totally involved in the plot, growling here, giving little yelps there.

'Excuse me,' said Stratton to the blind bloke.
'Your dog is quite astonishing. I just can't get over it.'

'Frankly, it surprises me too,' said the blind man.
'He hated the book.'

A Northern Territory publican was at a loss about
what to do with prospectors and ringers who would
turn up at his pub after midnight demanding service
and then drinking until dawn. He had just about had
it, and decided to take a holiday in Sydney, where
he stayed with his mate who was the head keeper at
Taronga Park Zoo. After discussing his problem with
his friend, the mate said, 'We've got an old gorilla
we're about to retire, why don't you take him back
with you and use him as a bouncer?'

The publican thought this a great idea, and the
gorilla was duly installed in a room next to the bar at
the pub.

Next night, the publican was ready to close up
at 11 p.m., when six ringers from out of town arrived
and started what was obviously a very serious bout of
drinking. After several attempts to get rid of them,
the publican eventually released the gorilla at about
2 a.m. A massive brawl developed, which spilled out
into the dust outside, accompanied by shouting and
screaming. The terrified publican, apprehensive about
what he might be responsible for, waited behind the

bar. After a while the leader of the ringers staggered back into the bar, covered in blood and with most of his clothing torn off, shouting, 'Who was the bloody idiot who bought that gin a fur coat?'

An ant and an elephant got married despite the advice of their friends. During intercourse, the elephant died of a heart attack and the ant said, 'Damn it, five minutes of passion. Now a lifetime digging the grave.'

The bear and bunny were sitting side by side, both having a crap. 'Do you have any trouble with shit sticking to your fur?' the bunny asked the bear.

'No, not at all.'

Whereupon the bear promptly picked up the rabbit and wiped his arse with him.

A well-to-do matron had long nurtured an ambition to own a talking parrot. So one day she plucked up courage and visited her local pet shop.

When she told the pet shop owner what she wanted he said, 'Madam, I do have a talking parrot, it is the only one I have. But unfortunately it has spent all its life in a bordello, and, as you are obviously a woman of taste, I fear that its language would be likely to offend you.'

'Not at all,' said the woman. 'It would be fascinating to own a parrot with such an interesting background.'

Despite further attempts by the pet shop owner to discourage the woman, she would not be dissuaded and finally bought the parrot.

Now the woman thought she would surprise her family with her acquisition, so she arranged for a cover to be put over the cage, which she then smuggled into her house.

The woman's family consisted of two nubile daughters and a husband. She duly summoned them into the lounge room, announced that she had a surprise for them and whisked the cover from the cage.

The parrot blinked its eyes in the sudden light, looked around, saw the woman and said, 'Ah, a new Madam.' Then it spotted the daughters. 'And new girls.'

Finally the parrot looked at the husband and said, 'But the same old customers.'

A grasshopper hopped into a pub and ordered a G&T. 'Did you know there's a drink named after you?' the barman asked.

'What?' said the grasshopper. 'Bruce?'

An elephant was drinking from the Murray River when he noticed a turtle asleep on a log. He ambled over and kicked it clear across the river.

'What did you do that for?' asked a passing wombat.

'Because I recognised it as the same turtle that took a nip out of my trunk 53 years ago.'

'What a memory,' said the wombat.

'Yes,' said the elephant, 'turtle recall.'

'**H**ow did you get on with that giraffe last night?' asked the monkey.

'Well, I'll never take her out again,' said the squirrel. 'She's a nympha. And what with kissing her and screwing her, I was up and down all night.'

A bloke wanted to go to Surfers Paradise for a holiday, but had a problem – his pet cat. So he asked the bloke next door to look after it. At the end of the first week he rang the neighbour from Surfers and asked, 'How's my cat?'

'Dead.'

The bloke was deeply shocked by the news and when he recovered, complained to the neighbour about how he had presented him with the bad news.

'You should have been more subtle, and said, "Your cat's on the roof and we can't get it down. Ring back tomorrow". Then when I rang back the second day you could have said, "The cat fell off the roof and we took it to the vet". And on the third day, you could have broken it to me gently that the cat had died. Then it wouldn't have come as such a terrible, terrible shock. Incidentally, how's my mother?'

'She's on the roof and we can't get her down . . .'

There once was a farmer who had a very sexually active cockerel. This bird was formidable, he stopped at nothing. After serving the hens he would leap into geese, then the turkeys – anything dressed in feathers, he fucked.

One day, after observing the cockerel screwing a duck, the farmer approached the cock and said, 'You silly young bugger. If you keep this up, your vital pieces will be used up in no time and you'll go to an early grave.'

The cockerel just laughed at the farmer and leapt on a passing moorhen. A few days later the farmer noticed a flock of vultures slowly circling in the sky above the farmyard. There, in the centre of the yard, lying on his back, completely still, was the randy cockerel. The farmer, believing the cockerel to be dead, walked over and addressed the corpse. 'You dopey bird, I told you what all that fucking would do for you.'

At that the cockerel slowly opened one eye and pointed a wing at the vultures circling above. 'Shush,' he said. 'Don't frighten them – they're coming down.'

A blind man and his labrador were walking down the street when an old friend approached. So they stopped for a chat.

A codger coming the other way saw the dog and moved to avoid it. 'It's quite all right,' said the blind man. 'He's a friendly dog. He won't bite.'

'I'm not worried about him biting. But the way he lifted his leg, I thought the bugger was going to kick me.'

Somewhere in the saltbush country was an old cocky who had five sheepdogs, all named Fuckya. When asked to explain, the cocky said that he would get up in the morning, step outside and yell, 'Come here, Fuckya.' And the five dogs would come running.

A flea was sitting at a table in a roadhouse cafe, having a cup of coffee, when one of his mates entered. The second flea was wet, cold and shivering so the first flea asked, 'What's happened to you?'

I just got a lift on a bikie's moustache, but didn't know that he'd be driving all through the bloody night through the mountains. It's the middle of winter, and the rain's absolutely pissing down . . .'

The first flea replied, 'That's really dumb. You should do what I do: saunter into the nearest women's toilet, hop up on one of the seats, and when the opportunity comes along, grab a ride in some nice, warm, soft pubic hair.'

The second flea agreed to take his friend's advice, and they went their separate ways.

A week later, the first flea is sitting in the same cafe when his mate comes in wet, cold and shivering, as before.

'Didn't you take my advice?' he asked.

'Look, I did everything just as you told me. I was happily ensconced in some really nice lady's pubic hair, but just my bloody luck. Five minutes later I was back on the bikie's moustache!'

A bloke and his mongrel dog went into a posh restaurant, famous for its gourmet food and its string quartet. The head waiter said, 'I'm very sorry, sir, but we don't allow dogs in this restaurant.'

'But this isn't just any dog,' said the bloke, 'he was trained by that fellow on the ABC. He can speak too. Look, if he tells you the name of the composer who wrote that stuff the string quartet is playing, will you let us stay?'

'Perhaps,' said the head waiter.

'Okay, Blue. Who's the composer?'

'Bach,' went the dog.

'That's nonsense,' said the head waiter, throwing both bloke and dog out of the restaurant.

As they hit the pavement, the dog said, 'Sorry about the mistake. It was, of course, Mozart.'

A penguin decides to shoot down to Phillip Island and visit his rellies, so he hops into his car. It was an automatic – manuals are too hard to operate when you've got flippers. He gets to the crest of the bridge across the island when, *snap, bang, kerplunk*, the car goes bung. Luckily he sees a service station at the base of the bridge, so he rolls the car down, pulls up by a bowser, hops out and waddles around to the counter. 'Scuse I,' he says, 'but the car's ratshit. Can you have a look at it?'

The mechanic looks down at him from over the counter. 'Yeah, mate, no worries. But I've got a bit of a job on for a moment. It'll be an hour or so before I can have a look and give you any sort of verdict.'

'An hour? What am I going to do here in the middle of nowhere for a bloody hour?'

The mechanic says, 'There's a milk bar over the road. Why don't you just waddle over there?'

The penguin does so and after half an hour waddles back.

'Scuse I,' he says. 'My car, what's the prob?'

The mechanic leans over the counter and sees the penguin. 'Oh, you. Well, it looks like you've blown a seal.'

'No,' says the penguin furiously wiping his beak. 'No, I've just had an ice-cream!'

Three legs. Right ear chewed off. Blind in left eye. No teeth. Recently castrated. Answers to Lucky.

How do you tell which end of a worm is the head? Bury it in flour and wait till it farts.

How do you titillate an ocelot? Oscillate its tits a lot.

'Can you give me a lift into town?' asked a bloke leading a cow.

'Yeah, I can give you a lift,' said the motorist, 'but what about your cow?'

'No worries. She'll just follow along.'

So off they went, with the motorist checking in his rear-vision mirror. To his astonishment the cow broke into a trot. They accelerated to 80 km/h but the cow was still there, galloping along like a thoroughbred.

'Amazing,' the motorist muttered, accelerating to 90 . . . 100. And the cow was still there, thundering along.

When he got to 120 the motorist took another decko in the rear-vision mirror. 'I don't like the look of your cow, mate,' he said to the passenger. 'Her tongue's flopping out of the side of her mouth.'

'No worries,' said the bloke, 'that just means she's going to overtake.'

It was the Gundy Agricultural Show and there was a competition for the strangest pet. There was a three-legged dog, a four-legged spider, a one-winged parrot and a calf with two heads. But a kid won second prize with a tin of salmon.

What is the difference between a duck?
    One of its legs is both the same.

What do you call a blind dinosaur?
    Do you think he saw us?

What do you get when you cross an elephant with
a kangaroo?
    Big holes all over Australia.

What type of shoes do koalas wear?
    Gumboots.

How do you stop a dog fucking your leg?
    Give it a blow job.

What do you call a fly without wings?
    A walk.

What's the difference between a goldfish and a mountain goat?
One mucks around the fountain . . .

Why did the wombat cross the road?
To see his flat mate.

A horse walks into a bar and the barman says, 'Why the long face?'

An old Afghan in the Northern Territory was showing some tourists how to top up a camel with water. 'That way,' he said, 'you get an extra day out of them between drinks.'
As it bent down to drink, the Afghan picked up two bricks and bashed them over the poor creature's testicles. The camel sucked in its breath and, in doing so, took on three days' extra water.
'Doesn't that hurt?' inquired a tourist.
'Only if you get your fingers caught.'

A Bumpy Playing Field

A city bloke was holidaying at a merino stud. The farmer he was staying with said, 'It's a beautiful morning. Why not take the dogs and do a bit of shooting?'

'Great! Thanks.'

At lunch the farmer inquired, 'How was the shooting?'

'Terrific. Got any more dogs?'

A bloke climbed up the Harbour Bridge and stood teetering high, high above the water. He opened his haversack and pulled out a couple of budgies. He stuck one on his left shoulder and the other on the right. Then he took a great leap into the void, hitting the water at 200 km/h.

'Jesus,' he said, when the police fished him out more dead than alive. 'That budgie jumping isn't what it's cracked up to be.'

A bloke is marooned on a desert island. But he survives as there are plenty of coconuts and fresh water. Months pass and he sees a ripple about a hundred yards off shore. It keeps getting closer and closer until, at last, a tall blonde in full diving gear appears.

'You poor man,' she says. 'How long have you been here?'

He replies that he's lost all track of time and doesn't know. What he does know is that he's dying for a fag.

'No trubs,' she says, unzipping a pocket on the arm of her wetsuit and pulling out a packet of Winnies and a lighter.

Puffing happily, the bloke says he's in seventh heaven and she asks him if he'd like a beer.

'Would I!' So she unzips the other pocket and pulls out a can of Tooheys.

With a fag in one hand and a beer in the other, the bloke reckons he's got it made. Then the blonde starts to unzip the front of her wetsuit.

'Having been here all this time,' she says, 'I guess you'd like to play around.'

And the bloke says, 'How on earth did you fit a set of golf clubs down there?'

At an outback racetrack the stewards had long suspected the owner of doping his horses. So before the main race the chief steward followed him to the stables.

Watching closely, the steward saw the bloke slip something into his horse's mouth.

'Gotcha, you bastard,' he said, grabbing the bloke. 'You'll get rubbed out for life.'

'What are ya talking about?' said the owner. 'These are only homemade lollies the wife makes. Look, I'll show ya.' And he swallowed one. 'Here, you try one. They're beaut.' And he gave one to the steward who, somewhat confused, ate it.

The owner then led his horse to the saddling paddock. 'Get in front from the start and stay there.'

'Is anything likely to pass me?' asked the jockey.

'Just me,' said the owner, 'and the Chief Stipendiary Steward.'

Three gay blokes are having coffee during the Mardi Gras and describing their greatest aspirations.

Bryce explains, 'I want to have a lovely little

hairdretherth shop with perfumeth and shampooth and lots of nithe ladieth to chat to all day.'

'Oooo, how nithe!' the others exclaim.

Bruce says, 'I would like to be a thtar on sthage and lithen to all the applauth when I deliver another great performanth.'

'Oooo, tho good!' the others agree.

Brian isn't to be outdone. 'I would like to be a thtar footballer and play for Canberra against Canterbury in the grand final with the scoreth tied and a minute to go.'

'Be still my beating heart,' chorused the others.

'Canterbury kickth the ball into the air and it comes whithling towards me and I do a mighty leap and take the ball ath all those big bwuteth try to tackle me. But I do a dance and a leap and, with the wind whithling in my hair, run towards the try-line. Other bruteth try to tackle me but I leap and thidethtep and beat them. And the wind ith till whithling through my hair when, finally, there'th no one to stop me . . .'

'What happenth?' squealed his friends.

'Just then, I stop a metre short of the line. Can you imagine?'

The others look puzzled.

'Well, as the thiren goeth, 20 000 Canberra fans are thcreaming "Fuck him!"'

A Pakistani cricket umpire rolls up to the Pearly Gates and finds two signs dividing the crowd. One says 'Heroes' and the other says 'Everyone Else'.

There is a queue in front of the latter sign but the cricket umpire slots himself into the 'Heroes' line. St Peter appears and asks him why he should be classified a hero. The umpire smiles and says, 'I gave Javed Miandad out LBW on his front foot in Karachi, and that's why I should be considered a hero.'

St Peter is quite astonished at the fact that this umpire broke the unwritten rule that *nobody* gives Javed Miandad out LBW on his front foot in Karachi, and asks exactly when the umpire made this heroic call. 'Five minutes ago,' came the reply.

St Peter was standing at the Pearly Gates when Cathy Freeman and Lionel Rose approached, but he told them to go away because heaven did not admit Aborigines. St Peter told God what he had done, but God said to him, 'The Heaven Olympics are coming up. Go back and see if you can get them.' Peter went off but came back yelling, 'They're gone. They're gone!'

God asked him, 'Cathy and Lionel?'

But Peter answered, 'No, the Pearly Gates.'

(Arthur Tunstall, at a meeting of the Commonwealth Gates Association Executive Board in Sydney.)

By the time the building was evacuated, the whole block of flats was ablaze. The fire brigade was losing the battle and everyone was enjoying the excitement. Then a woman appeared at a fourth-floor window, holding a baby and screaming for help. But the fire brigade's ladder wouldn't reach.

Whereupon, Jack Dyer stepped forward and said, 'I'm Captain Blood, once captain of Richmond, member of the AFL's Hall of Fame and greatest ruckman ever. Throw the baby down to me. I've never dropped a mark in my life.'

The mother had no choice. She threw the baby down. Jack jumped into the air, took a screamer of a mark, and kicked a goal.

'Thank you for the swimming lesson,' said the attractive young woman, 'but will I really sink if you take your finger out?'

An Irish Rugby Union player emigrates to Australia and looks around for a rugby club to play with. Nobody's very interested, because he is not much of a player. Eventually, he finds a club willing to give him a go. 'But listen,' the coach says, 'I can't give you a full game. I'll have to pull you off at half-time.'

'That'll be lovely, that'll be lovely,' says the Irishman. 'Back home, we only get oranges at half-time.'

On his very first parachute jump, Harry found himself heading towards terra firma tugging furiously at an unresponsive ripcord. To his astonishment he saw someone rocketing up towards him. Always ready to make polite conversation, he yelled, 'Do you know anything about opening parachutes?'

'Sorry, mate,' came the reply. 'Do you know anything about lighting gas barbecues?'

Who's this an impersonation of?

'Click, how's that? Click, how's that? Click, click, how am I doing? Click, is that right? Click, how's that?'

Give up? A blind bloke with a Rubik's cube.

'Do you play much footy up this way?' the salesman asked the local.

'Yeah, just last week we had a great game against the Snake Gully mob. Blood everywhere. Two multiple fractures. Three broken legs. A couple of broken noses. Busted teeth. Ribs cracked. It was

125

bloody lovely.' He took another sip of his beer. 'And one or two of the players got hurt, too.'

A businessman bought a racehorse. Being a businessman he couldn't afford to take it round the race meetings, so he employed a man called Sam Finnell to cart the horse around the country and race it. So the opposition wouldn't know how it was doing, he said to Sam Finnell, 'Let me know how it's going, but do it in some sort of code.'

So after the first race out, the businessman received a telegram from Sam Finnell, which said, 'SF, SF, SF, SF.' He couldn't understand the telegram so when Sam got back he asked him, 'What's this all about?'

'It's code,' said Sam. 'It stands for Started, farted. Stumbled, fell. See you Friday. Sam Finnell.'

Two loonies go for a pushbike ride. After a few miles one gets off and lets his tyres down. 'What did you do that for?'

'My legs are too short to reach the pedals!'

Whereupon the second gets a spanner and turns his own bike seat around. 'If you're going to fuck around, I'm going home.'

There was a very promising horse which ran away with all the races, so that Tommy Smith wanted him to run in the Melbourne Cup. A marvellous horse, he could do anything, even talk. In fact, he used to grumble at the strict training when he was kept away from mares. By the eve of the Cup he was thoroughly fed up and insisted that unless he had a mare for the night he would not perform on the day. Tommy argued, but the horse was adamant: he must have a mare. Giving in, Tommy said, 'I'll make a bargain with you. If I can find a mare, you must promise me that it will be no more than once.' Pawing and snorting, the horse agreed.

Tommy searched around, but the best he could find was a zebra at the zoo. 'Here she is, mate. Now remember, only once.'

The next morning, Melbourne Cup day, Tommy arrived at the stables to find the horse with head drooping, exhausted, and the zebra much the same. 'You bastard, you promised only once!' Tommy exclaimed.

'Only once!' snorted the horse. 'I've spent all night trying to get the bloody pyjamas off!'

It was a country cricket match. Bill was the club's fast bowler but knew he was going to have a bad day when he discovered that his father-in-law was to umpire the match. Bill's first ball caught the batsman LBW. 'Owzat!'

'Not out,' said the ump.

The second ball snipped the bat to be caught by the wicket-keeper. 'Owzat!'

'Not out.'

Getting really shitty, Bill bowled the fastest ball of his career. It not only hit the middle stump but splintered it, sending the bails into orbit.

'Nearly got him that time,' said Bill.

Pat Cash and Ivan Lendl played an exhibition match at Yalara. After the match they went for a walk together to see Uluru as the sun set. When they were out in the scrub a bit they were confronted by two dingoes. Cash was able to escape, but Lendl was caught by the dingoes, one of which began to eat Lendl as Cash ran for help.

Cash returned soon after with a couple of rangers. They found the dingoes still there, but there was no sign of Lendl.

'Which one was it that ate Lendl?' asked the rangers.

'That one there,' said Cash, pointing to the larger of the two dingoes.

'Now, you're sure? You're sure it was the male one?'

'I'm sure,' said Cash.

So the rangers killed the male dingo and split

open its belly. But there were no bits of Lendl in the dingo's stomach.

Moral: never believe a Victorian when he says the Czech's in the male.

A couple of blokes went fishing in the Gulf of Carpentaria. One had brought the grog and the other was supposed to have brought the bait. But, instead, they both turned up with grog. And no bait.

They were sitting on the beach drinking their grog and wondering about bait when they saw a dirty great carpet snake with a frog in its mouth. So they dribbled some grog on the snake's head and as its fork tongue reached out to lick it, they grabbed the frog. The frog made great bait and they caught a couple of barramundi. Trouble was, the frog was a bit past it, whereupon one of the blokes felt a tap on the shoulder – and there was the snake with another frog.

A duck shooter was banging away at ducks at a billabong between Albury and Wodonga. He'd just shot a couple of birds and was sloshing through the water to retrieve them when a game warden shouted at him from the Victorian bank.

'Hey, the duck season is over in Victoria!'

'So what?' said the shooter. 'I shot these in New South Wales.'

'Doesn't matter,' said the warden. 'They could be our ducks.'

'Come off it,' said the shooter, 'they're bloody wild ducks.'

'Don't argue with me. I'm an expert. Chuck me a duck,' said the warden.

Muttering imprecations the shooter tossed him one of the ducks. The warden caught it, parted its tail feathers and shoved his finger up its bum. He then withdrew his digit and sniffed it. 'Okay, that's a New South Wales duck. Now chuck me the other one.'

'What a load of crap,' said the sportsman. 'They were flying together, side by side. I shot them both with one blast.'

'Don't argue. I'm an expert. Did a three-year course in ducks. Toss me the other one.'

The shooter tossed the second duck.

Once again, the warden caught it, parted the tail feathers, shoved his finger up its bum and, retrieving it, took a long sniff.

'Gotcha,' he said. 'This duck is a Victorian duck.'

'Bullshit,' said the shooter.

'Don't argue with me,' said the ranger. 'I'm an expert and I'm going to write you out a ticket. What's your name?'

'Bill Smith.'

'Where are you from, Bill?'

'Richmond.'

'Richmond Victoria, or Richmond New South Wales?'

Bill undid his belt, dropped his daks, and said, 'You're the bloody expert. You tell me.'

A Fitzroy footballer went one Saturday night to a dance at the Richmond Town Hall, and because the local girls would not be seen dancing with him, eventually got into a conversation with a very beautiful girl in a wheelchair. When the dance had finished, she agreed that he could wheel her home. While walking through the park, she said to him, 'Just because I'm in a wheelchair doesn't mean I don't appreciate the finer things in life, you know – if you want to do something about it.'

The Fitzroy man was amazed. 'Yeah, okay. But how do you manage?'

'It's simple,' she said. 'In the boot of the wheelchair I keep this leather harness. All you've got to do is hang me up in a tree, and you can go for it.'

When he had finished and had put the girl back in the wheelchair, she said to him. 'You are a Fitzroy boy, aren't you?'

'Yeah,' he said, 'but how did you know?'

'Well, the Collingwood and Richmond blokes always leave me hanging in the tree.'

Two blokes decided that they would like a game of golf, and one suggested that it might be nice to invite old Charlie, who was known to like a game, but was a bit frail these days.

Well, old Charlie was delighted with the idea. So off they set. Somewhere approaching the fourth green, one bloke remarked to the other that he hadn't seen old Charlie for a while. The other replied that he had seen him heading for the rough after his tee shot, and that maybe they had better have a look for him, as he'd obviously lost his ball.

They fished around the rough for a while and eventually found old Charlie with the greenkeeper chock-a-block up him.

'What the hell do you think you're doing to old Charlie?' they yelled. And the greenkeeper said, 'He had a heart attack and stopped breathing.'

So the blokes say, 'You're supposed to give a bloke mouth-to-mouth resuscitation when he has a heart attack, not fuck him.'

A dignified English solicitor-widower with a considerable income had long dreamed of playing Sandringham, one of Britain's most exclusive golf courses, and one day he made up his mind to chance it when he was travelling in the area.

Entering the clubhouse, he asked at the desk if he might play the course. The club secretary inquired, 'Member?'

'No, sir.'

'Guest of member?'

'No, sir.'

'Sorry.'

As he turned to leave, the lawyer spotted a slightly familiar figure seated in the lounge, reading the *London Times*. It was Lord Parnham. He approached and, bowing low, said, 'I beg your pardon, your Lordship, but my name is Higginbotham of the London solicitors Higginbotham, Willingby and Barclay. I should like to crave your Lordship's indulgence. May I play this beautiful course as your guest?'

His Lordship gave Higginbotham a long look, put down his paper and asked, 'Church?'

'Church of England, sir, as was my late wife.'

'Education?'

'Eton, sir, and Oxford.'

'Sport?'

'Rugby, sir, a spot of tennis and number four on the crew that beat Cambridge.'

'Service?'

'Brigadier, sir, Coldstream Guards, Victoria Cross and Knight of the Garter.'

'Campaigns?'

'Dunkirk, El Alamein and Normandy, sir.'

'Languages?'

'Private tutor in French, fluent German and a bit of Greek.'

His Lordship considered briefly, then nodded to the club secretary and said, 'Nine holes.'

'**I**t took me bloody hours to play a round with Robbo today. He had a heart attack and died on the fifth hole. And it's bloody hard going drag, hit, drag, hit, drag, hit!'

The club secretary explained to the member that he couldn't play today because the course was fully booked. 'But I've been a member for 30 years.'

'Sorry, sir,' said the club secretary.

'If John Howard lobbed here for a game today, I bet you'd make room for him.'

The secretary conceded the point.

'Well, I just happen to know that the little bastard's in Canberra. So I'll take his place.'

There was a great outcry after Phar Lap's death. The doctors performed an autopsy to see if he'd been poisoned. Among other things, they were surprised to find splinters in the thoroughbred's bum. Finally the penny dropped. The horse had a very close association with young strapper Tommy Woodcock.

Three guys are playing golf. The guys playing ahead of them are so excruciatingly slow that the three are losing their temper. So they walk back to the clubhouse and scream at the manager, 'Can't you get those guys off the course?'

The manager says, 'They're blind.'

So the guy in the pink shirt says, 'Oh, holy Mother, how could I ever have had such thoughts? Everything I believe in. I'll never forgive myself.'

The second guy, a minister, says, 'I taught compassion and understanding and forgiveness all my life.'

And the rabbi says, 'Why can't they play at night?'

Some Australian tourists were in Barcelona for the Olympics and found themselves in a small restaurant in a side street. They were served magnificent meals of rissoles, two to a plate. Having scoffed them, they asked the waiter the name of the dish. 'Gonads,' he said, explaining that they were the testicles of two bulls killed in the Barcelona bullring the previous day. The first reaction of the Australian was to feel somewhat squeamish, but, after all, the dish had been delicious.

So the next day they decided to order it again. However, the waiter apologised, saying that he could only serve one of them. And this time the rissoles were a fraction of the size. 'Sorry, senor. But as you can see, yesterday a bull won.'

What has Princess Diana got in common with Gary Ablett?

They're both fucking good footballers.

A bloke's running a BB rifle range amongst the sideshows at the Royal Melbourne Show. There's a row of very battered tin ducks marching across the back of the tent. A drunk weaves into view and demands a go at the *bing, bing, bing*. After trying to talk the drunk out of it – pointing to the dangers of someone in his state having control of a rifle – the stallholder surrenders. After all, business has been slow.

To his astonishment, the drunk knocks three ducks over – *bing, bing, bing*. 'Shit,' says the stallholder, 'you've won a prize.' And he reaches under the counter and pulls a small live tortoise from a bucket.

'Bewdy,' says the drunk and, taking his prize, he staggers off.

A while later he presents himself, if anything slightly more inebriated, demanding another go. This time the stallholder is even more reluctant to hand over the rifle. But, bugger it, there's not exactly a queue of customers. So he pockets another deener and gives the bloke another go. Once again it's *bing, bing, bing*. Down go three tin ducks. 'Christ,' says the stallholder in astonishment, 'you've won another bloody prize.' And reaching down he presents the drunk with a kewpie doll.

'What's that?' the drunk asks.

'It's your prize. A kewpie doll.'

'I don't want a bloody kewpie doll. I want a meat pie, like last time.'

The local cop calls a mate. 'Bad news, cobber. We've just found your mother-in-law. Her corpse, that is. Wedged in the mangroves. All swollen and horrible, with four dirty great muddies having a go at her.'

'Four muddies! That's terrific. Two for you, two for me . . . and we can put the old biddy back for bait.'

A bloke drove off the first tee at Royal Melbourne and sliced right over the fence on to the road. Without bothering to look where his ball landed, he played another. After the round, the club pro approached him and said, 'You know that drive you sliced off the first tee? It hit a bloke on a motorbike who swerved in front of a truck which ran through the fence on to a railway line and collided with the Southern Aurora. They're still going through the wreckage but the death toll so far is 37, with more than a hundred in hospital.'

'Christ Almighty,' said the golfer. 'What should I do?'

'Turn your right hand over a bit,' said the pro, 'and don't grip so hard with your left.'

D ave, a very strong swimmer, well known to the local lifesavers, was out beyond the breakers when a shark appeared. He began waving frantically to the lifesaver on duty. The lifesaver gave him a friendly wave in return.

Meanwhile, however, the shark had removed one of Dave's legs. *Chompf!* Dave tried waving again. The lifesaver waved back.

Chompf! Off went the second leg. This provoked even more frantic waving, which, once again, elicited a cheerful response.

Chompf! Off went the right arm, leaving only the left arm to wave. He waved it, and the lifesaver, by now getting sick of waving, gave a token response.

Chompf! The last limb had gone. Now, belatedly, the lifesaver noticed a crimson stain surrounding Dave. He charged into the water.

He finally arrived by Dave's torso and told the poor bloke to balance on his back so that both his arms would be free for swimming. And with the shark circling them both, the lifesaver heroically, miraculously made it back to the beach.

'Jeez, I'm buggered,' he groaned.

Dave, still on his back, said, 'Sorry about that. But it was the only way I could hang on.'

In the Political Asylum

Liberal Party. Braille Party.
   Labor Party. Rort by a pal.
   Coalition. I-anti-cool.
   Democrats. Mad sect.
   Peter Costello. Lo, elector pest.
   Alexander Downer. Wander, axed loner.
   Gareth Evans. Hear gas vent.
   Cheryl Kernot. Tory hen-clerk.

The cocky went into town and bought a new colour
telly. He took it home in the back of his ute and
tried it out. Then he rang the electrical store
spewing. 'This bloody telly you sold. All I get on it is
politicians. No matter what channel I turn to, it's
only politicians.'

The store said they'd send a repair man out. When he got back to town the shopowner asked him what happened.

'The poor old bloke really did have a problem,' said the repair man. 'Nothing but politicians on every channel. You see, he was using his windmill for an antenna and had the thing earthed on his manure spreader.'

Why is Ros Kelly like Divine Brown?
Because they both know how to blow huge grants.

As the 1996 federal election campaign neared its end, Paul Keating was trying to remain cheerful and optimistic. 'Look. There are big crowds and they're still waving.'

'Yes,' says an aide, 'but they seem to be holding up less fingers.'

Wycheproof has a train line going right through the middle of town. And right in the middle of the town there is a town hall where a council meeting was going hammer and tong. Suddenly the door opened and a bloke rushed in. 'My mini-bus is stalled on the railroad tracks. I want to ask that it be moved.'

'I say move,' cried a voice from the back of the hall.

'I second it,' said another.

The mayor banged his gavel and said, 'You've heard the motion. All in favour say "aye".'

'Aye,' came the chorus.

'So ordered. Now let's get on with the other business that we were talking about.'

Bob Hawke and John Hewson are standing beside one another at the urinal in Parliament House. Hewson looks over at Bob and says, 'Bob, for such a small man you have a very large member. What's your secret?'

Bob says, 'Every time I go to see my mistress I take the member out, and as I walk up the stairs to where she awaits me in bed, I give it a knock against the wall. It gets big and swollen. It's a bit sore but the pain soon goes.'

That night Hewson decides to try this. As he walks up the stairs he takes out his member and knocks it against the wall. *Thwack! Thwack!*

Mrs Hewson leans out of bed and shouts, 'Is that you, Bob?'

Following the cancellation of a Canberra flight an Ansett ticketer was trying to handle a long queue of passengers when a formidable-looking woman, with a beehive hairdo, pushed her way to the front. 'Get me on this flight. First class.'

'Sorry, madam, you'll have to take your turn. As you can see, there's a long queue of people before you.'

Mrs Bishop was outraged. 'Do you have any idea who you're talking to?'

The ticketer smiled, reached for the PA mike and turned up the volume. 'May I have your attention please? We have a passenger here who doesn't know who she is. If anyone can identify her, please come to the counter.'

When Russ Hinze died, the mortician couldn't find a coffin big enough for the infamous pollie. His anguish was noted by a colleague who said, 'Well, you know what politicians are full of.'

So they gave Russ an enema and buried him in a matchbox.

If you had Idi Amin, Saddam Hussein and Paul Keating in a room with a gun with two bullets, who would you shoot?

Keating. Twice.

In Canberra rectal thermometers were banned when it came to light that they were causing brain damage to politicians.

I'm glad that I'm Australian
I'm glad that I am free
I wish I were a little dog
And Howard was a tree.

In a very small town in northern Queensland a local councillor, who everyone thought was a prick, proposed that a bridge be built over a local creek. It was clear that the bridge would be of little benefit – except to the councillor who happened to be in the bridge-building business.

So another councillor jumped up and said, 'Put a bloody bridge over the silly little creek? It hasn't had any water in it for 20 years. And I could spit halfway across the bugger.'

The first councillor called upon the mayor. 'He's out of order, Mr Chairman. Out of order.'

'I know that,' said the dissenting councillor, 'otherwise I'd spit right across the bloody thing.'

Alexander Downer lands at Washington airport carrying a personal letter for President Bill Clinton from the Prime Minister of Australia. Standing on the tarmac, he hands it to Clinton as the photographers capture the moment. What does the letter say? *Please ignore this man. He's an idiot!*

It was day one of the year at the one-teacher school at Condamine, and two of the new enrolments were twin boys who gave their names as Robert Hawke O'Brien and Paul Keating O'Brien. The teacher wrote a note to the mother:

Dear Mrs O'Brien, these names do not seem correct. Please verify.

Back came the reply: *If you can think of two better names for a pair of bastards, you tell me.*

The late Bob Katter, the father of the current Bob Katter of National Party fame, was once driving through the backblocks of Queensland during a drought. His Land Cruiser got stuck in wheel ruts on a narrow track, and he proceeded to bowl along them. It was the line of least resistance.

Suddenly a cloud of dust appeared on the horizon. It was an approaching vehicle, also stuck in the tracks. Katter decided to stay in his rut, forcing the approaching driver to swerve. It was a woman, who wound down her window and screamed, 'Pig!'

'Bitch!' Katter shouted back.

He accelerated into the cloud of dust only to run smack into the biggest wild pig in Queensland.

Having just died, a man is sitting in the devil's waiting room anticipating his pre-admission interview. He notices that all the walls are covered in clocks – and they're all running at quite different speeds. Wanting to know the significance of the clock arrangement, the dead man approaches the receptionist and asks her for an explanation. The girl explains that there's a clock for every person on Earth, that the more lies the person tells, the faster his or her clock runs. Being impressed by technology, the man wanders through long hallways looking at the names under the countless millions of clocks, and noting the various speeds at which they're running. After a few hours, he returns to the reception desk and tells the girl that he hasn't been able to locate a clock for Peter Costello. The girl looks at him and says, 'Oh, Peter Costello – the devil keeps Peter's clock in his office and uses it as a fan.'

Three blokes are in a boat surrounded by crocodiles. The boat breaks down. People on the shore yell out, 'Don't jump overboard, the crocs will get you.' But the first bloke ignores them. He swims bravely towards the shore and gets eaten halfway. The second bloke has the same fate. The third bloke disappears from sight in the bottom of the boat and re-emerges in the nuddy with something written on his bum. He dives overboard and makes it safely to the shore. 'What did you do?'

'I wrote, *Carmen Lawrence told the truth* on my left buttock . . . and the crocs wouldn't swallow that.'

'Your Majesty, make Australia a kingdom and make me the king.'

'Mr Keating, I'll make it a country and you can be what you are.'

At a political rally a heckler called, 'Clinton should be bloody well hung.'

Whereupon Hillary Clinton said, 'Unfortunately he is.'

'Mr Howard, have you heard the latest political jokes?'

'Heard them? They're all in the Cabinet.'

The Arab sheik asked his sons what they wanted for Christmas. The eldest son wanted a new Lear jet, the second son wanted a Lamborghini, and the third son wished for a cowboy outfit.

On Christmas day the plane and the car were delivered to the palatial tent. But there was no cowboy outfit. The little boy was very, very upset. At last a fax arrived saying that there was a package on the wharf in Kuwait.

So they climbed into the Lamborghini and drove into town. And there, on the wharf, was a big container wrapped in cellophane.

The sheik said to his son, 'Here, at long last, is your cowboy outfit.'

The kid opened the container and inside was the Queensland government.

Prime Minister Howard stood proudly on the dais beside the Governor-General on Anzac Day. Thousands upon thousands of old vets passed, each proffering the official party a snappy salute. They were followed by squadrons of jets, lines of tanks, heavy artillery and columns of infantry. Finally a group of men carrying briefcases, marching out of step, brought up the rear.

'Is that your secret service, Prime Minister?' asked a foreign diplomat.

'No, they're Treasury's economists. And they're more dangerous than the rest put together.'

One day, several years ago, a White House aide approached the President in a state of great agitation.

'Mr President, it pains me to tell you this, but I've just seen the First Lady cavorting naked as a jaybird with a fellow in the Oval Office.'

The President was aghast. 'Who's the guy – I'll kill him!'

'Sir, I can't remember his name, but you know him. The guy with the German name who's a diplomat.'

'You mean he's Kissinger!?'

'No, Mr President, he's fucking her!'

Law and Disorder

What's wrong with the design of police stations?
    They're above water.

What's 40 cm long and hangs from arseholes?
    Police ties.

What sort of animal has a cunt halfway up its back?
    A police horse.

Mr Plod is walking through the local park when he
sees a couple bonking near the little Anzac memorial.

''Allo, 'allo, 'allo,' he says, feeling somewhat stimulated. All the more when he recognises the woman as the district's most attractive prostitute.

Looking around to make sure no one's about, he says to the bloke, 'Hey, can I be next?'

'Dunno,' says the bloke. 'I've never fucked a copper before.'

Laurie Connell kicked the bucket in the middle of his trial. He left behind him a grieving family and a great many grieving debtors. At the funeral, the handful of mourners were surprised to see a security truck pull up outside the church and the guards hauling out dozens of gold bars.

The chief security guard explained, 'He stipulated in his will that he wanted to be buried with all the money he had hidden away in the Swiss banks and the Cook Islands. So we're here to load up the coffin.'

They finished putting all the bars in the coffin and the service was held. But when the pallbearers tried to carry it out, it was far, far too heavy to lift, no matter how hard they strained.

Suddenly the first pallbearer, Kerry Packer, opened the coffin and started taking out the gold bars and shoving them into his pockets. The other pallbearers, who were almost as famous, started grabbing gold bars too.

'Just a second,' cried the preacher. 'He wanted to be buried with his money.'

'It's okay,' said Kerry, 'we're leaving him a cheque.'

A pompous bank vice-president from one of the larger city banks was on holidays back of the black stump. Passing through a small country town, he decided to visit the local branch to see how things were going. The one-room bank was completely empty with the front and back doors wide open. Through the back door he could see the bank manager and teller and two stockmen playing cards on the verandah of the bank's residence.

He thought to himself, 'I'll throw a real fright into this sloppy operation', and leaned over the counter and turned on the bank's alarm, which echoed from one end of the town to the other.

The card players did not even look up from their game. But a minute later the publican from the hotel opposite the bank ran across the street into the front door and out the back door carrying four beers for the players.

'We're sacking the accountant.'

'Why?'

'He's too shy and retiring.'

'Is that a reason to sack him?'

'Yes, he's 200 000 shy. And that's why he's retiring.'

The local council decided to plonk a dirty great fountain in the middle of the local park, between the new brick loos and the barbecue area. They put the project to tender and got three quotes, from contractors in Melbourne, Sydney and Brisbane.

They interviewed the Brisbane tenderer first. 'How much?'

'Three thousand dollars.'

'How do you break that down?'

'Well, it's a thousand for the fountain, a thousand for me and a thousand for you.'

The Town Clerk called in the Sydney contractor. 'How much?'

'Six thousand dollars.'

'And how do you break that down?'

'Two thousand for the fountain, two thousand for me and two thousand for you.'

Next the clerk called in the Melbourne bloke who said that his price would be nine thousand dollars.

'And how do you break that down?'

'Well, it's three thousand each and we give the job to the bloke from Brisbane.'

A guy was out bush one day when his four-wheel drive broke down in the middle of nowhere. In keeping with accepted practice he stayed with his vehicle hoping someone would rescue him. After four or five days no one had arrived, and, having run out of food, decided to set off on foot and look for help.

Tired and hungry, he'd walked miles before he stumbled across a bush stream with a log straddled across it. As he attempted to cross the stream the log broke under his weight and landed on a platypus, killing it. Hungry, the man thought he may as well eat it.

Just as he was eating the platypus, a park ranger came along and pinched him for eating a protected species. He was subsequently hauled off to court.

'You are charged with eating an endangered and protected species. Have you anything to say for yourself before I pass sentence on you?' asked the judge.

'Well, as a matter of fact, sir, yes I have,' said the man indignantly. 'There I was, caught out in the bush with my broken-down four-wheel drive. I thought I'd do the right thing like they always tell us and I stayed by my vehicle for fair on nearly a week, but no one came. I thought, blow this, I'm off. So I head off into the scrub, tired and hungry, and suddenly came across this stream with a log over it. As I stepped onto the log it broke and fell into the stream and hit this poor platypus on the head. There wasn't much I could do about it; it was dead. I was hungry, so I thought I'd eat it. Just as I was eating it along came the park ranger – and I don't mind telling you, your Honour, I was very glad to see him.'

'Well, said the judge, 'that sounds like a reasonable story – case dismissed!'

'Thank you, your Honour,' said the man.

As the man was about to leave the courtroom the judge called out to him, 'By the way, tell me, what does platypus taste like?'

'Well, your Honour,' said the man, 'it sort of tastes like a cross between koala and dolphin.'

Three lads were roaring around the backblocks of Queensland in a panel van. They were doing wheelies outside the Town Hall when the cops pulled them over. 'Don't give your real names,' hissed the driver.

A cop asked the bloke sitting in the middle his name. He saw a neon sign over the cop's shoulder. 'David Jones,' he replied.

Now the cop turned to the other passenger. 'And what's your name?'

'Aaah, G. J. Coles.'

Now the cop circled the ute to the driver. 'Okay, name?'

'Aaah. Ken.'
'Ken? Ken what? I suppose you're Ken bloody
Myer. What's your last name?'
'Tucky Fried Chicken.'

What's the difference between a lawyer and a leech?
A leech drops off you when you die.

Why is it dangerous for a lawyer to walk on to a
building site?
Because they might connect the drain line to
the wrong suer.

A group of New Guinean headhunters set up a sales
stand in the Sepik River, advertising the following
menu:
Sauteed tourist, $20.
Roasted reporter, $25.
Diced diplomat, $15.
Lawyer shashlik, $200.
A customer, noticing the price differential, asked
why lawyers cost so much. The headhunter replied,
'Have you ever tried to clean one of those bastards?'

A lawyer returns to his parked BMW to find the headlights broken and considerable damage to the bonnet. There's no sign of the offending vehicle but he's relieved to see that there's a note stuck under the windscreen wiper. *Sorry. I just backed into your Beemer. The witnesses who saw the accident are nodding and smiling at me because they think I'm leaving my name, address and other particulars. But I'm not.*

What's the difference between a vulture and a lawyer?
The vulture doesn't get frequent flyer points.

The local magistrate had had a busy morning fining prostitutes and dealing with domestic violence cases. He was, as usual, dealing with the low-life of the city. So imagine his astonishment when he found himself with the most respectable-looking bloke he'd ever seen in his court.

And indeed he was respectable. He was a JP, Treasurer of the local Rotary Club, and worked as a chartered accountant.

'Sir, why did you climb to the top of the flagpole outside the Town Hall, shout abuse at people passing by and then fart "Advance Australia Fair"?'

The defendant thought about it for a moment or two. 'Well, it's like this, your Honour. If I didn't do something mad once in a while, I'd go crazy.'

'**H**ave you anything to say for yourself?' asked the judge.

'Fuck all,' said the bloke in the dock.

'What did your client say?' asked the judge.

The barrister approached the bench and whispered, 'He said, "Fuck all", your Worship.'

'Odd,' said his Worship, 'I was sure I saw his lips move.'

'**I**'m looking for a fugitive from the law.'

'Tell me what he looks like.'

'Well, his name is the Brown Paper Kid.'

'The Brown Paper Kid?'

'Yeah, he wears a brown paper Akubra, a brown paper shirt, brown paper jeans and brown paper boots. And he's got a brown paper holster which holds a brown paper gun that shoots brown paper bullets.'

'What's he wanted for?'

'Rustling.'

A Ford Fairlane was driving very erratically through the streets of Brisbane when it attracted the attention of a cop car. They flashed the lights and hit the siren and got the driver to stop. 'Would you mind blowing into this bag?' the police said.

'I can't,' said the driver. 'I'm a chronic asthmatic.'

'Well, sir, how about accompanying us to the station for a blood test?'

'Sorry, officer, I'm a haemophiliac.'

'Well, sir, surely you wouldn't mind stepping out of your vehicle and walking along a straight line?'

'No way. I'm too bloody pissed.'

Criminal in the dock: 'As God is my judge, I am not guilty.'

Judge: 'He's not, I am and you are.'

A young police constable was giving evidence about the defendant's language at the time of arrest. He was having some difficulty in giving the evidence and he hesitated before repeating the words the defendant was alleged to have said.

'Well, go on,' said the magistrate.

'But there are women in court,' replied the constable.

'They won't mind. Go on, tell us what the defendant said.'

'Perhaps I could write it down, sir?'

'He obviously didn't say that, did he, constable? Come on, get on with it . . .'

'Well, sir, he said, "All you coppers are cunts!"'

'Goodness! That's shocking! I didn't know the proportion was *that* high, but keep going,' said the magistrate.

Occupational Hazards

An historian at the War Museum in Canberra was trying to establish why General Monash had been so successful in the First World War, why his troops had been so successful in charging the Germans. Again and again, Australian soldiers had taken far more ground than the pommies. It turned out that Monash always used a special reserve unit made up of accountants. 'When it came time to order them to charge,' Monash wrote in his diary, 'boy, did they know how to charge!'

An accountant arrives at the office and, first thing every morning, unlocks his desk drawer to look at a small piece of paper. He then replaces it and relocks the drawer. He does this, every day, for years.

Eventually he retires and the accountant sitting at the next desk unlocks the drawer and reads the tattered piece of paper. It says, *Debit column is the one nearest the window.*

A hooker went off duty at the Cross and climbed into a cab. 'Would you take me home, please, to Coogee.'

When the cab stopped, she said, 'Bugger, I've forgotten my purse.'

'Well, how are you going to pay for the trip?'

She promptly lifted her skirt. 'With this?'

'Haven't you got anything smaller?'

An old magician who'd worked the vaudeville circuit for years was booked on the Titanic on its maiden voyage. His job was to amuse the first-class passengers during dinner. He was a bit down on his luck and couldn't afford the traditional leggy assistant. He had to make do with a parrot whom he taught to say funny things to the audience like, 'It's under his cloak', or 'It's up his sleeve'. They were halfway through their act one night when the Titanic hit the iceberg. And sank. With an immense death toll.

The magician clung to a piece of flotsam while

the parrot fluttered overhead. He managed to stay
afloat all next day, despite the freezing water, and
still the parrot fluttered. That night the parrot finally
landed on the magician's head.

'Okay, I give up. What have you done with the
bloody ship?'

A young actor walks into a famous talent agency
determined to be signed up. He bursts into song,
tells a few jokes and does a great tap dance.

'You're very good,' says the agent. 'What's your
name?'

'Penis van Lesbian,' says the young bloke.

'Sorry, we'll have to change that for a start.
We'll call you Dick van Dyke.'

A young guy went to a casting agency to do an
audition. While he waited to be called, he saw an
assortment of jugglers, fire-eaters and magicians.

When it was his turn, the casting agent said,
'Hurry up now, I'm a busy, busy man. So what is it
you do, exactly?'

The boy said, 'Well, actually, I do a bird
impersonation.'

The casting agent's face clouded over and he

said, 'Listen, boy, don't you realise this is the 1990s? You'll never get anywhere doing bird impersonations. Get out of here and stop wasting my time.'

So the boy said, 'Stuff you,' and flew out the window.

A couple of blokes from Delhi fronted the employment office to inquire about getting a job.

'Well, what were your previous occupations?' asked the assessment officer.

'I ran a street stall in a market. Did very, very good business selling ladies pantihose.'

'Mmmm,' said the assessment officer, 'you may have some difficulty in Australia. We already have lots and lots of street stalls and market traders. And what about you? What job did you do in India?'

'I was a diesel fitter.'

'A diesel fitter? That's excellent. There's a big demand in Australia for skilled diesel fitters. What company did you work for in India?'

'Oh, I worked with my mate on his stall in the market.'

'I don't understand. He sold pantihose. What role could a diesel fitter play?'

'Well, he'd run around the stall yelling out, "Pantihose! Pantihose!" And I'd yell out, "Diesel fit her. Diesel fit her."'

'The current generation of mobile phones is incredibly old fashioned. They're out of date already. As a matter of fact, I've been electronically wired. So when I want to make a call I simply do this. I talk into my thumb.'

'Fair dinkum?'

'Yes, allow me to demonstrate. "Hello, can you put me through to Frank Blount, the Managing Director of Telstra? G'day, Frank. Sorry to bother you, but I'm just demonstrating the new technologies to some blokes at the pub." Here, say hello to Frank.'

'Is that you, Frank?'

'Yes, this is Frank Blount.'

'Christ, that's amazing.'

'Ouch!'

'What's the problem? Why are you bending over like that?'

'Don't worry, it's just a fax coming through.'

The encyclopaedia salesman wasn't having much luck. No one in central New South Wales seemed all that interested in the 24-volume Britannica with year books and the little 'assemble-it-yourself' bookstand. Not when it cost a couple of thousand bucks.

One Friday night saw him sitting sadly in a country pub, nursing a beer. He realised he was down to his last $50. That was that. After spending that, he'd be flat broke. Then, glancing around at the other blokes in the bar, who looked inbred and stupid, inspiration struck.

'My set of encyclopaedias is worth a couple of grand retail,' he said. 'But if any of you blokes can answer three questions that I select from the information therein, I'll give the whole bloody set to you for a hundred bucks. And if you can't answer all three questions, it's a hundred bucks to me. What do you reckon?'

There was movement amongst the gathering and a few mumbled exchanges. Finally a big, slow-moving bloke moved towards the salesman. 'I'll have a go,' he said. There were any number of approving 'Goodonyas'. And he slapped a $100 bill down on the bar.

This will be money for jam, thought the salesman. 'First question: What's the capital of Liberia?'

The farmer put a finger in his ear, studied the ceiling, frowned for a few moments and, finally, said, 'Monrovia'. The salesman winced. Reassuring himself it was just a lucky shot – perhaps the bloke had been watching *Sale of the Century* – he asked the second question. 'Who was Malaysia's third Prime Minister?'

The young farmer frowned, looked at the ceiling again, looked at the barmaid, looked at his mates and, finally said, 'Jeez, I think it was Tun

Hussein Onn.' The salesman was astonished and leafed desperately through the pages of his encyclopaedia.

'All right, here's question three. How many people attended the closing ceremony of the 1956 Olympic Games in Melbourne and what were their names and addresses?'

The farmer hitched up his trousers, drank a beer, took a deep breath and said, 'Sixty-eight thousand, nine hundred and twenty-two, not including the sheila who had to leave early to have a baby.' Whereupon he began to chant a list of names and addresses.

It took him four days to get to the end of his answer. By then the salesman was devastated. 'How the hell do you know all this stuff?'

'Well,' said the farmer, 'I take smart pills.'

The salesman realised that these must be miraculous preparations. He'd be better off flogging them than encyclopaedias.

'Where can I get some of these smart pills?' he asked.

The farmer scratched his crotch and said, 'Me dad makes them, but he reckons I'm not allowed to tell anyone the recipe. The ingredients are a family secret.'

'But he didn't say you couldn't sell them, did he?' asked the salesman.

The farmer thought for a moment and finally

said, 'I suppose it would be okay if I charged you $50 and you swallowed a couple here and now.'

The salesman eagerly handed over his last $50 bill and watched as the farmer produced a matchbox from his back pocket. 'Take them all now with a midi of beer,' he instructed.

The salesman looked apprehensively at the pills but then, one by one, swallowed them. A look of disgust appeared on his face. 'Christ, these pills taste like sheep shit.'

'See,' said the farmer. 'You're getting smarter already.'

When he was on a roll, John Elliott was making frequent trips to Moscow. With the help of Mikhail Gorbachev he made some marvellous business contacts. Mikhail organised an invitation for Elliott to address a large group of influential Muscovites. He decided that he'd deliver the speech in Russian, by reading from a text that had been translated phonetically. Though he didn't understand the language, he'd give the illusion of speaking it.

But he'd forgotten to get the words for Ladies and Gentlemen. So he rushed through the National Hotel and wrote down the words that were on the two doors. Now he was ready to make the speech. It was a triumph.

But afterwards Mikhail Gorbachev was slightly puzzled. 'It went very well, John. But why did you start your speech by addressing the audience as Water Closets and Urinals?'

The carpet layers had just finished putting in the burgundy Axminster for a rich matron when they noticed a lump in the middle of the room. Taking out his hammer, one of the layers bashed at the lump, attempting to smooth it out. 'Oh, bugger,' he said, patting at his pocket, 'must be me smokes.'

'No, here's your smokes. But have you seen the old girl's budgie?'

A Macleans salesman was on the country run and found himself at a little store in the middle of nowhere. It was dusty, dirty, dilapidated, and he didn't like his chances of making a big sale. Nonetheless he went into his pitch, describing the wonders of Macleans, how the paste worked miracles on your choppers. The store owner watched the performance impassively. Then he said, 'Have a look under me counter.'

The salesman looked and saw shelves packed with Lady Scott toilet tissue.

'Now have a look in me cupboard.'

The salesman looked and there was a mountain of Sorbent toilet tissue.

'Now come and look out the back.' He took the salesman to a backyard shed, opened the door and revealed mountains of Kleenex toilet tissue.

'What's that got to do with me selling toothpaste?' the salesman asked.

'Simple. I've been running this store for 20 years. And if I can't get the locals to wipe their bums, I've got no hope of gettin' them to clean their bloody teeth.'

A Melbourne engineer and his female assistant were working on a new road system in a country area. The engineer told the assistant to go to the other end of the proposed roadway and that he would signal if he wanted anything, as it was very far to walk.

After a while he waved, attracted her attention and then proceeded to signal just what he wanted.

He touched his eye, then his knee and started hitting up and down with his right hand.

The woman at the other end was rather perplexed. Then she nodded her head and replied. She touched her eye. Then her left breast. Then her pelvic region.

The boss was perplexed. Whatever did she mean?

He signalled again. She signalled back exactly as before.

Finally, he waved to her to come towards him. They met in the middle. He said he was quite mystified by her actions.

'Did you understand what I asked?' he inquired.

'Yes,' she said, 'you said, "I need a hammer".'

He said that's exactly what he requested, but he couldn't understand her reply.

'It's very simple,' she said. 'My reply was, "I left it in the tool box".'

His night's work completed, Dan the dunny man was plodding towards the depot when the tumbrel wheel struck a stone and the whole shebang overturned. Unhurt, he stood there surveying the result. A passing motorist stopped long enough to call facetiously, 'Had an accident?'

'No,' yelled Dan, 'I'm stocktaking!'

In 1919 a stockman was taking a mob of cattle to the gulf country when he came across a rabbit-proof-fence man. This lonely fellow hadn't seen anyone for years, so they sat around the campfire catching up with the news. After a lull in the conversation, the stockman said, 'By the way, we won the War.'

'That's good,' said the rabbit-proof-fence man. 'I never could stand them Boers.'

The travelling salesman stopped at a lonely farmhouse and asked for a bed for the night.

'Sorry, I don't have a spare room,' said the farmer, 'but you can sleep with my daughter. Provided you leave her alone.'

The salesman gave the farmer his word and after dinner went to bed. Undressing in the dark, he slipped into the cot beside the farmer's daughter. Next morning, after a big brekkie, he asked for the bill.

'That'll be $5 for the food and $5 for the bed. Seeing as how you had to share.'

'Fair enough,' says the salesman. 'By the way, your daughter wasn't at all friendly. In fact, she was rather cool.'

'Yeah,' said the farmer, 'we're going to bury her today.'

The farmer was taking flying lessons so that he could get part-time work as a cropduster. As he was approaching the local airfield, the radio crackled and a voice said, 'Please give us your estimated height and position.'

'I'm five foot ten, and sitting in the front.'

Why did Dave get the flick from the orange juice factory?

Couldn't concentrate.

What's the difference between a magician's wand and a policeman's truncheon?

The magician's wand is for cunning stunts.

What's the difference between a milkmaid and a stripteaser?

The milkmaid is fair and buxom . . .

Why don't public servants look out of the windows in the morning?

If they did, there wouldn't be anything to do in the arvos.

What's the difference between a farm and a pigeon? A pigeon can still put a deposit on a tractor.

A bloke was driving a little van very slowly through the city. He was pulled over by a cop. 'Look,' said the policeman, 'it's not that you've broken the law, but I'm curious. Why is it that you keep pulling up, racing round the back of the van and thumping the back door?'

'Well, officer, I've two tonnes of budgies in there and this is only a one-tonne van. And if all the little buggers landed at once, they'd break the springs.'

'Is this the motor pool? How many vehicles are operational?'

'We've got five trucks, five utilities, two scout cars and a tank. And that Bentley the fat-arsed colonel drives around in.'

'Do you know who you're speaking to?'

'No.'

'It's the so-called fat-arsed colonel.'

'Well, do you know who you're talking to?'

'No!'

'Thank Christ for that.'

Dawn. The deserter is being frog-marched to the place of execution. All the way he complains to the members of the firing squad. 'Fancy having to march all this distance in this cold weather just to get shot.'

'And you're complaining,' said one of the squad. 'We've got to bloody well march back again.'

Pacing the poop deck of his proud vessel, Lord Nelson looked up at a lad high in the rigging and called, 'Keep a keen eye out for Spanish sail, m'lad. For today I feel like a fight.'

Soon the boy cried, 'Sir, ten Spanish sail on the starboard bow.'

Nelson turned to his first officer. 'Lieutenant, bring me my red coat. If I'm wounded the blood shall not show. Better for morale.'

Just then the boy in the rigging cried, 'Fifteen Spanish sail on the port bow.'

Nelson said, 'Lieutenant, whilst you're getting my red coat, would you also be kind enough to bring me my brown breeches.'

In the greatest days of the British Empire, a new commanding officer was sent to a jungle outpost to relieve the retiring colonel. After welcoming his replacement and showing the courtesies (gin and tonic, cucumber sandwiches) the protocol decrees, the retiring colonel said, 'You must meet Captain Smithers, my right-hand man. God, he's really the strength of this office. His talent is simply boundless.'

Smithers was summoned and introduced to the new CO. He was surprised to meet a toothless, hairless, scabbed and pock-marked specimen of humanity, a particularly unattractive man less than four feet tall.

'Smithers, old man, tell your new CO about yourself.'

'Well, sir, I graduated with honours from Sandhurst, joined the regiment and won the Military Cross and Bar after three expeditions behind enemy lines. I've represented Great Britain in equestrian events and won a Silver Medal in the middleweight division of the Olympic boxing. I have researched the history of –'

Here the colonel interrupted.

'Never mind that, Smithers. The CO can find all that in your file. Tell him about the day you told the witch doctor to get fucked.'

Bill had been a workaholic all his life and when he kicked the bucket his friends took up a collection for a headstone. It read: ERECTED IN BILL'S MEMORY BY HIS RELATIVES AND FRIENDS.

They installed the headstone before the ground had settled and within a couple of days it had started to tilt. As a temporary measure, the mason looped a piece of fencing wire around it and tied the other end to a nearby tree. Bill's mates visited the grave for the first time since the funeral. 'Christ, that's our Bill,' said one, noticing the wire. 'Work, work, work. Now he's got the bloody phone on!'

A travelling salesman is heading up the Hume Highway towards Albury when he sees a not unattractive young lady thumbing a lift. He pulls over and she tells him she's going to work as a waitress in Wodonga. Seeking to glamorise himself he tells her that he is, in fact, 2AY Albury's top radio announcer. 'A radio announcer!' The girl is wildly excited. 'Are you a disc jockey or do you do talkback?'

'I'm sort of the local John Laws.'

'Oh, I'd love to be in radio. I'd really love to be an announcer.'

'Well, I think I could arrange to get you an audition.'

'Really?' Her excitement is palpable.

Whereupon he unzips his fly and produces his

generative member. And the girl reaches for it, grabs it firmly and bends over it. 'Hello, Mum! Hello, Dad!'

The wharfie had the security guards puzzled. Every day when he left Station Pier at Port Melbourne he wheeled out a wheelbarrow full of rubbish. And every day the guards would sift through the rubbish, certain that he was nicking stuff.

But every day the guards found nothing but rubbish.

Finally the wharfie retired and the guards couldn't bear to say goodbye without knowing. 'Look, we know you've been nicking stuff but we don't know how. What was the secret? What were you stealing?'

As he headed through the gates for the last time, he said, 'Wheelbarrows.'

Just before Prince Charles married Lady Diana, two Australians, being short of a quid to tide them over, answered an advertisement for employment at the palace. The positions were for coachmen to ride on the royal coach to and from Westminster Abbey, and, as the occasion was so auspicious, Her Majesty had decided to do the interviewing herself. So the pair were ushered into the royal presence and she explained that she wanted the wedding to be absolutely perfect, with no faults or flaws, as the eyes and ears of the world would be watching the fairytale wedding.

Now she got down to details. 'Would you mind showing me your legs, as they will be wearing tight-fitting pantihose, and firm legs are important?'

The blokes obliged and the Queen seemed satisfied. She then asked to see their feet as they'd be wearing buckle shoes. Satisfied with the feet, she asked to inspect their manly chests and biceps, and seemed quite impressed.

'Very well, gentlemen, that will be all. Now if you'll just show me your credentials.'

Ten years later, still scratching their heads, the blokes were leaving Wormwood Scrubs and one said to the other, 'You know, I think we would have got that job if we'd been a bit better educated.'

The council's road-building gang had a major problem. They'd gone to work and forgotten to take their shovels. They phoned the foreman to ask advice. 'No need to panic,' he said. 'I'll send the van out with the shovels. But you'll have to lean on each other until they get there.'

Caltex were drilling for oil in northern Australia. They'd freighted in American technicians but had a few Aussies as labourers, one of whom dropped his hammer down the shaft. All drilling had to stop for days on end until, finally, it was removed. It must have cost Caltex a fortune.

The American manager then assembled all the men around the shaft, called the Aussie forward and presented him with the hammer. 'I want you to accept this as a memento,' he told the Australian, 'and hope that it will remind you of the trouble and expense you've caused Caltex through your carelessness. So take it and piss off.'

'Do you mean I'm sacked?'

'Exactly.'

'Well, it's no flamin' use to me,' said the Aussie. And dropped the hammer down the shaft again.

The union talks had gone pretty well and the spokesman emerged from the conference with the boss to deliver the news to his comrades. 'Okay, cobbers. We've won just about everything we wanted. Retrospective salary increases for two years, two months annual leave, fares to Surfers, a two-hour lunchbreak, decent percolated coffee and we only work Friday. Nine to five.'

'What?' one of the workers cried. '*Every* bloody Friday?'

An undertaker was very pleased with himself when he organised for his son to be apprenticed to one of the best. 'You'll learn a lot from him,' he told his boy. 'He's a master of the trade.'

A few weeks later the boy told his dad of a strange experience. 'We got a call from the Hilton to say that a couple had died in bed. Apparently they were lying side by side, naked, dead as doornails.'

'And what happened?'

'Well, the boss got us to put on our poshest gear and we went around to the pub in the best hearse. We introduced ourselves to the manager and then went upstairs. It was all very quiet and dignified.'

'What happened then?'

'We opened the door and entered in a solemn manner befitting the occasion. And there, on the bed, was a naked couple. The boss quietly pointed out to me that the bloke had a gigantic erection. Apparently it's not uncommon in rigor mortis.'

'What happened then?'

'Well, the boss gave it a mighty whack with his umbrella.'

'What happened then?'

'What happened then? A bloody riot. We were in the wrong suite.'

Australia's first astronaut addressed a press conference before blasting off in the shuttle. Yes, he was proud to be included in the NASA team. But he admitted to some disquiet. 'There'll I'll be, sitting on top of 500 000 moving parts, every one supplied by the lowest tenderer.'

A purser on a flight from Cairns to Brisbane asked a passenger in Business Class what he had in his bag.

'Crabs. Caught them this morning. They're still alive and kicking. I'll cook them tonight.'

The purser, a charming young woman, volunteered to keep them in the kitchen until the flight was over.

The flight was full and she was pretty busy. As the plane was circling Brisbane she realised she wasn't quite sure which passenger the parcel belonged to. So she called over the intercom, 'Would the bloke who gave me the crabs in Cairns come forward so that I can give them back to him?'

Toads in the Hole

What's the definition of suspicion?
When your hotdog's got veins.

The little country store had sawdust on the floor
and smelt of freshly ground coffee. The scrubbed
pine counter contained jars of boiled lollies, boxes of
beeswax candles and a shiny bacon slicer. It was the
middle of World War II and there was a shortage of
commodities. So you had to have your ration
coupons.

A domineering local woman walked into the
store and began placing an order with the shop
assistant. 'I would like three pounds of flour, one
pound of butter, half a pound of sugar, a bottle of
kerosene, four pounds of potatoes and two pounds of

brown Spanish onions – to be delivered by lunchtime.'

The assistant wrote the order in the book but, on reaching the last item, said, 'I'm very sorry, ma'am, but we have no brown Spanish onions, for the time being.'

'Course you have,' said the woman, glaring indignantly. 'I know you keep some under the counter for favoured customers. I insist on having some of those.'

The stand-off continued until the manager made an appearance. 'Good morning, madam. What seems to be the trouble?'

'I have asked for brown Spanish onions and have been told there are none. But I know you keep some for special customers and would like some. *If you please!*'

'Madam,' said the manager, 'you are an intelligent woman. May I ask you a few simple questions?'

'Certainly.'

'Take the word PARSNIP, madam. Without the 'P' and the 'NIP', what have we left?'

The lady replied, 'ARS.'

'Yes,' said the manager. 'Now, without the first four letters of the word BEETROOT, what remains?'

'ROOT, of course.'

'Very good,' said the manager. 'Now, on to the final question. Take the FUGG out of ONIONS and what do we have?'

The woman frowned at him and said, 'But there is no FUGG in ONIONS.'

'Quite right,' said the manager. 'That's what we've been trying to tell you for the last ten minutes.'

'**Y**ou want salt?' the bloke in the fish shop asked the customer.

'Yeah.'

The bloke reached deep into his hip pocket, pulled out a salt shaker and sprinkled some on the chips.

'Pepper?'

'Yeah.'

The bloke reached into his other pocket, pulled out a pepper shaker and sprinkled some on the chips.

'Vinegar?'

'Yeah. But if you piss on them, I'm not eating them.'

A bloke goes into a cafe for breakfast. He orders a boiled egg and toast. When the egg arrives it falls out of the eggcup and he notices, inscribed on the bottom of the egg in tiny writing, the following: 'I am beautiful, 22 years old, with a perfect figure. And I am looking for a boyfriend.' And there, below the message was a phone number.

So, having finished breakfast, he rings it. 'Thanks very much for calling,' said the young woman, 'but I was married 18 months ago.'

A Jewish bloke in Double Bay wouldn't, couldn't, go to bed without a bowl of mazo ball soup. He loved it and lived for it. One night he sat looking at the plate like a mummy. 'What's the matter? You don't feel good? Something bothers you?' said his wife.

There was no answer.

'Too hot? I'll blow on it.'

There was no reply.

'Too cold? I'll whack it back in the microwave.'

No word.

'For God's sake, what the hell is it?'

Very quietly he said, 'Taste it.'

'Orright, already. Where the hell is the spoon?'

'Exactly.'

It all depends on local custom. In Australia, a fly in one's soup results in it being sent back to the kitchen and a row with the management.

In England, the head waiter quietly, daintily, fastidiously extracts the fly and removes it beneath a serviette.

In France the soup is eaten, the fly left high and dry on the side of the bowl.

In the Orient, the fly is eaten first and washed down by the soup.

In Scotland, the fly is shaken over the bowl and carefully wrung out. Then the soup is consumed.

And there are places where the diner stares into the bowl and complains. 'What's this? Only one fly?'

A young man was standing outside a small suburban coffee shop. He stood there for ten minutes nervously peering through the window. Finally he went into the shop and sat at a table. The waitress asked him what he wanted and he said, very nervously, 'Just a cappuccino.'

When she brought the order to him, he asked if it would be possible for her to help him drink the coffee. The waitress was somewhat puzzled by his request, so he explained that, a few weeks earlier, he'd had a major operation on his intestine and gullet, and as a result was now only capable of drinking liquids through his anus.

'Your anus?'

'Yes, with the help of a funnel and some plastic tubing which I carry with me. All you have to do is pour the coffee slowly down the funnel.' And he inserted the tube into his rectum.

The waitress agreed to help but insisted that he go into the back storage room where no one could see them. Adjusting the tube, he handed the girl the funnel and she started to pour the coffee into it. Ever so slowly.

Suddenly he groaned as if in pain. 'Oh! Oh!'

The waitress became alarmed and said, 'Is it too hot for you?'

'No,' he said. 'Not enough sugar.'

First cannibal, 'I hate her guts.'

Second cannibal, 'Well, just eat the vegetables.'

A bloke went into a seafood restaurant which had been recommended by Leo Schofield, and asked for a lobster tail. The waitress smiled sweetly and said, 'Once upon a time, there was this handsome lobster ...'

A bloke goes into the Chinese restaurant in Bendigo and orders number 43. Chicken with Black Bean Sauce.

'Christ, this chicken is bloody rubbery,' he snarls to the waiter.

He replies, with a charming smile, 'Thank you very much.'

They do a lot of feral-pig shooting at Murrurundi. Half the shops have got stuffed boars' heads on the wall. A tourist calls into the local cafe and checks the menu.

Ham sandwiches, roast pork, pigs' feet, bacon and pork chops.

Being Jewish, he sighs heavily and asks for a glass of water. 'I better warn you, mate,' says the waitress, 'we only have bore water.'

'Bore water!' he replied. 'You don't waste much of a pig!'

The big rugby player was overweight so his coach sent him to the centre for sports medicine.

'Honestly, I've tried every diet under the bloody sun. And nothing shifts the weight.'

'Well, we can help you at the clinic. As a matter of fact we've had immense success with a new method. Mind you, it's not to everyone's taste.'

'Try me.'

'Well, it works like this. You can consume anything you like, anything at all, and as much of it as you like. But you must do so anally.'

'What? Bung it up me bum?'

'Exactly.'

The rugby player was somewhat horrified but agreed to try it. Three weeks later he came back and looked slimmer, stronger and very happy.

'I feel bloody great. No trouble with the tucker. I just it shove it up me arse.'

'Well, it seems to be working.'

A few weeks later he checked in again, even lighter and fitter. 'Doc, you wouldn't believe it, but just before I came in I had a whole pavlova. Just shoved the lot straight up the Khyber.'

The next time he arrived at the clinic he was jiggling up and down and sweating profusely. He seemed to be in considerable distress.

'What's the trouble? You haven't been overdoing it? There shouldn't be this twitching, this hyperactivity. I think we'll have to take you off the diet.'

'No, no, it's fine,' said the rugby player, wiping his brow. 'I'm just eating a packet of Minties.'

An Aussie who lives in Alice Springs wins a trip to Boston. His friends say that they heard that not only is Boston big, but the city sports the best seafood restaurants in the world. Upon arrival in Beantown our dusty friend freshens up at his hotel and then decides to sup. The city's so big he's overwhelmed. He decides to hail a cab and asks the cabby to take him to a good seafood restaurant. (Unbeknownst to him, the cabdriver is a graduate student from Boston College going for his doctorate in linguistics and grammatical syntax.)

'Hey, cabby, where can I get scrod?' asks our bewildered friend. Upon hearing this, the cab driver says, 'Sir, I have heard it asked for in many ways, shapes and forms, but never have I heard it asked for in the past pluperfect.'

What's orange and goes Ho-Ho-Ho?
Fanta Claus.

Villainous Vices

Two bats were hanging upside down in a cave. One turned to the other and said, 'I'm desperate for a drink. Gotta have a drink of blood. So I'm heading off for a while.'

'Well, you better hurry up,' said the other bat, 'it's almost dawn and you won't be able to see a damned thing when the sun rises.'

So the bat goes out like a bat out of hell and is back within a minute, blood dripping from its mouth.

'Well, that was quick. Congratulations.'

And the first bat says, 'Congratulations? Look, you see that dirty great gumtree over there?'

'Yes,' said the other bat.

'Well, I didn't,' said the first bat.

A white horse ambles into a bar and orders a beer. 'Funny thing,' says the barman, 'we've got a whisky named after you.'

'What?' responds the horse. 'Timmy?'

A bloke goes into a bar at Kings Cross and sees a big sign reading: TWO THOUSAND DOLLARS CASH PRIZE. ASK THE BARMAN.

So he goes over and asks the barman what he has to do to win the dosh.

'You have to do three things, and it's all yours,' the barman says.

'Just three?' the bloke asks. He can feel the money in his kick already. 'What are the three things?'

'Well, first you have to go over to that huge bouncer who works outside the Pink Pussycat Club and knock him out. Then we've got a savage dingo in the back room that needs a tooth pulled. Then you have to go upstairs and screw an 80-year-old sheila.'

'No worries,' says the bloke. He wanders over to the bouncer and says, 'Hey, mate, your shoelace is untied.' When the bouncer looks down at his Doc Martens, the bloke flattens him with a solid upper cut.

Then he heads for the back room and the dingo. The barman hears a huge noise – it sounds like the dingo has gone mad.

A few minutes later the bloke emerges from the back room bleeding. His clothes are torn and he's breathing heavily. 'Okay,' he says, 'now where's the old lady that needs a tooth pulled?'

A bloke went to a great party. Smoked some dope, drank a lot of grog. Woke up in the morning and realised he'd lost his watch, a really good fake Rolex. Bugger it. He must have dropped it at the party, but he couldn't remember where the party was, or who'd thrown it. All he could remember was that the house had a red front door and a gold-plated dunny. So he looked all over town, looking for houses with red doors. But none of them had a gold-plated dunny.

Finally, just as he was going to chuck it in, he spotted another house with a red door. And it looked like they'd had a party. There were empty stubbies all over the lawn and a pair of knickers dangling on a rosebush.

He knocked at the front door, which was opened by a woman who obviously had a big hangover. 'Did you have a party here last night?'

'Christ,' groaned the woman, 'did we ever.'

'Well, I think I was here last night. And I lost my watch. All I can remember is this red front door and a gold-plated toilet.'

The woman stared blearily at the bloke, then shouted down the hallway. 'Bruce, here's the dirty bugger who pissed in your saxophone.'

A couple of technicians were fuelling a rocket at Woomera when they noticed that the stuff smelt pretty good. 'And it seems to have a bit of a kick in it,' said one, as he licked a drop off his finger.

'Let's siphon off a couple of gallons for the canteen party,' said the first.

The party was a considerable success.

Next morning the first bloke rang the other, 'How do you feel?'

'All right, so far.'

'Have you been to the dunny yet?'

'No, not yet. Why do you ask?'

'Just to warn you. I'm ringing from Adelaide.'

A drunk at the new Sydney casino stumbled into the loo and started feeding coins into the condom vending machine. Slowly but surely he filled his pockets with them. A bloke was waiting behind him.

'Excuse me, can I have a turn?'

'Not,' said the drunk, 'when I'm on a winning streak.'

Every week a bloke visits the TAB and every week he loses all his money. The woman behind the counter feels sorry for him and decides to help. 'Look, we get some very, very good tips here,' she whispers to the bloke. 'Watch me every week and I'll do something physically to give you a hint.'

That week she scratches her nose. He backs Proboscis and it comes in at ten to one.

Next week she scratches her head. He backs Heir Apparent and it wins by a furlong.

Week three, she scratches between her legs. But he fails to place the winning bet.

'Didn't you see me signal Short 'n Curly?' she says the next time he's at the window.

And he says, 'Yeah, but I thought the cunt was scratched.'

Three blokes are at a country racetrack having a bad day. They've only got $50 left between them. They decide to share a bet, to put all on one horse, in the hope of getting square. But they don't know which horse to back.

The first bloke says, 'Let's go to the toilet, measure the length of our dicks, add them up and back the horse of that number.' They agree and the first bloke comes in at six inches, the second bloke at four inches, and the third bloke at two inches. So they put $50 on number 12 at 100 to one. It wins brilliantly and there's money to burn. Trouble is, they can't decide how to split it up.

The first bloke says, 'I get half because I had six inches of the 12.'

The second bloke says, 'I get a third because I had four inches of the 12.'

And the third bloke says, 'That's not fair. I don't get enough.'

The first bloke says, 'Look, if I didn't have six inches and he didn't have four inches, we wouldn't have backed number 12.'

And the third bloke says, 'And if I hadn't had an erection, we would have backed number 11.'

The colonel didn't drink much, but at a regimental dinner got pissed, stuffed himself and finished up getting the fright of his life when another drunken officer challenged him to a duel. He was rescued by his mates and sent home in a cab.

Next morning he tried to explain to his batman why there was such a mess on his jacket. 'Some bounder bumped into me and I was sick all over my tunic. I'll give him a month's detention when I find him.'

The batman said, 'I'd make it two months, sir. The bastard also shat in your trousers.'

Two blokes are standing at the bar having a glass of beer. 'You look miserable, cobber,' said one. 'What's the matter?'

'Well, my cheese and kisses has just fallen down the stairs and broken both her legs. I just wish it was closing time so that I could go home and pick her up.'

A bloke is standing at the bar having a quiet beer when someone bursts in and belts him across the back of the neck. He feels a blinding pain as he passes out. The assailant tells the bartender, 'When he wakes up, tell him it was a karate chop from Japan.' Then exits.

The following day, the poor bloke is drinking at the bar again when the same yahoo rushes in, kicks him in the neck and, once again, knocks him out. 'When he wakes up,' says the ratbag, 'tell him it was a tae kwon do kick from Korea.' He leaves.

The next day the expert in karate and tae kwon do is sitting at the bar having a beer. All of a sudden his victim bursts in and belts him on the scone. He slips off the bar stool, unconscious. The bloke tells the bartender, 'When the bastard wakes up, tell him it was a piece of four-by-two from the back of the ute.'

A drinker sees a jar full of coins on the bar. 'What's that for?' he asks the barmaid.

'A competition,' she replies. 'Guess how many dollar coins are in the jar and it's yours!'

'Three hundred dollars,' he says. He was right, and won the jar full of money.

Feeling happy, he gets pissed and on the way home trips on his front step and drops the jar. The coins go everywhere. 'Bugger it. I'll clean it up in the morning,' he thinks. In the morning his wife wakes him up. 'Guess what's on the front step?'

Being a smartarse, he says, 'Three hundred one dollar coins.'

'No,' she says, 'two hundred and fifty litres of milk!'

A stuttering drunk approached the barman and said, 'Will you give me a fu, fu, fu ...'

The barmaid glared at him until he completed the sentence.

'A fuff-fuff-few matches. I bub-bub-bub-bet you thought,' the drunk continued, 'I was going to ask you for a fu-fu-fu-fu- ... full box.'

A Melbourne-born man and a Brisbane-born man met one night in a pub. The two found they had

much in common, and soon became friends.
However, when they offered to shout each other, a
dispute broke out as to what beer to order. The
Melbourne man wanted to order VB, while the
Brisbane man wanted to order XXXX. Eventually
they decided to let an impartial judge decide which
was the better beer, and so sent a sample of each
beer off to the CSIRO. When the results came back,
neither was able to claim victory, as they read, 'Sorry
to inform you, but both horses have jaundice.'

An old drunk staggers up to a young bloke whose
head's under the open bonnet of a car.
'What's wrong?'
'Piston broke.'
'Me too.'

'**L**isten, mate,' said the drunk to the taxidriver.
'Have you got room in the front for four dozen beers
and a couple of pizzas?'
'Sure,' said the driver.
'Thanks, mate,' said the drunk, as he chundered
on the front seat. 'Now drive me home to Bondi.'

A drunken punter lifts his head from the bar and notices a sign reading LUNCH 12 to 1. 'Not bad odds. Excuse me, barman, I want to put a tenner on Lunch.'

'Yer pissed. Now bugger off or I'll throw you out.'

So the drunken punter staggers down the street to another pub, where he saw a sign saying LUNCH 11 to 2. 'Christ, the odds are down already. I better hurry up and place a bet. 'Hey, barman, I want $10 on Lunch at 11 to 2.'

'Yer drunk,' said the barman, and threw him out.

The punter staggered down the road to the next pub. Outside there was a sign reading LUNCH 1 to 2. 'Odds on,' thought the punter. 'That's no good. Anyway, I'll go inside and see the race.'

As he walked in the door, the barman shouted out to the cook, 'Sausages, one'.

'Thank Christ,' the punter said. 'I didn't back Lunch.'

A drunk lurched out of a pub and tumbled into the gutter. He woke up a few minutes later with a cop bending over him. 'Where the fuck am I?'

'At the corner of York and George Streets,' said the policeman.

'Never mind the bloody details. Which city?'

A tourist arrives at the Linga Longa pub in Gundy. 'It's a long time since I've seen sawdust on the floor of a pub,' he said approvingly.

'Sawdust? That's not sawdust, mate. That's yesterday's furniture after the whiteants got it.'

Five bikies walked into a country pub and, having ordered their beers, told the lone drinker at the other end of the bar to shout them. When he told them to get stuffed they punched him up and chucked him out the door.

'Not much of a fighter,' said one of the bikies.

'Not much of a driver, either,' said the barman. 'He's just driven his truck over five Harley Davidsons.'

A shearer stopped at a pub with his huge pay cheque. It was a pub used to shearers.

After a couple of rip-roaring days, the shearer was settling up with the publican. 'What's the damage, mate?'

'Well, your room with ensuite down the other end of the hall was 30 quid. You drank 20 quid worth of beer and two quid worth of whisky. You had $25 worth of steaks.'

'Yeah, that's right.'

'And you spent the night with one of the girls. That's another 20 quid.'

'Fair enough.'

'Oh, and there's 25 cents for hay for your horse.'

'That fuckin' horse is gunna ruin me.'

A bloke went into the pub in Murrurundi for a beer, and when he came out there was no sign of his horse. He went raging back into the pub. 'I'm giving youse blokes fair warning. If my fuckin' horse isn't back by the time I finish this beer, the same thing's gonna happen as happened in Gundy.'

When he finished his beer he slammed the glass down and went outside. And there was his horse, just where he'd left it. As he put his boot in the stirrup, a couple of the drinkers came out of the pub. 'By the way, mate, just what did happen in Gundy?'

'I had to walk home,' said the bloke.

A stockman walks into a pub. 'Look, my cobber will be in here soon,' he says to the barman. 'He's a bit of a dill. Short of a few kangaroos in the top paddock. And he'll try to pay for his drinks with bottle tops. So do me a favour, take the tops and I'll come in tomorrow and settle up.'

The barman is not too thrilled but is finally persuaded to go along with it.

A few minutes later, a bloke comes into the pub, orders a beer and plonks down a few bottle tops. And he keeps doing it all afternoon – paying for drinks with bottle tops. He shouts everyone in the pub, hands over more bottle tops and finally staggers off into the darkness.

Next day the stockman returns. 'Did my cobber come in yesterday? Did he pay you with bottle tops?'

'Yep,' says the barman. 'He bought a lot of drinks. It's gonna cost you.'

'No probs,' says the bloke, heaving a hub cup onto the bar. 'Got change for that?'

A little bloke was approaching a pub in Port Melbourne, a bit of a bloodhouse frequented by wharfies. Just as he threw a left to go in the door, he slipped on a pile of dog shit and landed flat on his back. Picking himself up, he staggered to the bar and was having a curative beer when he saw a big docker coming through the door. And he slipped in the same dog shit. As the dazed docker picked himself up, the little bloke walked over and said, 'I just did that.' And the docker punched him right in the face.

'Yes, sir, what's your pleasure?' inquired the barman.

'A scotch and a box of matches,' said the bloke.

He drank the scotch and put ten cents on the counter. 'This is for the matches. I didn't really want a drink, but when you were so nice about it.'

'Don't come the raw prawn. Cough up for the scotch!'

'Get stuffed.'

'Then bugger off!'

A week passes. 'Hey, I told you last week you were barred from this bar.'

'I've never been here before. You must have me mixed up with someone else.'

'Then you must have a double.'

'That's very nice of you. And a box of matches.'

A man was drinking at the bar when the bloke next to him said, 'Tickle your arse with a feather.'

'What did you say?'

'Particularly nasty weather,' said the bloke, with an amiable smile.

He thought this was pretty witty and would try it out. After a few drinks another fellow fronted the bar alongside him – a huge Hell's Angel covered in tattoos. Now somewhat inebriated, the bloke said, 'Stick a feather up your arse.'

The Hell's Angel turned to him, snarling, 'What did you say, you little bastard?'

Whereupon our hero said, 'Cunt of a day, isn't it?'

Two old ladies had been trying to give up smoking for years and used to meet every month or so to check up on each other's progress. Sadly, their habit persisted, until the following conversation took place.

'Well, I've finally done it.'

'Done what?'

'What do you mean, done what? I've given up smoking.'

'I don't believe it.'

'It's true. And it was quite easy. You see, each time I was about to light a cigarette I stopped and sucked a Lifesaver instead.'

'That's easy for you … You live at Bondi.'

A drunk, having spent all his money, was chucked out of the local pub. Whereupon he walked in front of a ute and was killed instantly.

Next thing he knew he was standing in front of the Pearly Gates being greeted by St Peter.

'Where's the nearest pub, Pete?'

'Fourth cloud to the right,' said St Peter, 'but before you drown your sorrows, let me tell you that up here, we count a million years as a minute, and a million dollars as a cent.'

The drunk thought about this. 'Look, I'm a bit short at the moment, Pete. Could you lend me a cent?'

'Sure,' said St Peter, 'just wait a minute.'

A venerable member of the Melbourne Club had invited the Anglican archbishop to dinner. In preparation he had his butler whiz down to the Toorak Village to fetch a bottle of whisky, a box of Davidoff cigars and a few ounces of snuff. He knew that the bishop enjoyed his snuff.

The butler went to the village, procured the whisky and cigars but forgot the snuff. On arriving back at the gates of the mansion, he realised that he'd had a lapse of memory. But fortunately there were three dry lumps of dog shit on the nature strip which had blanched white in the sun. All he'd have to do was grind it into powder.

The dinner went very well and, afterwards, the businessman and the archbishop were enjoying their whisky and their cigars. But the host could smell dog shit. It was quite distinct.

'Do you smell dog shit?' he asked of the
archbishop.

'No, I can't say that I do. But I am having some
sinus trouble.'

'In that case, take a pinch of snuff.'

The archbishop took two pinches, sniffing one
up each nostril. 'Aah, dear chap, that's splendid snuff.
It's absolutely cleared my nasal passages. And you're
right – I can smell dog shit.'

A bloke was waiting in the arrivals hall at Mascot
Airport. Lots and lots of international passengers
were coming through with their luggage. Suddenly a
very beautiful woman appeared, and the bloke
started calling out, 'F. F., F. F.'

The woman, waving cheerily, shouted, 'E. F.,
E. F.'

'F. F.' and 'E. F.' were bandied back and forth
until a fellow passenger asked the woman what it
meant. 'I'm telling him I want to Eat First.'

An old Aussie took his pet giraffe into a country
pub and ordered two schooners. In fact, they drank
about eight apiece. Then they both staggered to the
door. But on the way out the giraffe went arse over

head. As the old Aussie reached the door, the barman yelled out, 'Hey, old timer. Don't leave that lyin' on the floor. Take him with you.'

And the old Aussie slurred back, 'That's not a lion, you drongo, that's a giraffe.'

The Body Beautiful?

They were at the pictures. An old bloke sat in front of them and, after a few minutes, there was a terrible odour. They gave him a tap on the shoulder. 'Did you shit yourself, you old bastard?'

'Yep.'

'Then why don't you move?'

'Haven't finished yet.'

How do you make a skeleton?

Hose down a leper.

An Australian executive visits Tokyo. His mission is to sell some Australian components to Toyota.

Unfortunately he's not feeling too well and has an attack of flatulence. So his meeting in the Toyota boardroom becomes an immense embarrassment to all concerned. He can't stop farting. And worse still, his farts sound eerily like a Honda. A Honda at Toyota? There is an immense loss of face.

Worried that he's going to blow the business deal, the bloke goes to the Australian Embassy, who refers him to an English-speaking dentist. The dentist takes one look in his mouth and finds an abscess, which he insists is the cause of the problem. And to the Australian's astonishment, after a simple treatment, the farting stops.

'But I don't understand,' he said to the dentist. 'What has an abscessed tooth got to do with farting?'

'Ah, as you people say, "Abscess makes the fart go Honda".'

'**I**s your bum asleep?'
'No, why?'
'I thought I heard it snoring.'

A bloke had a very, very bad problem. Smelly feet. He'd tried everything. Nothing worked. It undermined his self-confidence, particularly in romantic affairs. He learned, from painful experience, that no woman would come within a mile of his smelly feet.

So he signed up with a computer dating service and they eventually fixed him up with a girl who described herself as 'absolutely desperate'.

He prepared for the date very carefully. He almost boiled his feet in hot water, covering them with talcum powder, wore clean socks and a big, heavy pair of Doc Martens boots. He laced them as tightly as possible so that no hint of odour could escape.

The girl was very, very quiet. She mumbled a few things but didn't actually say anything and never mentioned his feet. Gaining confidence, he suggested they go to a motel. The girl nodded, and off they went.

Inside the room the girl, still silent, went to the bathroom. He undressed. But when he took off the Doc Martens his feet smelt to high heaven. He threw his socks out the window but it didn't help.

At that moment the girl appeared from the bathroom and the bloke, too scared to face her, ran inside it and slammed the door.

What he didn't know was that the poor girl had a problem as bad as his – the world's worst breath. Which is why she kept her mouth shut.

When he finally came out of the bathroom, she flung her arms around him and started kissing him wildly, passionately, hungrily.

'Darling,' she said, 'there's something I must confess.'

'I know,' he gasped, 'you've eaten my socks.'

A journo is visiting a mental asylum to interview the director. He's running late and as he walks up the driveway passes a patient sitting in his pyjamas and a dressing-gown on a bench in the sunshine. The journo asks the patient the time. He takes out his penis, lays it on the palm of his hand and says, 'Ten to twelve.'

Saying nothing, the journalist goes to his meeting. He leaves an hour later and passes the same man on the same bench. Out of curiosity he asks him the time again. And the man again takes out his penis, lays it across his hand and says, 'Ten to twelve.'

'But you said it was ten to twelve an hour ago,' said the journalist.

The man immediately begins masturbating, saying, 'Damned thing must have stopped!'

A young bloke applies for a job as a salesman. He's interviewed by the manager who can't help but notice that he has a serious stammer.

'Have you had a selling job before?'

'N-n-n-n-n-o. Th-th-th-this will be my fir-fir-fir-first j-j-j-j-j-job.'

'That's a bad stammer you've got. Nonetheless I'll give you a go.'

'Wh-wh-wh-what will I be s-s-s-s-selling?'

'Bibles.'

'B-B-B-B-Bibles?'

'Yes, I'll give you five Bibles, and if you can sell them in a week I'll keep you on.'

A few hours later the stammering salesman comes back.

'I s-s-s-s-sold the five B-B-B-B-Bibles,' he tells the boss.

'Marvellous. Now I'll give you a box of 50 and if you can sell them in four weeks I'll make you head salesman.'

Three days later he's back. 'I s-s-s-sold the 50 B-B-B-Bibles,' he tells the boss.

'Incredible. What's your sales pitch?'

'What's a s-s-s-s-sales p-p-p-pitch?'

'Well, what do you say to your customers?'

'I just g-g-g-g-go up to the f-f-f-f-front d-d-d-door and when the l-l-l-l-lady comes out, I say "W-w-w-w-would you like to b-b-b-buy a B-B-B-B-Bible off of me, or w-w-w-would you rather me r-r-r-r-read it to you?"'

A couple of furniture removalists were lugging a piano into a Toorak mansion. As they wheezed and gasped their way along the corridor, they heard a voice coming from the cupboard under the stairs. 'When I find you I'm gonna get you, and when I get you I'm gonna eat you.'

Nervously they put down the piano. 'Shit, the place is haunted.'

Whereupon they heard the voice again. 'When I find you I'm gonna get you, and when I get you I'm gonna eat you.'

Slowly, tentatively, they opened the cupboard door – to find the owner's son sitting in the dark picking his nose.

A young bloke, fresh out of a school from the big smoke, has just arrived to begin work as a jackeroo on a cattle station out past Inverell. The truck from town drops him of just after lunch and one of the other jackeroos spends the afternoon with him, showing him round and telling him what has to be done and when.

By the end of the day everything's been covered, he's been fired up with a horse, a saddle and a bunk and he's looking forward to his first full day as he scrubs up for dinner. On his way there, however, he realises that the first-day nerves have cramped his guts up a bit, so he makes a detour to the dunnies: four long-drop holes, side by side, enclosed by three sheets of corrugated iron with a fourth as the roof. A length of old tarp strung across the fourth side acts as the dunny door.

Pulling the tarp aside and stepping in, the young bloke notices another occupant. Squatting over one of the holes is a weather-beaten old cocky with a rollie hanging out of one corner of his mouth. Not being a social situation, the two acknowledge each other with a nod of the head, and the young bloke proceeds to drop his strides and squat over one of the other holes. As he does so, the old bloke finishes, wipes himself with a bit of newspaper and pulls his own strides up. The young bloke can't help but notice a $5 note sticking out of the old bloke's pocket. Before he can say anything, however, the note falls out and flutters down the hole. The old bloke sees this, but being busy tucking in his shirt and buttoning himself up, he's unable to do anything about it.

Without saying a word, he turns around and stands there, staring down the hole. After a while, and with great deliberation, he reaches into his pocket and pulls out his roll. Slowly, he removes a $50 note, puts the rest back in his pocket, then drops the note down the hole to join the fiver.

The young bloke is now staring wide-eyed and open-mouthed at the old cocky. He can't believe what he's just seen.

Without even looking over the old bloke says to him out of the corner of his mouth, 'Well, yer don't expect me to go down there for five bloody dollars, do yer?'

Yorke's Peninsula, although not far from Adelaide, had only a few settlers before 1875 because there are no streams and the ground water is saline. It was originally covered with dense woodland. By 1922 it had been extensively cleared for agriculture, but the country roads all had the original mallee trees on either side.

A Mr Tossell was the editor and proprietor of the newspaper *The Yorke's Peninsula Farmer*. He was also a member of parliament.

One beautiful warm day in early September when the snakes and sleepy lizards were emerging from their hibernation, Tossell was driving his trap along a tree-lined road, calling on farmers to seek their votes.

He had to stop and get down to answer a call of nature, unaware that where he did his business there was a sleepy lizard, which awoke and waddled off.

His companion, sitting in the trap, said, 'Well, Tossell, that's the first time I've ever known one of your motions to be carried!'

What did one tampon say to the other tampon?
Nothing. They were both stuck-up cunts.

Did you hear about the Australian who had a penis transplant?
It didn't take. His hand rejected it.

For years the couples had been playing cards every week, but as they grew older the pace slackened. While the wives were out of the room, one bloke said to the other, 'I usually have to remind you what cards have been played, but tonight I didn't need to. Why not?'
'I've been to memory school.'
'Yeah! What's the name of the school?'
'Let me see … what do you call that red flower, with thorns on the stem?'
'A rose?'
'Yeah, that's it. A rose. Hey, Rose,' he yelled towards the kitchen, 'what was the name of that memory school I went to?'

During the last war a young digger was posted to a remote part of the Western Desert. Being a dutiful son, he wrote to his mum regularly, and received the following reply. 'John, it is wonderful getting your letters and hearing of your activities, but we've almost forgotten what you look like. Could you send us a photograph.'

Well, there was something of a shortage of photographers in the Western Desert. But he did have a photo that a mate had taken – of him standing starkers except for his slouch hat and desert boots.

He had an inspiration. He'd cut it in half and send mum the top bit. Which he did.

Soon after, another letter from his mother arrived.

'Thank you, darling, for the letter and for the marvellous photo. You do look well. But could you forward one to Granny. She's always asking after you.'

He wondered what to do. He only had the bottom half of the one photograph. Well, the old dear was practically blind and probably wouldn't be able to see the details. So John sent Granny the bottom half.

In due course he got a reply from Granny. 'Dear John, how wonderful of you to send me a photograph. Do you know you're getting to look more like your father all the time. You have bags under your eyes. You need a shave. And what's more, your tie isn't straight.'

The colonel of a commando regiment was forever boasting how tough his men were, to such an extent that the high command got jack of this and decided to send one of their generals to check out his unit.

The general arrived at the army camp one icy-cold day and ordered the colonel to turn out his troops at 6 a.m. next morning for inspection. At 6 a.m. next day, with snow on the ground and an icy wind blowing, he insisted that, because the commandos were so tough, they should parade naked. So that is what they did.

The general strode along the rows of naked men and struck one across the buttocks with his swagger stick.

'Did that hurt, soldier?'

'No, sir!' said the soldier.

'Why did it not hurt?' asked the general.

'Because I am a commando, sir!' replied the lad.

Next soldier was struck a resounding blow to the cheek.

'Did that hurt, soldier?'

'No, sir!'

'Why?'

'Because I am a commando, sir!'

Then the general saw this commando standing to attention with a large erection. *Whack!* went the general's swagger stick, right on the erect organ.

'Did that hurt, soldier?' inquired the general.

'No, sir!' said the lad.

'Why did it not hurt?' asked the general.
'Because it belonged to the soldier behind me, sir!'

Two elderly, retired brigadier-types are in their club having a nightcap, reminiscing on their subaltern days, and their most embarrassing moments.

'It was the First War,' said one, 'and I was in pommyland and invited to the lord of the manor's ball. Tried damned hard not to be an uncouth Aussie. I was dancing with a girl with a very low-cut dress and saw it starting to slip down. I cried out, "Look everybody, out of the window". They did, thus giving the girl a chance to pull her dress up and save her from embarrassment. But damn it, man ... unbeknown to me, there were two dogs fornicating on the lawn. Well, what was yours?'

'Mine? Well, it was when my mother caught me masturbating.'

'But, that's nothing. All us boys got caught sooner or later.'

'Damn it, man, this was last Sunday!'

A bloke went into the pub's dunny and was bitten by a redback on the toilet seat. In the most painful of places. To make matters worse, he knew that the story of his intimate injury would get around the small country town.

Sure enough, when he was in the town a few weeks later he was fronted by an old lady who said she'd heard all about the injury.

'But where exactly did you get bitten?'

There was an embarrassed silence until an old chap sitting at the end of the bar said, 'Well, Edna, if you'd got bit where he got bit you wouldn't have got bit at all.'

Five blokes had been drinking for a while and were starting to get philosophical. One said, 'I wonder if a wink would be the fastest thing in the world?'

The second bloke said, 'I think a blink would be faster.'

The third bloke said, 'What about a think, that's quicker than a wink or a blink.'

The fourth bloke said, 'An electric light switch! You've only got to touch it and the light comes on straight away.'

The fifth bloke said, 'You're all wrong. Diarrhoea.'

'Why diarrhoea?' they chorused.

'Well, I had diarrhoea last night,' he said, 'and before I could wink, blink, think or turn on the light, I shat myself.'

'Jeez, mate,' said the little bloke to the fellow having a piss beside him in the hotel loo. 'You've got a big dick there.'

'And you've got a bloody big arse,' came the response.

'Yeah. It takes a big hammer to drive a big nail.'

'Let me shout you a stout. I hear that drinking stout puts lead in your pencil.'

'I don't know about you, old mate, but I don't have that many women to write to.'

A stranger in a small country town has been breasting the bar for a couple of hours when nature calls. He wanders round the back of the pub and finds a rickety dunny. It is listing slightly to port and the door is held shut with a piece of baling twine. He goes inside and, on finishing the job, looks around for the toilet roll. All he finds is a bare cardboard tube dangling on a piece of fencing wire. Nor is any substitute on offer – no sheets of newspaper hanging from a nail. Finally he sees a sign. 'To our customers. Owing to a shortage of dunny paper, we must ask you to use your finger to clean your bum. However, if you stick it through the knot hole to the left it will be sucked clean.'

The stranger follows the distasteful instructions and sticks a shitty finger through the knot hole. Where upon it is immediately hit by a hammer. Screaming he pulls the finger in – and sucks it!

At 20–30 years   Tri-daily
  At 30–40 years   Tri-weekly
  At 40–50 years   Try weakly
  At 50–60 years   Try oysters
  At 60–70 years   Try anything
  70 years and over   Try to remember

What to do when you get old:
  Never pass a toilet
  Never waste an erection
  Never trust a fart

His bride was a buxom 20-year-old. But he, despite his millions, was past it. He tried everything to encourage an erection but nothing worked.

Finally he went to a hypnotherapist who, to his astonishment, managed to implant a post-hypnotic suggestion.

'All you have to do is say "Ding!" In that second you'll get a terrific erection. And it will last until you say "Ding, Ding". Then it will go down again. But it will take a huge amount out of your system. I must warn you that you'll only be able to use this approach three times. Now, let's see if it's working. "Ding!"' Instantly a giant erection.

'Ding! Ding!' said the hypnotherapist. Instantly it went down. 'Now you've got two times left,' he said. 'Be very, very careful.'

On the way home the bloke passed the Town Hall clock as it reached 1.30. A giant 'Ding!' rang out and, voila, a huge erection. He swerved his car to the side of the road and sat there palpitating. Half an hour later the clock struck two. 'Ding! Ding!' And his erection disappeared.

He drove the rest of the way home as fast as he could. Rushing inside he said, 'Darling, get your clothes off and jump on the bed.'

Though unconvinced, she obliged. 'Ding!' he yelled. And, there it was, a giant erection.

'Hey, that's really something,' she said. 'But what's all this ding, ding crap?'

The pommy was not long in Australia before he heard that the duck-shooting season was about to start. He decided that he had to join in, so went out and bought all the things he was told he would need: double-barrel shotgun; waders; decoy ducks; hunting cap, etc. You name it, he had to have it.

On the opening morning, he took off into the swamp. He loaded the shotgun just in case he saw something on the way. When he came to a barbed-wire fence he rested the gun on the top strand and proceeded to throw his leg over. The gun was dislodged and went off. His old fellow copped the lot.

He managed to stagger into the nearest town and ask for a doctor. The doctor was horrified at the sight of the multi-holed member, but told the man he would do what he could. On the operating table, the doctor pulled out pellets one by one with tweezers and dropped them into a tray. *Ping, ping, ping.*

Eventually the doctor said that he thought he had the lot out. The pommy asked if he would be all right in his future. The doctor said, 'I think you will be okay, but before you go I suggest you see my brother next door.'

'I sure will, doc. Is he another doctor?'

'No, he's not a doctor, he's a musician. He will show you where to put your fingers so you don't piss in your eye!'

'You show me yours and I'll show you mine,' said the little boy to the little girl behind the shelter shed.

So she pulled down her knickers.

'Look, I'm growing feathers.'

'Then cop this,' said the little boy, as he lowered his pants.

'Christ, you've grown the neck and giblets as well,' she wailed.

Smarten up your act or I'll give you a Blundstone enema.

In fifth dynasty Egypt, a couple of scribes were quilling hieroglyphs onto papyrus, loudly proclaiming the merits of the Pharaoh Cheops. One tapped the other on the shoulder. 'How do you spell macho, mate? One testicle or two?'

'Doctor, I've got five penises.'

'How do your pants fit?'

'Like a glove.'

A bloke went to the doctor. Told him about his farting problem. 'The noise is bad enough,' he says, 'but it's the smell, doc. My farts stink to high heaven. They're ruining my social life.'

'Don't worry,' says the doctor, 'it'll just be a small internal problem. I'll be able to fix you up.'

Just then the bloke lets another one go.

'Christ!' the doctor says, fanning the air with a prescription pad. 'That's the worst-smelling fart I've ever smelt. And that's saying something.' And he gets up, goes to a cupboard, and returns with a long, long bamboo pole, with a sort of metal hook on the end. The patient takes one look and whispers, 'What the fuck are you going to do with that?'

'I'm going to open the skylight.'

Sin-shifters

What's white and hangs off clouds?
The coming of the Lord.

The Morgan Gallop Research organisation was conducting a poll on Australian sexuality. The pollster knocked on the door of a manse. 'Excuse me, sir, how often do you do it?'

'Oh, about seven or eight times a year,' replied the distinguished man who'd half opened the door.

'That doesn't seem very often,' said the researcher.

'Well, it's not bad for a 65-year-old priest without a car.'

Why wasn't Jesus Christ born in Perth?

Because God couldn't find three wise men from the east.

Have you heard of the atheist dial-a-prayer service?

When you phone, nobody answers.

What do you get if you cross a Jehovah's Witness with a Hell's Angel?

Somebody who knocks on your door and tells *you* to fuck off.

A young Irish girl in Dublin went to confession. 'Bless me, Father, for I have sinned. It has been two weeks since my last confession.'

There was a pause. 'Go on, my dear.'

There was silence.

'Come on, come on!'

More silence.

So the priest went out of his side of the confessional and joined her in hers. 'Is it about a boy?'

She nodded.

He kissed her. 'Did he do that to you?'
'Yes, Father. And much worse.'
He fondled her breasts. 'Did he do that to you?'
'Oh yes, Father, and much worse.'
He undressed her and began fornicating in the confessional. When he was finished, he asked, 'And did he do that to you?'
'Oh yes, Father, and much worse.'
The priest yelled, 'What worse can he do to you than that?'
'He gave me the clap, Father.'

A couple of Irishmen were digging up the road outside the local brothel when they saw a C of E vicar approaching. To their astonishment, he ducked through the door. 'That dirty Protestant. What a hypocrite.'
A few minutes later they spotted a rabbi making a sudden detour. 'Did you see what I saw? The Jews are no better.'
And shortly thereafter they spotted a Catholic priest doing the exactly the same thing. 'Mick, take off your hat,' said the other. 'One of the poor girls must be dying.'

One night in an Irish village two revellers were wending their way home when they met the local priest.

'Ah me, lads,' said the priest. 'You look like you've been having a good time.'

'We have, indeed,' said the revellers.

'And what might you have been up to?' said the priest.

'Well, Father,' said one of the revellers, 'we've been down at the pub and everyone has been playing this great game. The women are blindfolded, the men put their willies on the bar and the women have to tell who it is by the feel of their willies.'

'That's disgusting!' said the priest. 'I'll go straight down there and stop that.'

'Oh, I wouldn't do that if I were you, Father,' said the revellers.

'And why not?' asked the priest.

'Because your name has been mentioned a couple of times already.'

The doctor explained to the young patient that he was suffering stress, which, if he didn't do something about, could well lead to depression. 'Take life easier,' was his advice. 'Do you drink?'

'No, I don't.'

'Well, there's no harm in a few drinks. And

although I don't usually recommend smoking, I reckon a few cigarettes wouldn't hurt you. They'd help you relax. As would sex, at least once a week. In fact, given your symptoms, that's essential.'

A few months later the patient returned and was obviously in better health. He told the doctor how much he enjoyed his glass of beer each night and, as well, the odd cigar.

'And what about sex?'

'Hard to find it every week,' said the patient, 'especially for a parish priest in a small country town.'

A prostitute had been visiting a psychiatrist for many, many years, principally to discuss the sexual guilts caused by her profession.

He tried to maintain a professional distance but, suddenly, they were in each others arms and then bonking on the couch.

When it was over they lay quietly, side by side. Then both said simultaneously, 'That'll be $100.'

'Trouble with you, Hymie Goldstein,' said St Peter at the Gates, 'is that you've got a perfect record. Not a blemish. A life of good deeds.'

'So what's the problem?' asked the puzzled Hymie.

'Trouble is, you're too good to be true. We've dozens of popes up here that don't come near you for good deeds. And we'd have to place you above them in the heavenly hierarchy. We follow strict protocol up here, particularly when it comes to good deeds.'

'Sorry,' said Hymie.

'Look,' said St Peter, 'seeing that you're such a good bloke why don't we send you back for another hour or so. Maybe you could do something a little bit naughty in that time. And with your record, you'd still be in the upper echelons. But we wouldn't have the protocol problem with the popes.'

Reluctantly Hymie agreed.

'So here's the deal. You've got an hour, and no more good deeds.'

Instantly Hymie was back in his house as the clock was striking 11. What am I going to do? he thought. I don't drink, I don't gamble. I've never had sex. How am I going to commit even a venial sin? After wasting the first 30 minutes worrying, he thought of the middle-aged lady in the flat next door. And he remembered, decades earlier, lusting after her. Finally he plucked up courage and knocked on the door.

'Oh, how nice to see you. I heard you were ill.' Plucking up all his courage he rushed at her, threw her on the couch, ripped off her knickers and put an end to both their virginities. At that very moment, the clock started to strike 12. As the room began to blur and he heard the faint sound of an angel's chorus, he could hear a woman's voice. 'Oh, thank God! Thank God! Only God and I will know what a good deed you've done!'

Two nuns were riding on their bicycles through a French provincial town. 'I haven't come this way before,' said one nun.

'Must be the cobblestones,' replied the other.

The Hare Krishna rushed into a Catholic church in the middle of Mass, calling out, 'My karma has run over your dogma!'

'Excuse me, sir, for interrupting you, but we've a very, very good reason for knocking on your door like this. We want to invite you to become a Jehovah's Witness.'

'No fuckin' way. I didn't even see the accident.'

And old couple were watching the telly one Sunday morning. An American televangelist was jumping up and down, raving and ranting and Bible-bashing, and punctuating proceedings with constant demands for donations. Suddenly he changed tempo and became terribly, terribly sincere. He brought the camera very close to his face and told his viewers that he would transmit some spiritual healing. 'What you must do is place one hand on your heart and the other on the organ that needs a miracle.'

The old lady put one hand on her heart and the other on her arthritic elbow.

The old bloke put one hand on his heart and the other on his withered genitals.

'For God's sake,' said the old lady, 'he said he was going to heal the sick, not raise the dead!'

A bloke was at the Gap, down on his luck, and about to end it all. As he approached the edge, a voice out of nowhere said, 'Don't jump! Don't jump! Cardinal Gilroy will save you!'

The bloke stepped back, looked around, but couldn't see anybody. He approached the edge once more and was about to leap when the voice called out, 'Don't jump! Don't jump! Cardinal Gilroy will save you.'

He jerked back, spun around and looked behind him. No one was there. No one was anywhere in sight. He frowned and once more approached the edge, when the voice once again cried out, 'Don't jump! Don't jump! Cardinal Gilroy will save you!'

And the bloke shouted back, 'Who the hell's Cardinal Gilroy?'

And the voice replied, 'Jump, you Protestant bastard, jump!'

The Archbishop of Canterbury was sitting in the back of St Paul's Cathedral quietly fondling himself beneath his habit. He was so preoccupied that he didn't hear a tourist approach him. But the flash of the camera brought him back to Earth with a jolt.

'Please, please, sell me the film,' he begged. 'In fact, I'll buy the camera.'

Later the Dean noticed that the Archbishop had a new camera. 'How much did you pay for it?'

The Archbishop said, very glumly, 'Two thousand pounds.'

'Christ,' said the Dean, 'somebody saw you coming!'

Taosim: Shit happens
Protestantism: Let shit happen to someone else
Catholicism: If shit happens, you deserved it
Judaism: Why does shit always happen to
                   us?
Atheism: No shit
TV Evangelism: Send more shit
Buddhism: If shit happens, it is not really shit
Zen Buddhism: What is the sound of shit
                   happening?
Jehovah's
   Witnessism: We can only take so much shit
Hinduism: This shit happened before

Zen and the office party
Taoist: Office parties happen
Hindu: This office party has happened
                   before
Freudian: I dreamt I had an office party
Hare Krishna: Partyrama, rama, rama
Cartesian: I office party. Therefore I am
Protestant: I've worked hard for this office party
Catholic: I deserve this office party
Jehovah's
   Witness: *Knock, knock.* Where's the office party?
Jungian: Let's analyse this office party
Zen: Let's contemplate this office party

Buddhist:	When is an office party not an office party?
Mormon:	Office parties happen again and again and again
Jewish:	Why do office parties always have to happen to me?
Muslim:	Fundamentally, it's an office party
Rastafarian:	Let's smoke this office party

The Council of Adult Education decided to have a series of courses on comparative religion. The most attended course turned out to be on reincarnation, with various would-be Buddhists and local New Agers sitting in rapt attention listening to an account of the Dalai Lamas in Tibet. But there was one bloke in the class who just didn't seem to fit in. During the intense discussion of theological matters he burped, farted and scratched himself. He didn't seem to be paying the slightest attention and, in fact, was disturbing the others.

Finally, the lecturer said, 'Sir, we seem to be boring you. What brought you to a class on reincarnation?'

'Well,' he replied, 'you only live once.'

A really bad bastard who was into drugs, grog, prostitutes and foul language – whose favourite expression was 'fuck the coppers' – was listening to the Salvos in Fortitude Valley. For a while he stood there grinning and chiacking them. But after a while he started listening more seriously. And then he felt tingly and funny all over.

In that moment he decided to mend his ways and join the Salvos.

They were thrilled with their new recruit, and because he was such a big bloke, gave him the big bass drum to bang. After basic training in drumming and oratory, it was his turn to preach. And by an amazing coincidence, the scene took place outside what had been his favourite pub. 'Here I stand before you, ladies and blokes of the Valley. I, too, was like you doing the normal things. I was lecherous, debauched, sodden with booze and dopey with drugs … and the Salvos showed me the light. And now my days of vice are behind me. I'm swelled up – bursting with the joys of Jesus! I'm so full, I could burst this fucking drum!'

A new priest at his first Mass was so scared he could hardly speak. After the service, he asked the Monsignor how he had done.

'Fine, but next week it might help if you put a

little vodka or gin in your water to relax you.'

The next week the new priest put vodka in his water and really kicked up a storm. After Mass he asked the Monsignor how he had done this time.

'Fine,' he said, 'but there are a few things you should get straight:

1. There are Ten Commandments, not twelve.
2. There are twelve disciples, not ten.
3. David slew Goliath, he did not kick the shit out of him.
4. We don't refer to Jesus Christ as the late JC.
5. Next Saturday there will be a Taffy pulling contest at St Peter's, not a Peter pulling contest at St Taffy's.
6. The Father, Son and Holy Ghost are not Big Daddy, Junior and the Spook.
7. Moses parted the water at the Red Sea. He didn't pass water.
8. We do not refer to Judas as El Finko.
9. The Pope is consecrated, not castrated, and we do not refer to him as the Godfather.'

'**Y**ou can go home and tell your husband he's going to be a daddy,' said the doctor.

'But, doctor, I'm not married.'

'Well, you can give the good news to your boyfriend.'

'But I haven't got a boyfriend. I have never been out with a man.'

The doctor looked out the window at the night sky. 'Last time this happened there was a big star in the east.'

The bush parson decided to retire from his duties and announced his intention of selling his horse. Knowing that it was a tough little pony, great for the high country, a farmer immediately offered the reverend $200. They shook on it. But when the farmer climbed into the saddle the horse wouldn't budge.

'Oh, I neglected to point out that he's a very, very religious horse. He will only go when you say "Jesus Christ" and will only stop when you say "Amen".'

The farmer thanked the reverend and said, 'Jesus Christ', whereupon the horse took off at a trot. They were travelling back to the high country when a storm started brewing and a bolt of lightning split a nearby tree. The horse bolted and a low branch struck the farmer in the face, momentarily blinding him. As it galloped wildly through the scrub, he tried to think of the word to make it stop. Finally he remembered. 'Amen!' The horse skidded to a halt. And when the farmer regained his vision, he saw that they'd propped right on the edge of a thousand-metre cliff. 'Jesus Christ!!' he said.

A parson, who always read his sermons, placed his carefully prepared text on the pulpit about half an hour before the service. A young member of the congregation thought it would be funny if he removed the last page.

Preaching vigorously, passionately, the minister came to the following words on the bottom of the page '... so Adam said to Eve ...' Trouble was, there was no next page. The minister was horrified to discover that it was utterly and entirely missing. He looked down at his feet, riffled through the other pages, and gained a little time by repeating, 'So Adam said to Eve ...' Then, in a low voice, which the amplifying system carried to every part of the church, he added, 'There seems to be a leaf missing.'

A new Australian lady entered a tram and sat next to a Salvation Army lass. She turned to the Salvo and said, ''Scuse, please. You are vearink a uniform. Vot is it?'

The Salvation Army girl said, 'I work for the Lord Jesus.'

'Very intelesting,' said the new Aussie. 'I'm a verken for the Kraft cheeses.'

A young novice was climbing up the hill towards the grim-looking convent. She carried a little cardboard case in her hand, containing the few items she'd be permitted once inside the walls. Halfway up the hill she stubbed her toe on a rock. 'Oh, shit!'

Standing still she looked around. 'Oh, fuck, I said shit.'

She bit her lower lip. 'Oh, shit, I said fuck.'

Whereupon she turned around and headed down hill. 'Stuff it, I didn't want to be a nun anyway.'

After years of training in the seminary, three young priests were assigned to parishes in and around Tottenham. The girl in the ticket box was uncommonly mammiferous and the priests were somewhat nonplussed.

'Three tickets to Titterston,' stammered the first, prior to blushing and retreating.

'Here, I'll have a go,' said the second priest. 'Three titties to Tockerton.'

'Christ, you're making a real mess of it,' said the third. He snatched the money and approached the window. 'Three tickets to Tottenham, Miss,' he said very, very formally, 'and unless you dress more demurely St Finger will point his Peter at you.'

The Pope was rapidly declining and medical experts, called in from all over the world, argued over the best approach to the crisis. Finally there was consensus – a lifetime of celibacy had built up a huge store of seminal fluid that was choking the Papal arteries. The only cure? An urgent course of intercourse.

The Pope crossed himself and shook his head.

But the physicians were convincing. 'Your Holiness, if you persist in celibacy you'll condemn yourself to death. That is suicide, a mortal sin.'

The Pope asked for three days so that he could pray and consider the theological implications.

On the third day he called the doctors to his bedside. 'I've come to a decision. I will be guided by your advice. But make sure she has big tits.'

A priest was doing the rounds of the Belfast prison. 'What are you in for?' he asked one.

'Murder.'

'And what did you get for that?'

'Life.'

The priest asked a second man what he'd done.

'Forgery. And I got ten years.'

'And what are you in for, my man?'

'Pouring petrol over Protestants and setting them alight.'

'And what did you get for that?' asked the priest.
'About 20 to the gallon,' said the prisoner.

The young novice, on arriving at the convent, was assigned the job of sweeping the steps of the chapel. 'You must keep the entrance immaculately clean,' said the Mother Superior.

Trouble was, the pigeons kept shitting all over them. Every time she got the steps clean, they'd crap on the marble.

'Fuck off! Fuck off!' she'd scream at them.

The Mother Superior said to the novice, 'My dear, your language is unseemly. Just swipe at them with the broom and say "shoo-shoo". Then they'll fuck off.'

Two young nuns went to the supermarket in the convent's mini minor. They couldn't find a parking space so one said she'd keep circling the block while the other ducked into the store.

Returning with a full trolley, the nun could see no sign of her colleague. 'Have you seen a nun in a red mini?' she asked a policeman.

'Not since I stopped drinking,' he replied.

The Mother Superior was addressing the graduation ceremony. 'In the outside world you will be confronted by many temptations. You must remember what you've been taught here. You must cling to your ideals. You must resist all temptation. For example, a man might try to take sexual liberties with you. Remember that one hour of pleasure could ruin your whole life. Any questions?'

'Yes, Mother. How can you make it last an hour?'

The cardinals met in the Sistine Chapel to elect a new Pope. After the first round there was no agreement, so they moistened their ballots and set fire to them, sending the traditional puff of black smoke out of the little vent in the roof. Unfortunately the small fire ignited an old tapestry and within moments the entire chapel was ablaze.

Cut to heaven where the cardinals are lining up for admission. 'Hang on. Don't just go charging in,' roared St Peter. 'You've got to go through the same tests as anybody else. Now, before you're barbecued, how many of you committed sins of the flesh?'

After an awkward silence, 49 cardinals raised their hands. Only one didn't. 'Right,' said St Peter, 'off to Purgatory, you 49. And take the deaf bastard with you.'

At a Catholic school a little girl asks, 'Do angels have babies?'

Whereupon the little boy in front turns around and sneers at her, 'Do they fuck in hell?'

And the nun says, 'Please, please … one question at a time.'

The vicar prepared a beautiful sermon for his Presbyterian church, describing the plight of the poor. 'Is it the charitable duty of the rich to share their wealth?' he said.

Asked how the sermon went, the vicar replied, 'Well, it was a partial success. I convinced the poor.'

The Pope and Don Juan arrived at the Pearly Gates on the same day. Whilst the Pope lingered near the entrance shaking hands with old friends, Don Juan went straight in. When the Pope finally entered, he bumped into Don Juan. 'My son, I want nothing more than to kneel at the feet of the Virgin Mary. Do you know where I can find her?'

'Yes, holy Father, but you're just a bit late.'

A priest from Brunswick who was suffering from depression went to see a psychiatrist. 'I think you should go overseas, to some place where nobody knows you, and have a very, very good time. Why not try Las Vegas?'

So the priest went to Las Vegas and found himself in the front row of a strip show. And when a pneumatic dancer cavorted past him he leant out and stroked her bum.

'No you don't, Father,' said the dancer.

'How do you know I'm a priest?'

'Because I'm Sister Bridget from Footscray and we've got the same shrink.'

A priest was walking through Sydney's Botanic Gardens when he saw a sad-looking frog sitting on a rock in the middle of a pond. 'Why are you so unhappy?' he asked.

'Well, I wasn't always like this. I used to be a happy, normal boy of eleven, a choirboy at St Patrick's church. But one day I was walking through the gardens and I met a witch. "Go away wicked witch", I said. Whereupon she turned me into a frog.'

'My poor child,' said the priest. 'Can the witch's curse ever be reversed?'

'Yes,' said the frog, 'if a nice, kind person were to take me home and give me a hot meal and put me in a nice warm bed and make sure I was kept warm all night. Then, next morning, I'd wake up as a little boy once more.'

The priest put the frog in his pocket, took him home, gave him a bath and a hot meal and put him into his bed. When the priest woke up the next morning, beside him in the bed was an 11-year-old choirboy.

And that, Royal Commissioner Wood, is why I'm innocent of paedophilia.'

At a Christian Revival meeting the evangelist invites anyone who wishes to be healed to speak up. Way up the back of the hall a hand waves frantically. 'Do you wish to be healed?' asked the preacher.

'Yes, preacher.'

'What is your name?'

'My name is Michael.'

'Well, Michael, come down here to the stage.'

So Michael, with callipers and on crutches, struggles down to the stage.

'Go behind the screen, Michael. Who else wants to be healed?'

And from the audience a voice with a severe cleft-palate impediment says, 'Yeth pleathe, I want to be healed.'

'And what is your name?'

'My name'th Patrick.'

'Well, Patrick, come to the stage and go behind the screen. Now, brothers and sisters, let us pray for Michael and Patrick.' And there's much praying and choral singing.

'Now, Michael,' cries the preacher, 'throw out your crutches.' One crutch comes sailing over the screen and lands on the stage at the preacher's feet. Then the second crutch comes sailing over the screen as well.

'Now, Patrick,' says the preacher, 'speak!'

And we hear Patrick's familiar voice saying, 'Michael'th fallen over.'

An Australian hellfire preacher wanted to impress his congregation. He arranged for a boy to get above the pulpit in the loft and let a lit piece of paper flutter down when the preacher reached the great climax of his sermon. 'When I shout "Send fire from heaven", light the paper and let it flutter down.'

The great day came and the thunderous sermon was given. He shouted, 'Send fire from heaven.' Nothing happened. He shouted again, 'Send fire from heaven!' Nothing happened. He shouted again.

The voice of the boy could be heard, 'I can't. The cat's pissed on the matches.'

What do you get if you cross a Jehovah's Witness with an atheist?

Someone who knocks on your door for nothing.

Jesus Christ was having a great deal of trouble raising money for the cause so he called a meeting of his twelve business advisers for a little supper and commercial input.

'I need ideas,' he said. 'Ideas that must raise money quickly or we all go to the wall.'

'What about the hitting of the rock with the staff and bringing forth the wine?' offered John.

'No, no, no!' JC exclaimed. 'Been done to death all over town.'

'Well, there's the feeding the masses with fish and bread,' said John.

'No, no,' said JC, mildly upset.

'What about the walking on the water bit,' said Luke.

'That's it,' said JC, with gusto. 'Rehearsals tomorrow. Sea of Galilee early morning. Be there!'

So the next morning the 13 were down by the sea to rehearse for the big show. They proceeded to walk out into the water without much trouble, except for one. For him the water came up to his shins, then his hips, then his chest.

John turned to JC and asked, 'Do you think we should tell Judas about the sandbar?'

Two swaggies called in at the presbytery in a country town hoping for a handout. The good father gave them a note and said, 'Take this to the Shamrock Hotel and give it to the proprietor. He'll let you each have a meal and a bath.'

Clutching the note, the swaggies ambled off in the direction of the Shamrock. Then one stopped and said, 'Hey, Bill, what's a bath?'

'How would I know?' replied the other. 'I ain't a Catholic!'

There was a conference of cannibals in New Guinea before they had made progress and learnt how to kill each other with guns. They discussed the different missionaries they had eaten. Some said they liked Methodists. Some said they liked Baptists. Some said they preferred Catholics and some, the socially upward mobile, said they liked the Church of England. One cannibal said they had had a tough one the other day. They had boiled him and boiled him and boiled him, but he was still very tough. They asked what his denomination was. He said he didn't know, but that he was dressed in a brown habit with a cowl and had a fringe of hair round his bald head. The president of the cannibal conference said, 'You should not have boiled him. He was a friar.'

When does life begin?

Roman Catholics say, 'At the moment of conception.'

Anglicans say, 'When the child is born.'

Jews believe differently: 'Life begins when the kids are married, the dog has died and the mortgage has been paid off.'

A couple of teenagers decided it was time to graduate from heavy petting to intercourse.

'Come round tomorrow morning. It's Sunday and my parents will be at church. But don't forget a condom.'

Next morning the boy arrived at the front door just as her parents were leaving for church. 'We're coming with you,' said the boy.

During the sermon the girl whispered, 'I can't believe what you did. Since when have you been religious?'

'Since I discovered that your dad's the chemist.'

A young bloke confessed to the priest that he'd just had sex with a striptease dancer. 'Her name is Pussy Pink, Father, and she's very, very beautiful. But she's also a good Catholic and I'm bringing her to church on Sunday.'

The priest granted absolution and could hardly wait for Mass. The following Sunday he saw a spectacular redhead sitting in a mini skirt in the front pew. He nudged his organist and said, 'Hey, is that Pussy Pink?'

'No, Father,' said the organist. 'It's just the way the sun is shining through the stained-glass windows.'

The young bride sought advice from the priest in the confessional.

'Father, is it all right to have intercourse before receiving communion?'

'Certainly, my dear. Provided you don't block the aisle.'

A drunk lurched into church, meandered down the aisle and then turned left at the confessional. He sat down and immediately started snoring.

After a few minutes he was woken by the priest banging on the partition.

'No use banging,' said the drunk, 'got no paper here either.'

Two mates arrived in a country town. They didn't know a soul. 'So we're going to confession,' said one.

'To confession?'

'Follow me.'

And he squeezed into the confessional and said, 'It's been a week since my last confession, Father, and I'm sorry to say that I've sinned of the flesh again.'

'Was it Mrs Bridges from the general store?'

'No, Father.'

'Was it one of the Briggs twins from the dairy?'

'No, Father.'

'Don't tell me it was that naughty widow Paterson?'

'No, Father.'

'Well, do your usual penance and be off with you.'

'Well, I've got the names,' said the bloke to his mate. 'Now let's look up the phone numbers.'

Two tramps met. One had in his hand a steaming, fresh meat pie. 'Jesus,' said the other, 'where did you get that, and how did you get it?'

'Easy,' said the first. 'This part of Belfast is very strictly religious and I just demonstrate my Bible scholarship. I go to a house and say, "Good morning, missus. I am a God-fearing, Bible-reading beggar. In fact I know my Bible backwards. I know all about Jonah who spent 40 days and nights in the belly of a whale. I know all about Lot's wife who was turned into a pillar of salt. I know all about Esau who sold his birthright for a mess of pottage and I know all about Samson, that strong man, who killed 40 000 Hittites with the jawbone of an ass. Can I have something to eat?" And there you are, it works every time.'

His friend said he would try the same thing. But next day he needed some courage to try it, so only approached a house when suitably fortified.

He knocked on a convenient door and addressed the owner thus, 'Good morning, missus. I'm a God-fearing fucking beggar. I know my Bible arsewise. I know all about Jonah who spent 40 days and 40 nights on the belly of Lot's wife. I know all about Seesaw who sold his wife's afterbirth for a tin of porridge, and I know all about that strong bastard Sando who killed 40 000 Shittites with the arsebone of a giraffe. Give us a pie.'

Black holes are where God divided by zero.

A nun from the Sisters of Mercy was traipsing around the outback in northern New South Wales. It was in the middle of the drought and she was doing whatever she could to help isolated families.

On her way back to Sydney on a lonely bush track she ran out of petrol. She was at her wit's end and as it was growing dark she knelt in the dust and prayed. A few minutes later an old farmer came bouncing along in his rusty Land Cruiser. Having determined the problem, he asked if she had some sort of container – and all she had was a standard-issue, Sister of Mercy bedpan.

The farmer headed for the nearest town to get some petrol. On his return he thumped down the can and apologised that he'd have to leave immediately as he was in the middle of calving. She assured him she'd be all right – she could decant the petrol into the car.

When she'd almost completed her decanting task, and was down to the last few drops, another farmer came along in an equally rusty Land Cruiser. He looked down from his cabin and said, 'I admire your faith, Sister. But, to be perfectly honest, I don't reckon that will work.'

Doctor Crock

It'd been a really tough drought and a drover had mustered cattle up and down the long paddock. And although he was as tough as old boots, he finished up being saddle sore. So a mate told him to try a folk remedy that a bloke from Cooma had told him about. 'Pour the old water out of the billy and shove the tea-leaves up your arse.' So he did.

And it didn't help much. In fact, his backside was hurting so much that he decided to go and see the doctor.

'Hmmm,' said the doctor. 'Hmmm.'

'Something wrong?' asked the drover.

'Not at all,' replied the doctor. 'You're going to take a long trip and you'll meet a tall, romantic stranger.'

What are three good things about Alzheimer's disease?
1. You can hide your own Easter eggs.
2. You make a new friend every day.
3. You can hide your own Easter eggs.

The scene is the nurses' room at St Vincent's, a meeting place for both sacred and secular staff members. An elderly nun whispers to a non-religious co-worker, 'May, do you happen to know the new patient in bed seven?'

'No, I don't, Sister Mary. Why do you ask?'

'Well, when I was giving him a sponge bath I couldn't help but notice that he has your name tattooed on his penis.'

'Really? I'll go and have a look.' Whereupon she heads for the ward. A few minutes later she returns looking a little disappointed. 'I thought it said May at first,' says May, 'but as soon as I touched it I realised it read, "Matrimony".'

The little bloke was born without a penis. 'No probs,' said the doctor, 'thanks to microsurgery we can do a transplant. All we need is three inches – if we can find a compatible donor.'

The family discussed the matter and agreed that Dad would provide an inch, as would Uncle and Grandpa. The operation seemed entirely successful.

Twenty years later, the door of the surgery burst open and in came an enraged young man.

'Excuse me?' the doctor asked.

'Remember that dick operation you did 20 years ago? Well, I was the kid.' And he belted the crap out of the doctor.

'Why did you do that?' said the doctor as he lay bleeding on the floor.

'For putting Grandad's inch in the middle.'

Lacking confidence in traditional medicine to give her much-desired larger breasts, a young woman consulted a faith healer, Dr Sophius. He told her that the treatment was quite simple, but that she would have to follow his instructions implicitly. This she readily agreed to do.

'Well, three times a day, at precisely 9 a.m., 12 noon and 3 p.m., you must say the following words, "Hooby, dooby, dooby. Give me bigger boobies".'

'Is that all? Are you sure it will work for me, Dr Sophius?' she inquired hopefully.

'Yes,' he replied, 'it will work, but only if you say the spell at the exact times. And have faith in me.'

Off she went. The next day at precisely 9 a.m., nobody near, she uttered the words given by the faith healer, and immediately her bustline increased by 5 cm. Delighted, she waited impatiently for 12 noon. Again, completely alone, she spoke the incantation, and again her breasts increased in size.

As 3 p.m. approached she was at a bus stop near a park. Concerned at the presence of others, she walked into the park until she found a quiet spot near a hedge. There, at precisely 3 p.m., she said, 'Hooby, dooby, dooby. Give me bigger boobies.' Two things happened at once: Her breasts popped out another 5 cm, and a bloke bobbed up from the other side of the hedge. Excitedly, he said, 'You beaut! You and I are patients of the great Dr Sophius!'

'How do you know that?' she asked, embarrassed.

'Watch this,' he said, unzipping his fly as he continued with great confidence. 'Hickory, dickory, dock ...'

A bloke goes to see a psychiatrist. 'I've got a problem, Doc. When I go to bed at night I can't sleep because I've got this feeling that there's somebody under the bed. So I get out of the bed to check and while I'm peering under it, I get this strange feeling that somebody's on top of it. That goes on all night. On top. Underneath. On top. I'm going to have a breakdown.'

'I can cure you,' said the shrink, 'but it will take years. Two visits a week at $100 a visit.'

The bloke never returned. But a year later the psychiatrist saw him in the street. 'Why didn't you come back?'

'At 200 bucks a week? Not when the carpenter next door cured me for $5.'

'How did he do that?'

'He told me to saw the legs off me bed.'

A middle-aged cocky went to his doctor complaining, 'The missus and I have a problem. I'm too tired at night to do any good, and only get horny when I'm on the tractor during the day. But by the time I turn off the motor, jump into the ute and drive back to the house, I've gone off again. Can you give me anything for the problem?'

The doctor thought for a while, then said, 'There is nothing I can give you. But I suggest you take a shotgun with you on the tractor, and when you get the hots, fire a few blasts, jump into the ute and meet your wife, who will have heard the shots and who'll come to meet you by car.'

A couple of weeks later, the doctor saw the guy

in the street and remarked on his happy and contented appearance. 'Doc, your suggestion really works. Thank you, thank you.'

Some time later, the doctor ran into the farmer again and remarked on his miserable and unhappy demeanour. 'Isn't it working any more?'

The farmer replied, 'I'll say it's working. But I haven't seen the wife since the duck season started!'

A bloke goes into hospital for a vasectomy. Afterwards the surgeon tells him there's good news and there's bad news. The bad news is that the hospital mixed up the documentation and they've cut off both of his legs. The bloke is horrified. 'Christ! That's dreadful. What's the good news?'

'The chap in the next bed wants to buy your shoes.'

The bloke went to his doctor and said, 'Look, I've got a problem. Every morning at six o'clock I've got to go to the toilet.'

The doctor said, 'Well, it's good to be regular.'

'Yeah, but I don't wake up until seven.'

A doctor is walking the streets of Dublin when he sees two heroin addicts in the process of injecting each other. He goes up to them and says, 'Look, using heroin is bad enough, but you shouldn't be sharing needles these days. Not with AIDS around.'

And one of the heroin addicts replies, 'Oh, we're safe. We're both wearing condoms.'

A man was committed to Callan Park for many years. One day he was taken before a panel of doctors to see if he was fit to be released. 'If you were let out, what would you do?' asked a doctor.

'I'd make a shanghai and shoot little birds,' said the patient.

The doctors looked at each other, shook their heads and locked him up again.

A few years later he was taken before the panel again.

'What would you do if you were released?'

Once again he said he'd make a shanghai and shoot little birds. Once again he was locked up.

A few years later he was taken before the panel for a third time.

'What would you do if you were released?'

'I would walk down the street until I found a pretty girl,' he said.

The doctors looked at each other, venturing

small nods of their heads. Things looked promising.
'Yes, yes. What would you do then?'

'I'd put my arm around her and walk her down
to the beach.'

'Yes, yes. What would you do then?'

'I'd lay her down in the sand.'

'Yes, yes! What would you do then?'

'I'd take her pants off.'

'Yes, yes! What would you do then?'

'I'd take the elastic out of them, make a
shanghai and go and shoot little birds!'

A bloke arrives at the local surgery and tells the
receptionist that he has an appointment with the
doctor. He's ushered into a consulting room and,
after a few minutes, a rather flustered medico
appears. The man says, 'Well, tell me about the tests.'

The doctor replies, 'I've confusing news for you,
Mr Jones. We did the test on your wife, and the
result was mixed up with another test. Consequently
your wife has either AIDS or Alzheimer's.'

'But that's a terrible situation, doctor,' said the
bloke. 'What should I do?'

The doctor thought about it for a moment. 'The
best solution for you is to go home and send your
wife down to the shop for a newspaper,' he said.
'And if she comes back, don't fuck her.'

A female dwarf goes to a doctor complaining of an embarrassing itch in the groin area. The doctor looks her up and down, picks her up and stands her on his desk. He lifts up her skirt and puts his head under. A little perplexed, she hears, *snip, snip, snip, snip, snip.* The doctor emerges from under her skirt.

'How's that?'

'Well, it's a lot better, actually. But … it's still there.'

Undaunted, he dives back under the skirt. *Snip, snip, snip, snip.* Out he comes.

'How's that?' he asks again, more confident.

'That's wonderful! What did you do?'

'Trimmed the top of your ugg boots.'

'Now, what seems to be the problem?'

'I have this recurring dream about having sex.'

'Well, that's not so unusual.'

'Yes, but I have sex with biscuits.'

'Biscuits?'

'Yeah, biscuits.'

'Wholemeal biscuits?'

'No, not wholemeal.'

'Chocolate biscuits?'

'No, not chocolate.'

'Milk Arrowroot?'

'No.'

'Nice?'

'No, not Nice.'

'Well, what sort of biscuits?'

'Ryvita. Always Ryvita.'

'Then you are fucking crackers.'

After meeting at various IVF clinics in their quest to become pregnant, two women bumped into each other at David Jones. 'My dear, look at you! You must be seven or eight months pregnant!'

'Yes, I finally gave up on science and went to a faith healer.'

'Oh, my husband and I tried that. We went to one for months.'

'That's not how you do it. You've got to go alone.'

'I'm sorry, my old friend. But at this stage of your life I have to advise you of the following. There'll be no smoking, no drinking and no sex.'

'But, doctor, life would be meaningless without smoking, drinking and sex.'

'Okay, but only one cigarette after dinner. That's after dinner, not lunch and breakfast. Dinner only. And no more than one glass of wine a day. No spirits, no beer.'

'What about sex?'

'Very, very occasionally. And only with your wife because it's essential to avoid excitement.'

Princess Di was visiting the repatriation home at Heidelberg. In the first bed she was introduced to a bloke with no arms.

'What a wonderful sacrifice you've made for your country,' said the princess.

'That's nothin', your Majesty,' said the bloke. 'If I'd had four arms, I'd gladly have given them.'

In the next bed there was a bloke with no legs.

'What a wonderful sacrifice you've made for Australia,' said the princess.

'Yep,' said the bloke with no legs, 'and if I'd had ten legs, I'd gladly have given them.'

The next bed had a screen around it. When pulled aside it revealed a head on a pillow. Nothing else, just a head.

'What a wonderful sacrifice one has made for one's country,' said the somewhat dismayed Diana.

'Crap,' said the head.

'We do apologise,' said the doctor accompanying the princess.

'Please excuse him. He's got a bit shitty because he's going to the dentist this afternoon.'

In an attempt to lower medical costs, the Kennett government has introduced a new phone-in strategy for the Department of Health. When you ring up, a voice says, 'If you are an excessive compulsive, press number one. Then press number one again. Then again, then again, then again. If you are a manic depressive, press button one, then button nine, then button one, then button nine, then button one, then button nine. If you are a schizophrenic, press all the buttons. If you are paranoid, don't press any button. We're coming to get you.'

A doctor tells his patient, 'I've got good news and bad news. The good news, you've got 24 hours to live.'

'That's good news? What's the bad news?'

'I forgot to call you yesterday.'

A woman goes to the IVF clinic to be artificially inseminated. She's lying with her legs in the stirrups and the doctor comes in, carrying his trousers over his shoulder.

'I'm sorry, madam, but we're out of the bottled stuff,' he said. 'You're going to have to have draught.'

The doctor placed his stethoscope on the young woman's chest. 'Big breaths, my dear.'

'Yeth, and I'm only thixteen.'

A doctor was trying to write out a prescription, but something was wrong. The fingers moved but no trace was left on the page.

Whereupon he realised that what he had in his fingers was a thermometer.

'Bugger it,' he said to the nurse, 'some bum's walked off with my Biro.'

'I've got bad news for you, Mr Briggs. We've just got the tests back and they confirm that you have a comparatively new illness known as RASH.'

'RASH?'

'Yes, RASH. It combines rabies, AIDS, syphilis, and herpes.' Mr Briggs paled visibly.

'We'll have to put you in strict isolation, Mr Briggs,' the doctor said. 'You'll be locked up in a special RASH ward and fed on a diet of flounder, pancakes and pizza.'

'A diet of flounder, pancakes and pizza? Will that cure me?'

'No. But it's easy to slide under the door.'

A 75-year-old woman decides she wants a baby. She goes to an IVF doctor and asks to be put on the program. The doctor tells her she's too old. She promises to donate $100 000 to further research if he lets her join the program. She gets pregnant and has the baby. Some time later friends call round to see the baby. She tells them to wait until it wakes. So they wait. And wait. Hours pass. They ask again if they can see the baby. She says you'll have to wait until it wakes up. 'I've forgotten where I've put it.'

A bloke who thought he was a dog went to a psychiatrist. When invited to lie down he said, 'But I'm not allowed on the couch.'

The doctor shouts at his hard-of-hearing patient, 'What's it today, Mrs Briggs?'

'Oh, doctor, I'm breaking wind all the time,' she replies. 'It doesn't worry me a lot. In fact, it feels quite nice. But there's no smell and no sound.'

'Take this prescription and come back in a week,' says the doctor.

Seven days later he converses with his patient quite normally. 'How are things now?'

'Oh, doctor, I'm still farting,' she said, 'but at least I can hear it happening.'

'Excellent, Mrs Briggs. That's the ears fixed. Now for the nose! And give your Medicare card to the receptionist on the way out.'

'**D**octor, why is the nun in the waiting room crying like that?'

'I just told her she's pregnant.'

'Oh, poor thing.'

'Actually, she isn't pregnant at all. But I've completely cured her hiccups.'

A senior nurse in a Sydney hospital was instructing a new girl in her duties. 'Now go down to bed 12 and give the gentleman there, Mr Wong, a bed bath. Make sure you do him all over. And, dearie, don't you worry when you see it, but he's got his name tattoed on a certain very private part of his anatomy. Just ignore it. Now, off you go.'

Some time later, the senior passed the girl in the ward and asked, 'How did you go with Mr Wong?'

The girl said, 'Fine thanks, sister, but you made a mistake. His name's not Wong, it's Wollongong.'

A new female patient comes into a psychoanalyst's office and he says, 'Take off your clothes and get on the couch.' Surprised, the woman gets undressed and lies on the couch. Whereupon the analyst removes his trousers and climbs on top of her. Afterwards he says, 'You can get dressed now and sit in that chair.' She does so and the analyst says, 'Okay, we've taken care of my problem. What's yours?'

'I'd like to see an outtern.'

'You mean an intern?'

'Whatever you call him, I want a contamination.'

'An examination? In a maternity ward?'

'I don't know what you call it, but I haven't demonstrated for months and I think I'm stagnant.'

A woman rang the family doctor. 'Please come around, doctor. My husband says he's ill.'

'I'm not coming around again, and that's flat. He only thinks he's ill.'

Next day she rang again.

'What is it this time? Does he still think he's ill?'

'No,' she said, 'he thinks he's dead.'

A bloke woke up in a bush hospital and asked why the room was so dark. 'Well,' said the nurse, 'there's a bushfire outside. And we didn't want you to think the operation had been a failure.'

'**Q**uick! I want a tooth pulled. Really fast. We've got to catch a plane. So just rip it out, will ya? Never mind an anaesthetic. We haven't got the time.'

'It will be very, very painful without an anaesthetic.'

'Never mind about the pain. Just do it.'

'Well, that's a very brave attitude. Now, which tooth?'

'Beryl, get in the chair and show the dentist your bad tooth.'

A young bloke goes to his local GP. 'I can't explain very well why I'm here to see you, doctor, but I just feel weak all the time and I've lost interest in all the things I used to enjoy.'

'That's a bit hard to diagnose,' said the doctor, 'but I read only this morning in the *British Medical Journal* that a return to childhood ways and the diet of your early years can work miracles for many people.'

'What's the treatment, doctor?'

'To be brief, you should start drinking mother's milk from its original source.'

'Wherever could I get that?'

'You're lucky, I've just made contact with a young lactating lady who can start your treatment right now. Here is her address.'

The patient knocked at the front door of the apartment and a beautiful young blonde in a diaphanous negligee ushered him into the lounge room. 'Just sit on the couch with me and then lie your poor head on my lap,' she said.

John obeyed, lay his head in her lap and looked up at a descending nipple with a gentle pink areola. He suckled it and blissfully closed his eyes like an infant.

Of course, he rolled his tongue around the nipple and after a few moments the blonde's feelings changed from maternal to amorous. She squirmed somewhat on the lounge and said huskily, 'Is there something else you'd like?'

He pulled his head back and the nipple popped noisily from his lips. 'Yes,' he said dreamily, with his eyes still tightly closed, 'have you got a bikkie?'

An old bloke came gasping into his doctor's surgery. 'I'm frantic, Doc,' he said. 'I've been making love to an old dear at the twilight home and I've got this big erection that won't go away. It's now twice the size it used to be and there's a slight discharge.'

The doctor examined him. 'Congratulations,' he said, 'you're about to come.'

A very old bloke came to see his doctor. 'I'm going to marry a 20-year-old.'

'Well, at your age I think you should take things easy,' said the concerned medico. 'In fact, it might be a good idea for you to take in a young, energetic lodger.'

A year later he bumped into the old bloke. 'How's married life?'

'Wonderful. The wife's pregnant, I'm proud to say.'

'And did you take my advice about the lodger?'

'Yes, I did. She's pregnant too.'

It was visitors' day at the funny farm and all the inmates were standing in the garden singing 'Ave Maria'. And they were singing it beautifully. But the strange thing was that each of them was holding a red apple and tapping it rhythmically with a pencil.

A visitor listened in wonderment to the performance then approached the choir. 'This is one of the best choirs I've ever heard,' he said, 'and I know about choirs. I used to sing with the choir at St Paul's.'

'Yes, I'm very proud of them,' said the conductor.

'You should take them on tour,' said the visitor. 'What do you call them?'

'Surely that's obvious,' said the conductor. 'They're the Moron Tapanapple Choir.'

Struck Dumb

A chemist employed a new girl and left her in charge while he went out for lunch. When he came back he asked if there'd been any customers.

'Yes, a man came in and wanted some Macleans toothpaste. But we didn't have any.'

'Well,' the chemist said, 'you should have sold him something else. You should have tried to get him to buy the Colgate, the Pepsodent or the tooth powder. Make sure that doesn't happen again. If we haven't got exactly what someone wants, try to sell them something else.'

The next day, when the chemist was out at lunch, the same customer came in and asked for some toilet paper.

'Sorry,' said the girl, 'we're right out of toilet paper. Can I interest you in wrapping paper, brown paper, fly paper, sandpaper, or confetti?'

There was a bloke in Sydney who couldn't afford personalised numberplates. So he changed his name to TLX 126.

What's the difference between a magician's act and a bunch of blondes?

The magician's act has a cunning array of stunts.

Why don't blondes breastfeed their babies?

It hurts too much when they boil their nipples.

What do you call a blonde wearing a leather jacket on a motorcycle?

Rebel without a clue.

Why did the blonde want to become a veterinarian?

She liked kids.

What does a blonde do if she's not in bed by ten?
   She picks up her purse and goes home.

A blonde and a brunette are skydiving. The brunette jumps out of the plane and pulls the cord. Nothing happens. She pulls the emergency cord and still nothing. Whereupon the blonde jumps out of the plane yelling, 'So you want to race!'

What do you call it when a blonde gets taken over by a demon?
   Vacant possession.

What's a blonde's idea of safe sex?
   A padded dash.

What do you do when a blonde throws a pin at you?
   Run like hell – she's got a hand grenade in her mouth.

Why did the blonde stare at the orange juice can for two hours?

Because it said 'Concentrate'.

Two blondes were driving along a road by a wheatfield when they saw another blonde. She was in the middle of the wheatfield sitting in a rowboat pulling energetically at her oars. One blonde turned to her friend and said, 'You know, it's blondes like that that give us a bad name.'

And the other blonde said, 'Yes, and if I knew how to swim I'd go out there and drown her.'

A blonde rang the local police station. 'We need help. We're three blondes changing a light bulb.'

The policeman said, 'Look, this is not really a police matter. But have you put in a fresh globe?'

'Yes.'

'The power is on?'

'Yes.'

'And the switch?'

'Yes, yes.'

'And the globe still won't light?'

'No, the globe's working fine.'

'Then what's the problem?'

'We got giddy turning the ladder around and
fell over and hurt ourselves.'

Two blondes were walking through the woods when
one looked down and said, 'Oh, look. Look at the
deer tracks.'

The other blonde said, 'Those aren't deer tracks.
Those are wolf tracks.'

'No, they're deer tracks.'

They kept arguing and arguing and half an hour
later, they were both killed by a train.

How do you plant dope?
Bury a blonde.

What do you call a pimple on a blonde's bum?
A brain tumour.

Why did the blonde keep a coathanger on the
back seat?
In case she locked the keys in her car.

Why does a blonde insist on men wearing condoms?

So she can have a doggy bag for later.

How can you tell that it's a fax from a blonde?

There's a stamp on it.

A policeman pulled over a blonde after she'd been driving the wrong way up a one-way street. 'Don't you know where you're going?'

'No, but wherever it is, it must be unpopular because all the people were leaving.'

Did you hear about the blonde who shot an arrow into the air?

She missed.

Did you hear about the blonde who stayed up all night to see where the sun went?

It finally dawned on her.

A blonde was driving up the highway to the Warner Brothers theme park when she saw a sign saying HOLLYWOOD ON THE GOLD COAST LEFT.

After thinking for a minute she said, 'Oh well,' turned round and drove back to Brisbane.

A brunette is drying herself after a shower when, in her full-length bathroom mirror, she notices a single grey pubic hair.

'Good heavens,' she says. 'I know that you haven't been getting much lately, but I didn't know you were worrying about it!'

Why do blondes have see-through lunchbox lids?
    So they'll know if it's morning or afternoon.

Why did God create blondes?
    Because sheep can't bring beer from the fridge.

What did the blonde name her pet zebra?
    Spot.

Did you hear about the blonde dingo?

Got stuck in a trap, chewed off three legs and was still stuck.

What does a blonde say when she gives birth?

Are you sure it's mine?

Why do blondes take the pill?

So they know what day of the week it is.

What happens when a blonde gets Alzheimer's?

Her IQ goes up.

What's the first thing a blonde does in the morning?

Introduces herself.

What's it called when a blonde blows in another blonde's ear?

Data transfer.

How do you know when a blonde reaches orgasm?
    She drops her nail file.

Why did blondes vote for the GST?
    Because they could spell it.

What did the blonde think of her new laptop?
    She didn't like it because she couldn't get
Channel Nine.

What do you call it when a blonde dyes her hair
black?
    Artificial intelligence.

Why don't you give blondes coffee breaks?
    It takes too long to retrain them.

How do you get a blonde's eyes to twinkle?
    Shine a torch in her ear.

Mick's dog died. So he borrowed Paddy's shovel and went out in the back garden to bury it.

After a while Paddy came out to see how Mick was going, and saw that he'd dug one, two, three holes.

'Why three holes for one dog?'

'Well, you see, the first two weren't deep enough.'

Three builders were working on a Grollo Brothers skyscraper. There was an Australian, an Englishman and an Irishman. The Australian peeled open a sandwich. 'Christ, bloody Vegemite again,' he said. 'If I get Vegemite sandwiches tomorrow I'll jump off this bloody building.'

The Englishman opened his lunch. 'Not cheese again! If I get cheese sangas tomorrow, I'll jump with you.'

The Irishman opened his lunch. 'Not jam again. If I get jam sandwiches again tomorrow, I'll jump too.'

The next day the Australian took one look at his sandwiches. 'Fucking Vegemite,' he said, and jumped off the building.

The Englishman opened his lunch. 'For Christ's sake, cheese!' He jumped too.

Very, very tentatively, the Irishman opened his lunch. 'Bugger me dead, jam again.' And he jumped as well.

At the triple funeral the widows sobbed in each

others' arms. 'If only I'd known that he hated Vegemite,' said the Australian.

'I didn't know he hated cheese so much,' lamented the Englishwoman.

The Irish widow was also deeply shaken. 'I can't figure it out. Paddy always made his own lunch.'

And Englishman, an Irishman and a Scotsman were visiting Luna Park and decided to try the slide. As they lined up to collect their mats, the attendant said, 'Remember that whatever you say on the way down you'll land in at the bottom.'

The Scotsman went first. As he sat on his little mat he began to murmur, 'Money, money, money!' And lo and behold, he landed in a great pile of bank notes.

The Englishman shouted, 'Money, money, money!' too. And he, too, landed in a pile of bank notes.

Then it was the Irishman's turn. He sat on his little mat and launched himself down the long, bumpy slide. 'Weeeee!' he shouted.

An Irishman went ice fishing. He bought himself a hammer, a saw, a stool and a fishing rod. And off he went.

He bashed a hole in the ice with his hammer

and trimmed it with the saw. Then he sat on his stool and started fishing. Whereupon a mighty voice boomed out, 'There are no fish down there!'

The Irishman looked around in astonishment. 'Is that you, God?' he asked nervously.

'No,' boomed the voice. 'It's the manager of the ice skating rink.'

Paddy was very proud of himself. 'I've just finished a jigsaw puzzle, Mick. It was very, very hard and it took me five days to finish it.'

'Five days for a jigsaw puzzle? How many pieces?'
'Forty.'

'Forty pieces. You're telling me that it took you five days to fit 40 pieces together?'

'That's why I'm so pleased with myself,' said Paddy. 'Look. On the box it says five to six years.'

A professional photographer was taking a group photo of workers and machinery in a Belfast factory. He adjusted the tripod and draped the black cloth over the camera and himself. Two factory girls watched with great interest and one said, 'What's he doing?'

The other replied, 'He's going to focus.'
'What? All of us?'

It was a quiz show on telly and the Irish contestant had to complete the following sentence. 'Old McDonald had a ...'

The Irishman yelled out, 'Farm!'

The compere said, 'Great, you're doing very well. Now spell that.'

The Irishman said, 'E-i-e-i-o.'

An Irishman walks into a railway station and presents himself at the ticket counter.

'I'd like a return ticket.'

'Where to?'

'To here!' says the Irishman.

An Irish surgeon has just been admitted to the *Guinness Book of Records*. He was the first medical man to separate a Siamese cat.

An Irishman applied for a job as a strawberry picker. The farmer asked if he had any experience.

'Lots,' said the Irishman. 'I'll show you how good I am. Just lend me a ladder.'

The Irishman went to a brothel, and, seeing a BYO sign on the door, went home to get his wife.

An Irishman was having sex with a Scottish lass and when it was all over she expressed some dissatisfaction. 'Aren't Irishmen supposed to be big and thick?'

'Aren't Scots meant to be tight?'

An Englishman, an Irishman and an Australian were being conscripted into the army. None of them liked the idea.

The procedure began with a medical exam. The Australian was first to be called in, and after a few minutes, returned with a huge grin. 'They've rejected me! They won't have me because I've got FF.'

'What's FF?' asked the Irishman.

'Flat feet,' said the Aussie.

Next it was the pom's turn. And he came out grinning from ear to ear. 'They won't take me. I've got KK.'

'What's KK?' asked the Irishman.

'Knock knees.'

It was the Irishman's turn. After an hour he came out looking very, very pleased.

'I can't go either. They told me I've got TC.'
'TC? What's TC?'
'Terminal cancer,' said the Irishman.

Mick entered the pub, proudly fronting the bar with a handful of dog shit. 'Look what I nearly trod in,' he said.

An Irishman opened a factory in Dublin – to bottle goldfish farts for spirit levels.

An Irishman lost a hundred dollars on the Melbourne Cup. And another hundred on the replay.

An Irishman on Anzac Day: 'Was it you or your brother who got killed in the war?'

An Irish duck overflew his mark and ended up in Australia. He was exhausted from the trip but made extra effort when he saw a pair of native ducks on the horizon. He flew and joined them. However, they travelled a good half hour before anyone broke the silence.

'Quack!' said the first duck.

'Quack!' said the second duck.

'Give us a break,' the Irish duck puffed. 'I'm goin' as quack as I can!'

Two Irishmen from a little village went to Dublin for the first time and decided to go to the cinema, also for the first time. When they got inside, the film had started, so they had to fumble their way down the dark aisle. Seeing their plight, an usher with a torch approached to help them. 'Watch out,' said one to the other. 'Here comes a bike!'

A large Irishman was holding up a telegraph pole while a little Irishman stood on his shoulders with a tape measure. A passer-by said, 'Wouldn't it be easier to lay it on the ground to measure it?'

And the big Irishman said, 'Look, we already know its length.'

And the little Irishman said, 'Now we want to find its height.'

Reilly always slept with a gun under his pillow. Hearing a noise at the foot of the bed, he shot off his big toe. 'Thank the Lord I wasn't sleeping at the other end of the bed,' he said at the pub. 'I would have blown my head off.'

The attendant at the car wash chatted to an emerging customer. 'I bet you're Irish.'

'Now how on earth did you guess that?' said the customer.

'Well, to tell the truth, we don't get too many people coming through here on motorbikes.'

An Irishman is on a quiz show, and the compere, in his very best Kenneth Williams accent, asks him, 'Can you name three famous people from history?'

And the Irishman is there thinking and thinking. 'Ah, tree famous people from history, eh? Oh dat's a hard one? Oh, yes. Joan of Arc, Alfred da Grate, und Dick da Shit.'

The audience is aghast. The compere is beside himself, and just as the studio manager is about to eject the Irishman from the set, his mate in the back row stands up and yells, 'I tink he means Richard da Turd!'

An Irishman decides to go on a quiz show and the compere asks him, 'Tell me, can you give the first names of these three famous people from history: Churchill, Hitler and Gandhi?'

'Ah, Churchill, eh? Arr, Winston. Yus, dat's it, Winston. Now, Hitla. Oh, dat's a hard one. Hitla. Yus. Oh! A-dolf. Yus, dat's it, A-dolf. And Gandhi, eh. Gandhi. Oi know, oi know. Goosey Goosey.'

Irish aphrodisiac: a crate of Guinness and a housebrick.

'You know,' said the Irish farm labourer to his boss, 'I feel very guilty working for you.'

'How so?' asked the farmer, surprised.

'Sure, I have the feeling that I'm doing a pair of horses out of a job.'

'The train for Edinburgh will leave from platform three at 20 minutes to four,' said the fella over the intercom at Victoria Station. 'The Birmingham express will leave from platform two at half past five. And those of you who are going to Dublin, listen

closely. Keep an eye on the clock and when the big
hand's pointing straight to the top and the little
hand's right at the bottom, then you go and get on
your train, which is the big green one.'

'**P**addy', said the farmer, 'go out and see if it's raining.'
'Aw, Da,' answered his son, 'can't you call in the
dog and see if it's wet?'

The new police officer found a dead horse in
Chichester Street, Belfast. 'How do you spell
Chichester?' he asked the group of onlookers, but no
one knew, or was game to assist a policeman in front
of witnesses.

'All right then. Some of you give me a hand to
pull the animal into Mary Street.'

An Irishman, an Englishman and an Australian are
at the local pub, lamenting their woes. The
Englishman says, 'Old chaps, I think my wife is
having an affair. I came home yesterday to find the
room in disarray, and when I checked under the bed
I found a whole lot of pipes and wrenches. I think

she's having an affair with a plumber.'

His companions feel his pain, and the Australian takes a swill of his beer before telling his own sorry story. 'That's nothing. I think my wife is having an affair too, but with an electrician. I checked under the bed and found a tangle of insulation wires. She's doing the dirty on me.'

They sit in silence for several minutes, before the Irishman confesses, 'My wife, I'm sure, is having an affair with a horse, and I'm right upset about it. I came home one evening and found our bedroom all messed up. And when I checked under the bed, I found a damned jockey!'

Identity Crises

In many outback cattle properties, stock work would have been impossible without a ready supply of cheap Aboriginal labour. And cattlemen, given the opportunity, liked to breed a few extra stockmen for themselves.

During the worst of a hot summer, Missus went down to Brisbane until the temperature dropped. Her husband would go down for a few days at Christmas but spent most of his time with the herd.

On return in the autumn, Missus would resume command of the household and smarten up the domestic staff, mostly lubras, questioning old Betty on how things had gone in her absence. And Missus was determined to obtain all the facts. All of them.

'When Missus away, boss muck about a bit?' she would ask.

'No, Missus,' came the sing-song response. ''E no muck about. 'E fair dinkum.'

A black-faced bloke is sitting at the bar in a pub in Surfers Paradise. The local drinkers have never seen an Abo there before and can't help but notice that he has a very white middle finger. Later the black-faced bloke goes into the gents' for a piss, and one of the other drinkers follows him. He notices that the blackfella has a white penis – and comes out and tells his mate. 'He's got a white finger and a white dick,' he whispers to the barman.

'No worries, mate,' the barman says, 'he's just another bloody Cessnock coalminer up here on his honeymoon.'

Why are local Abos migrating to Thailand?
They want to be Thai coons.

An Aborigine goes to heaven. St Peter is pretty impressed to see a blackfella from Australia. 'I'm so impressed that I'm going to send you back to Earth so you can spread the glad tidings to other

Aborigines. What would you like to be reincarnated as?'

'A piece of dog shit.'

'Why a piece of dog shit?'

'Well, you lie around in the sun and go whiter and whiter and the cops don't pick you up.'

Captain Cook arrives in Australia and is astonished by the flora and fauna. Seeing a native standing on one leg, leaning on his spear, he asks, 'What's that funny animal jumping around, going boing, boing?'

'Kangaroo,' comes the reply.

'What did you just tell that pommy bloke?' asks another Aborigine who'd been watching the scene.

'Kangaroo. Which means, as you know, I haven't the foggiest idea what you're fucking well talking about!'

Jacky is walking down the main street when he spots another well-known Aborigine leaning against a light pole. He walks over and says, 'Hey! You jist the fella I wanna see. I need some advice from yuh.'

'Yeh, what's the problem, mate? Tell uz all 'bout it.'

'Well, last month I bought a colour TV and

yesterdy I got this here bit of peper in the mail an it sez I owe them munney for the TV. I got the munney, what I got to do wit it?'

Wilf takes the piece of paper from Jacky, glances at it, and says, 'Whitey calls this thing a beel but you dun hav to worry 'bout it cos wese on weelfahr and the guvmint look after us blackfellas. You got the munney, eh? Good, we can go and get a coupler phaglons uv red and hev a party.' Which they proceed to do.

Some two months later Jacky is in town again and sees Wilf, walks up to him and says, 'Eh, Wilfey, I got another pise of peper in the mail yesterdy. This wun called a summens as they wan more munney. I got the munney, what I do, Wilfey?'

Wilf takes the paper and says, 'Gise a look at it. I tol you last time that wedon hev to wurry 'bout things like this cos wese on weelfahr the guvmint look after us. Got the munney, eh! This time we can get tree phaglons uv red and hev a bigger party than las time!'

Some three months later Jacky spots Wilf in the community store and says, 'Some mate you are. Your advice ain't worth a piece uv crow shit. I now go anudder pise uv peper this wun called a subpena. It's for a lot more munney. What the hell is a subpena?'

Wilf takes the subpoena from Jacky and scans it. 'Eh, Jacky, this in Letin. I dun read Letin. Hey hang on. Member wen we wuz goin to the coven

and them nuns wuz tring to learn uz them things at
the beginnin and end uv words. Well, they wuz
Letin. Well, sum uv it coming bek. Let me tink. If I
remember right now. Sub mean under. Pena, dat
probably mean penis. Sub, under, penis. Under
penis. Hey, Jacky, I tink dey got you by the balls und
you bitter pey.'

A blackfella goes to a doctor. He's got a parrot
sitting on his head and the parrot looks at the doctor
and says, 'Hey, how can you remove this blackhead
I've got on my foot?'

An Aborigine goes into his local employment
office. Says he wants a job. Bloke checks the cards.
'Got one here – Managing Director of Grace
Brothers, just down the road.'

The Abo looks at him with astonishment,
bewildered.

'And what about this? Chief of the Reserve
Bank. Or Managing Director of the Nine Network?'

'Oh, stop bullshitting,' says the Abo.

'You started it,' says the employment officer.

How do we know that Adam and Eve weren't
Aboriginal?
　　Because if they were they'd have eaten the
bloody snake.

How do we know that The Man from Snowy River
was Aboriginal?
　　If he was white, people would have remembered
his name.

What do you call ten Aborigines in one cell?
　　A chandelier.

An elderly Aboriginal couple were on a pedestrian
crossing in Darwin when a drunken hoon in a four-
wheel drive, doing a good 100 km/h in the 60 zone,
skittled them. One was thrown violently into the air
and landed metres away in a bush. The other crashed
through the windscreen, finishing up on the Toyota's
back seat.
　　'Will there be any charges, mate?' slurred the
tattooed redneck driver when the cops arrived.
　　'Bloody oath,' said the cops, 'we'll charge the

one in the bush with leaving the scene of an accident without giving his name and address, and we'll get the other on breaking and entering.'

A tourist goes up to an Aborigine in the Kimberleys. 'They're very nice sunglasses,' he says.
'They're not sunglasses. They're my nostrils.'

Two Aborigines were discussing the new Northern Territory government's policy on Aborigines.
'They're paying us to have these injections. You only need one and it turns you white. And they give you 500 bucks in return.'
'Well, let's get them.'
'No, let's one of them try it and see if it works. Then we can meet later, have a beer and talk about it.'
So one had the injection, got the $500 and met his mate at the pub.
'Cripes, it works. You've gone all white, man. Come on, let's have a drink.'
'Wait a minute. You don't expect me to be seen drinking with a blackfella!'

It was a hot day in north Queensland and a traveller came to an inlet where there was an Aborigine sitting on the bank. The traveller asked, 'Are there any sharks in here, mate?'

'No sharks, boss.'

So the white joker stripped off and dived in. After a while he asked the Aborigine why he wasn't swimming.

'Too many crocodiles, boss.'

The boss and the Aboriginal stockman go shooting. They agree to share the bag. They shoot a turkey and a crow.

Back at the station the boss says, 'Well, Albert, we agreed to share the bag so I'll let you decide. Either I'll take the turkey and you take the crow, or, if you prefer, you take the crow and I'll have the turkey.'

Albert thought for a while and said, 'Funny thing, boss, but which ever way we share, I seem to cop the crow.'

A whitefella is driving in the outback. He gets utterly, hopelessly lost. He sees an old Aboriginal bloke sitting under a tree. He pulls over and asks, 'Hey, mate, can I take this road to Sydney?'

'Might as well. You've taken every other bloody thing.'

A hungry Kakadu crocodile was waiting on a bank of a river for a boatload of plump American tourists. Days passed, no tourists. Finally an Aborigine came down to the river to spear barramundi, and although he was pretty skinny, the crocodile decided that he'd be better than nothing. So he lunged at him, grabbed his feet and began to gulp him down, bit by bit. Whereupon the long-awaited boat of American tourists came into view. One of them spied the head sticking out of the croc and said, 'Look! Look!'

Another tourist, a woman, said, 'I thought they said Aborigines were poor. Well, there's one with a Lacoste sleeping bag.'

An Aborigine went to the doctor and explained that no matter how many times he and his wife had intercourse, they couldn't conceive. Could the doctor possibly help?

'Well, the best thing for you to do is bring me a specimen of your semen. Here's a container for that very purpose.'

Two days later the Aborigine returned to the

surgery and plonked the specimen container down on the table. The doctor stared at it and said, 'But there's nothing in it. It's empty.'

'I couldn't manage it,' said his patient. 'You don't know the trouble we had, trying to do what you told me to do.'

'What happened?' asked the doctor.

'Well,' said the Aborigine, 'I held it in my right hand, then I held it in my left hand. Then my wife held it in her right hand, then her left hand. Then my mother-in-law tried it with her teeth in. And then with her teeth out.'

'And, and . . .?'

'And we still couldn't get the bloody lid off!'

A large Aboriginal lady went to the doctor and told him of the aches and pains she had all over her body. The doctor told her to go behind the screen, remove all her clothes and squat under the window. He then told her to move to one corner of the room and squat there. Looking thoughtful, he asked her to move to another corner of the room and squat down. 'Can you tell what's wrong if I squat down?' asked the extremely large lady.

'No,' said the doctor, 'but I'm thinking of buying a black leather sofa and was wondering where the best place to put it was.'

Two women, one black and one white, were standing outside Long Bay Prison. The white woman said, 'My son got life for rape and murder.'

The black woman said, 'My son got death for drunk and disorderly.'

A whitefella went fishing with an Aboriginal mate who caught all the barramundi while he didn't get any. 'How come you're catching all the fish and I'm not?' he asked.

'Well, it's an old Aboriginal custom. This morning I woke up and my wife was sleeping on her right side, so I've been fishing on the right side of the boat. Yesterday I fished out of the left side of the boat because she'd been sleeping on her left side.'

'And what happens if she's been sleeping on her back?'

'I don't go fishing.'

An old Aborigine was explaining the origin of the term 'boong'. 'It started off a while back when it was still legal to run us over, and the noise off the roo bar was "boong".'

An Abo was walking down the Swan River near the power house when he found a flagon. He dusted it off and there was a big puff of smoke. 'I'm your genie. I grant you two wishes.'

'Okay, I wish I was white.'

So she made him white, adding, 'Hurry up, I haven't got all day. What's your second wish?'

'I wish I was rich and never had to work any more.'

And puff, he was black again.

What three things can't you give an Aborigine?

A fat lip, a black eye and a job.

An Aborigine went to the supermarket and asked the checkout lady, 'Excuse me, where can I get two dozen cans of cat food?'

She said, 'Get out of here. I know what you're like, you coloured people. You're going to feed that to your kids.'

'No, no, no,' he said. 'I've got a cat.'

And she said, 'Well, you're not getting the cat food until I see your cat.'

So he went off and came back with a cat. And she said, 'All right then, here's half a dozen cans.'

Next day he came back and said he wanted some dog food.

'No, you can't pull that on me. I know you're going to feed that to your kids.'

He said, 'Look, I've got a dog.'

She said, 'Bring it in.'

So he went home and brought in his big kangaroo dog, Blue. So she gave him the dog food.

The next day he walked in and presented the checkout lady with a heavy plastic rubbish bag. She said, 'Christ, this smells disgusting.'

'Yeah,' he said, 'could I have half a dozen rolls of toilet paper?'

An Aborigine was driving down the highway in his four-wheel drive when a cop pulled him over. 'Look, you shouldn't be driving in your drunken condition, but I'm only going to give you a caution.' So the Aborigine took off. Only to discover that the copper was alongside him again. 'Bugger this,' said the Abo, 'I'm not going to talk to this bloke again.' So he really put his foot down. But there was the copper alongside him still. So he slammed on the brake and said, 'What's the matter this time?'

And the copper said, 'I've got my handcuffs caught in your door handle.'

An Aborigine went into a whitefella butcher shop and said, 'Crikey, look at those funny things there! What are those legless lizard things?'

The whitefella butcher said, 'They're sausages.'

'Well, I'd better have some of them. How do you cook them?'

'Just like fish,' said the butcher. 'You fry them in the frying pan.'

'So give me a kilo of those things called sausages.'

He came back an hour later and said, 'Boss, give me another ten kilo of them sausages.'

'By God, that's a lot of sausages,' said the butcher, 'you must have a very big family.'

'No, it's not that. But by the time I cleaned and gutted them, there wasn't much left.'

Two Aborigines got married and went to a motel room. He took off his trousers and she said, 'Crikey, you sure got some small knees.'

'Yeah, I know. When I was a kid I got kneemonia and my knees ain't grown since.'

With this he took off his shoes. 'Crikey, you sure got small toes.'

'Yeah, I know. When I was a kid I got toemain poisoning and my toes ain't grown since.'

Next he took off his underpants. 'Crikey, I'm glad you never got dicktheria!'

What do you call two Abos in an overturned car?
Tenants.

'I've got an identity crisis,' announced the eight-year-old, coming home after school.

'What do you mean?' said his mum. 'You're only bloody eight.'

'Yeah, but Mum, you know the problem. You're Aboriginal and Dad's Jewish.'

'So what?'

'I'm confronted by an ethical dilemma,' said the kid. 'You see, there's this terrific bike at school that a kid wants to sell me for $20. And I don't know whether to offer him $10 – or to pinch it.'

A group of English cabinet makers were in Australia looking for interesting timbers. At a timber mill in Victoria they were inspecting some newly sawn timbers and asking for information.

'Now this,' said the Aussie, 'is hardwood, and it's used for makin' kegs for beer.'

'He means barrels for ale,' a posh voice announced from the back of the group.

'And this one is hard, hardwood, and it's used for makin' coffins for stiffs.'

337

'He means caskets for corpses,' said the posh voice up the back.

The Aussie let the remark pass and pointed to a third example of local timber.

'And this one is hard, hard, *hard*wood and it's used for makin' piles for piers. And for the benefit of the bloke up the back, I don't mean haemorrhoids for aristocrats.'

A Kiwi farmer counting his sheep: '303, 304, 305, hello darling, 307, 308 . . .'

A Welshman and an Englishman were arguing politics in the pub. The pommy, a left-winger, said, 'Margaret Thatcher has a face like a sheep's arse.'

Whereupon the Welshman punched him in the moosh.

'Christ, I didn't know you were a Conservative,' said the pom, spitting out a broken tooth.

'I'm not,' said the Welshman. 'I'm a shepherd.'

Two women were standing outside a little supermarket in Alice Springs wondering what to do with their noisy kids. The white woman decided to plonk hers in the kids' seat on the trolley and went into the supermarket. The black woman's trolley didn't have a kids' seat so she called her son over. 'What am I going to do with you?' she asked.

A white redneck was walking past. 'Why don't you lick his lips and stick him to the shop window?'

A New Zealand couple had been living in a *ménage à trois* but it was creating serious tensions. So they ate the sheep.

Why do seagulls have wings?
  To beat the Abos to the tip.

Why do Abos have big nostrils?
  Big fingers?

What do you call an Abo with dandruff?
  A lamington.

How does an Irishman have a bubble bath?
Sits in a puddle and farts.

How do you get a pom out of the bath?
Turn on the water.

What did the Irish dingo do?
It ate the pram.

What do you call an Abo with a gun?
Sir.

An Italian man fishing on Port Phillip Bay found
that his aluminium dinghy was sinking. He grabbed
the radio and yelled, 'Maya Daya, Maya Daya, I sink.
Quick, help! The little bambinos hava no papa ifa no
one helpa!'

'No worries, mate,' said a crackly voice. 'We've
received your call and are immediately despatching
our Fokker Friendship to assist you.'

'I no want your fokker friendship. I want your
fokker help!'

How do you stop Fijians from jumping on your bed?
Stick velcro on the ceiling.

A migrant, just off the boat from Italy, walks into a
country pub. He tells the drinkers, 'My name isa
Luigi. I'm a new Australian and prouda to be here.'

Whereupon he walks to the bar and asks for an
empty glass. He pees into it and drinks the lot. He then
leaves the pub and heads for the cattleyards with a
number of puzzled fellow drinkers wandering behind.

To everyone's astonishment, he squats on the
ground and starts talking to some cow manure.

He then hops over a side fence, grabs a chook
from a backyard pen, and attempts to have sex with it.

Finally one of the drinkers says to Luigi,
'Whaddaya think ya doin'?'

Luigi says, 'I wanta be a good Australian. I
wanta be justa like you. I wanta drinka the piss, talka
the bullshit, fucka the chicks.'

A n Italian started work on a building site and his
foreman said, 'We've lots of ethnics here so we give
everyone a nickname, according to their country of
origin. Since you're from Italy, we're going to call
you Wog.'

Noticing that the Italian bloke was insulted, the foreman said, 'Look, I'll introduce you to the other fellas and you'll get the picture. This is our Greek. We call him Nick the Greek. Nick the Greek, meet Wog the Italian.

'This bloke's from Edinburgh. He's called Mack the Scot. Mack the Scot, this is Wog the Italian.

'This bloke's from Dublin. He's Paddy the Irishman. Paddy, meet Wog the Italian.

'Finally, this is our one home-grown Australian. We call him Whacker the Australian, or Whack for short. Whack, meet Wog.'

Having finished the introductions, the foreman left them to get on with it.

On his return he was horrified to see the others kicking the shit out of the Italian. He yelled out, 'Nick, Mack, Paddy, Whack, leave the Wog alone.'

A new Australian, with a reasonable command of English, starts his first job. It's on a building site, and within a few minutes, he's offended when a co-worker, albeit in a friendly tone of voice, calls him a bastard. The new Australian complains to the foreman, proclaiming his legitimacy. In an attempt to build a bridge of understanding, the foreman calls out, 'Okay, which one of you bastards called this bastard a bastard?'

A businessman in India visits the local store and
buys a few groceries. Pappadams, curry, rice,
vindaloo paste. He then asks the bloke behind the
counter for a roll of toilet paper. He presents him
with a lovely 600-sheeter, Lady Scott two ply, with a
very discreet design deriving from the Willow
pattern.

'How much?'

'Ten rupees.'

'Too much, too much. Something cheaper.'

Out came a roll of Sorbent. 'Heavenly soft and
most absorbent,' said the shopkeeper.

'How much?'

'Six rupees.'

'Too much, too much. Waste of money. Got
anything else?'

'Well, only the house brand.' And he reached
under the counter to produce a rather bleak-looking
roll of paper, somewhat off-white in colour and
unevenly rolled on the spindle.

'How much?'

'Two rupees.'

The businessman hands over the coins and
departs. He returns the next day with what was left
of the roll.

'Lady Scott, Sorbent, what do you call this?'

'It doesn't have a name,' says the shopkeeper.

'You should call it John Wayne.'

'Why John Wayne?'

'Because John Wayne, he take no shit from no Indian.'

Did you hear about the New Zealander who thought the Canning Stock route was an annual event?

Two Englishmen, two Scotsmen, two Welshmen and two Irishmen were stranded on a desert island. The Scotsmen started the Caledonian Club to celebrate all things Scottish – tossing the caper, playing the bagpipes. The two Welshmen started an eisteddfod. The two Irishmen formed the IRA and agreed to blow up anything built by the English. The two Englishmen went to opposite ends of the island and would not talk to each other as they had not been introduced.

In Italy a poll was taken to determine why men got up at night. Here are the results:

10% to raid the fridge;
15% to have a pee;
75% to go home.

Soon the Japanese will own so much of Queensland that visitors will have to leave their shoes at the New South Wales border.

A New Zealander was wandering along Bondi Beach when he saw an Australian bloke jumping up and down on a manhole cover.

He was shouting, 'Twenty-nine, twenty-nine, twenty-nine.'

'Uxcuse me,' says the Kiwi, 'bit why are you doing thet?'

'Exercise,' the Australian said. 'Stress relief. Great for getting rid of the tension. You should try it.'

So the Kiwi starts jumping up and down on the manhole cover. And just when he's got himself going, the Aussie yanks the manhole cover away and the Kiwi disappears.

The Aussie slides the manhole cover back into position and starts jumping up and down again. 'Thirty, thirty, thirty.'

A Chinese couple were having a mildly inventive bout of sexual intercourse when he asked his wife for a sixty-niner. She indignantly replied, 'If you think

I'm getting out of bed at this hour to cook you Beef and Black Bean Sauce, you've got another thing coming.'

A Kiwi living in Sydney walked into a shop and said, 'Fush and Chups.'

The shopkeeper replied, 'You'd be a Kiwi, wouldn't you, mate?'

Disgusted, the Kiwi stormed out of the shop, muttering to himself, 'U've gotter git some ilocution lissons so these blddy Ozzies wull live me ulone.' Which he duly did, practising every day, saying over and over, 'Fish and Chips' until he had it word perfect, the vowels no longer strangulated.

Right, he thought, entering the same shop, now I'll show this Aussie bastard. 'Fish and Chips,' he demanded of the shopkeeper in his best Ocker.

'You'd be a Kiwi, wouldn't you, mate?' replied the shopkeeper.

'How the bloody hell did you know?' howled the distraught Kiwi. 'I've just had six months of elocution lessons to get rid of my Kiwi accent.'

'Nothing to do with your accent, mate,' said the shopkeeper. 'It's just that this is a furniture shop.'

An Australian bloke's definition of foreplay:
   'You awake love?'

Why is the Australian bloke like a wombat?
   Because he eats, roots and leaves.

Why do Australian blokes make love with their
eyes closed?
   Because they can't stand to see women enjoying
themselves.

Australian foreplay: 'I'll make you a cuppa after.'

Australian foreplay: 'Brace yourself, Raelene.'

A young English migrant's first job in Australia was
on a cattle station in the far north. After a few
months he asked the blokes what they did for female
company. They said, 'We use a goat.'

347

He was horrified, but after another three months found the thought acceptable. So he joined the other blokes as they went in search of a goat herd. Selecting one, the Englishman was taking his pleasure when he realised that the other blokes were laughing their heads off.

'Why are you laughing?'

Still pissing themselves, they said, 'You picked the ugly one!'

How do you know when a Vietnamese robs your house?

Because your dog is missing and your homework's done.

The shearers had been giving the Chinese cook buggery. They'd put snails in his boots, spiders under his pillow and a dead snake in his coat pocket. Finally they felt a bit sorry for the poor bloke and said that they wouldn't do it any more.

'No more spiders?'

'No,' they promised.

'No more snails? No more snakes?'

'No, no more tricks,' they said.

'Okay, then I stop pissing in soup.'

How can you tell when an Australian's getting better?
    He tries to blow the froth off his medicine.

How can you pick a Kiwi in a shoe store?
    He's the one standing at the ugg boot display
with an erection.

Why is British beer like bonking in a boat?
    They're both fucking close to water.

Why did the Arabs shoot down the Concord?
    Because with a nose like that, it had to be Jewish.

How do you get a one-armed Irishman down from a
tree?
    Wave to him.

What's the difference between a pommy cricket
team and a 747?
    The 747 stops whining when it gets to Sydney.

What's the difference between an Australian wedding and an Australian funeral?
 One less drunk.

Why do Queenslanders call their beer XXXX?
 Because they can't spell beer.

What's the difference between making yoghurt and making an Australian baby?
 With yoghurt you have to start with a bit of culture.

What words are written on the walls of an English brothel?
 PLEASE TELL THE GIRL WHEN YOU'RE FINISHED.

An Irishman walked into a pub in Sydney and asked the barman for a pint of Guinness for himself and a thimbleful of whiskey for his friend. He then pulled a tiny little bloke out of his breast pocket and plonked him on the bar.
 'Is that a leprechaun?' asked the barman.

'No,' said the Irishman. 'It's an Australian with all the bullshit squeezed out.'

How do you get a hundred Vietnamese refugees into a Vegemite jar?
Tell them it floats.

The Nine Network decides that Ray Martin should host a weekly quiz. The contestants are required to guess the identity of a particular object by asking no more than 20 questions, to which the answers must be either Yes or No.

For week after week there's one woman who invariably wins. She becomes the Barry Jones of 20 Questions. No matter how obscure the object, she nails it down in four or five questions. It's like watching a demonstration of Einstein's 'intuitive leap'.

Martin insists there must be a way to catch her out. So he chooses an object himself. 'A nigger's cock,' he says to the studio audience while the champion is out of earshot in a special soundproof room. 'I will repeat that: a nigger's cock.'

The champion is brought into the studio confident and smiling. 'Okay,' says Mr Australia, 'you have 20 questions and three minutes to guess the object starting . . . now!'

'Is it animal?'

'Yes.'

'Is it alive?'

'Usually.'

'I know. A nigger's cock.'

It was a quiz program where contestants were required to answer three questions on chosen topics. An expert could squeeze into the booth with the contestant and assist with the last answer if the contestant had got that far.

Not unexpectedly, one contestant had chosen the topic of sex, and had a Frenchman in the booth with him as his adviser. The first question was, 'You're in bed with a 20-year-old virgin. Where do you kiss her first?'

The man advanced the correct answer, 'On the mouth.'

The second question was where he would kiss her next, and he again tentatively proffered an answer, 'On the breast.'

'Now for $60 000,' demanded the quizmaster, 'where do you kiss her next?'

The man turned eagerly to the French expert and demanded, 'What's the answer?'

'Don't ask me,' quipped the Frenchman. 'I got the first two wrong.'

During the Pacific War a wealthy Melbourne hostess phoned the American military command in Melbourne and offered to entertain several American officers for dinner. Being of racist leanings she added that she would prefer it if there were no Jews among the officers.

On the appointed evening, her butler ushered in three coal-black army captains.

'It's very good of you to invite us over for dinner like this, ma'am,' one of them said.

Clutching a chair for support, the hostess said, 'I'm awfully afraid that there must have been some mistake.'

'Oh surely not, ma'am,' the captain replied, 'Colonel Cohen never makes mistakes.'

An Australian, a Jew and an Irishman were so broke they were sitting in a rubbish tip where they'd been scavenging, even though a cold southerly was blowing. The Aussie touched a bottle of the grog beside him. Out came the magic bunyip and granted them one wish each.

The Australian said he never wanted to be without a beer for the rest of his life. The Jew said he never wanted to be without money. The Irishman thought, then whispered something in the bunyip's ear. 'Granted,' said the bunyip and dissolved back into the bottle. They headed for the pub to celebrate their luck.

The Aussie ordered a schooner, and glugged it in one go. As he banged the glass down, it miraculously refilled itself. The Jew went to the door, took his last $5 note from his tattered coat and held it up to the wind. The wind plucked the note away. He put his hand in his pocket and found the note replaced. He did this several times, then closed the door, delighted that he would always have money in his pocket.

There was a pounding at the door, and it burst open. Standing there were two men in white nighties and funny pointed white hoods.

'Okay, y'all,' drawled one of the hooded figures, 'which one of you guys wanted to be hung like a nigger?'

An Englishman was driving through the backblocks of Australia. As he passed a paddock he noticed a little girl running from a huge Herefordshire bull. Despite her best efforts the bull was rapidly gaining on her. The Englishman jumped out of the car, and, ignoring the agonising shocks, clambered over an electric fence. He then ran like mad towards the bull. Unbeknown to him, a journalist from the local paper was driving by and witnessed his courage. The Englishman reached the bull, grabbed it by the horns and stopped its charge just inches from the child. He flipped the bull over and, wrenching at the horns, broke its neck.

'Christ, that was great, mate,' said the journo. 'I've never seen a bloke with so much strength and courage. It makes me proud to be an Australian. Look, this story's going right on the front page of the *Gundy Advocate*. Now, just give me a few details about yourself. I take it you're a local?'

Next day the *Gundy Advocate* had a big headline on the front page. POMMY BASTARD KILLS CHILD'S PET.

A Barry McKenzie-type arrives in London and starts a pub crawl. He finishes up in a posh pub in Knightsbridge. The barman was quite impressed with his drinking capacity. He downed beer after beer after beer. Even though he kept complaining that it was 'warm as piss'.

After a while the barman suggested that he might need to go to the toilet. 'Nah, I'll be apples. Pour me a few more.' And he continued to drink, showing not the slightest desire to point Percy at the porcelain.

Finally it was closing time. 'Last orders, please,' said the barman. The Bazza-type ordered three more and downed them in a flash.

He was the last to leave the pub, and, as the barman ushered him out the door, he saw Bazza pause on the pavement and undo his fly. 'Sir,' the barman said, 'you can't do that here!'

'I ain't gonna do it here,' said Bazza, 'I'm gonna do it wa..a..a..a..a..ay over there!'

An Englishman is looking for the subway. He walks up to an Australian and, looking at him somewhat fastidiously, says, 'I say, excuse me – would you tell me how I can get underground?'

The Australian says, 'Sure thing. Drop dead, you pommy bastard.'

An Englishman, a Scot and an Irishman were on the Titanic the night she struck the iceberg. As she started to sink, the chaplain shouted, 'We are doomed. We're about to meet our maker. I urge you to do something religious.'

So the Englishman murmured a prayer. The Irishman sang a hymn. The Scot took up a collection.

A Scot met a Scottish doctor on the street and hoping for some free medical advice asked, 'What should I do for a sprained ankle?'

'Limp.'

A Scottish gentleman is one who gets out of the bath to piss in the handbasin.

The Scot went for his annual check-up and, as usual, proffered the doctor a large bottle of urine.

After the test, the doctor announced that the analysis had been reassuring. There was absolutely nothing abnormal in the specimen. The Scot returned home to tell the family the good news. 'My dear, you and I and the kids and Grandpa are all in good health.'

The Scot had been sitting beside his dying wife for days and nights. Having looked more and more uncomfortable for some time, he finally leaned over and said, 'I have to go for a while. I have to go to the toilet. But I'll be back as soon as possible. However, my dear, if you feel yourself slipping away while I'm out of the room, would you mind blowing out the candle.'

A Scot went to a clinic for a check-up and was told that he was pre-diabetic. 'You've got too much sugar in your urine.' Next morning he pissed on his porridge.

'Is this your first time in Sydney?' the taxidriver inquired of a Scotsman wearing the full cossie of kilt and sporran.

'Ai,' he said, 'and not only that, I'm on my honeymoon.'

'Then where's your wife?'

'Oh, she's been here before.'

A Scotsman was touring Australia, and a bloke invited him to the Leagues Club. He watched the people playing the pokies for a while and realised that he needed to piss. Trouble was that you needed 20 cents to get in. His friend gave him the coin but just as the Scot was about to use it he saw someone leaving the loo, grabbed the door and got to pee free.

So he decided to put the 20 cents in one of the pokies. And to everyone's astonishment, won the $20 000 jackpot. 'If it hadnae been for you, laddie,' the Scot said to his friend, 'I'd not ha' won. You deserve to be rewarded. Here, have your 20 cents back.'

Two Jews had planned to assassinate Hitler. They learned that he drove by a certain corner at noon each day so they waited for him there with their guns well hidden. At exactly noon they were ready to shoot, but there was no sign of Hitler. Five minutes later, nothing. Another five minutes went by but no sign of the fuhrer. By 12.15 they'd started to give up hope. 'My goodness,' said one of the men, 'I hope nothing's happened to him.'

During the early days of the Hitler regime, Goebbels maintained that Jews were, in reality, clever people and that Hitler was making a mistake in being so tough on them. Hitler said, 'On the contrary, they're stupid.'

To settle the argument the two men disguised themselves and went shopping. They first entered a china shop run by a German, where Goebbels asked for left-handed teacups. The poor German had never heard of such a thing. He stammered, apologised and finally admitted that he hadn't any.

Next Goebbels and Hitler went into a shop run by a Jew. The Jew scratched his head, smiled and cried, 'What a lucky thing. I have just six left-handed teacups left. Naturally I carry them in stock, although they're very hard to get. And, you understand, being so rare, they're a little more expensive than ordinary teacups.' Goebbels paid up and picked up the package.

'Any time you want more I'll be very glad to order them,' the Jew called after them.

When they reached the street, Goebbels turned to Hitler. 'There, didn't I tell you? The Jews are a lot smarter.'

'What do you mean smarter?' snarled Hitler. 'He was just lucky. He had some in stock.'

Not being a religious man, Hitler was inclined to consult his astrologers about the future. As the tide for war worsened, he asked, 'Am I going to lose the war?' Answered affirmatively, he then asked, 'Well, am I going to die?' Consulting their charts, the astrologers again said yes. 'When am I going to die?' was Hitler's next question.

'You're going to die on a Jewish holiday.'

'But when? On what holiday?' he asked in agitation.

The reply, 'Any day you die will be a Jewish holiday.'

Rosenblum was on his way to the market in Munich with a chicken under his arm. He was accosted in the street by a Nazi bully who demanded, 'Jew, where are you going?'

'I'm going to the market to buy some feed for my chicken.'

'What does he eat?' the Nazi snarled.

'Corn,' replied Rosenblum.

'Corn? The nerve of you Yids. German soldiers go hungry while you Jews feed your chickens on native German corn.' He then belted Rosenblum and continued on his way. A moment later another Nazi stopped Rosenblum. 'Where are you going, Jew dog?'

'To the market to buy some feed for my chicken.'

'What does he eat?'

'Wheat.'

'Wheat? Of all things, the Jew's chicken eats wheat while German children go hungry.' And he promptly knocked Rosenblum to the ground.

He picked himself up and continued on his way but he was approached by yet another Nazi.

'Where are you going, kike?'

'To the market to buy some feed for my chicken.'

'Feed for your chicken? What does he eat?'

'Look,' said Rosenblum, 'I don't know. I figure I'd give him a couple of pfennigs and he'll buy whatever he wants.'

Hitler sometimes disguised himself to visit public places in order to hear the people's reaction to his appearances and speeches. One day he shaved off his moustache, donned a hat and a long coat, and went to the pictures. Every cinema had to flash Hitler's photo on the screen and everyone would rise and proclaim, 'Heil Hitler'. When the fuhrer's likeness appeared and the crowd saluted, Hitler remained in his seat. The man next to him prodded Hitler and said, 'Look, friend, we all feel the way you do. But you're taking your chance by not standing up.'

A Jew arrives in hell. He wants to learn about his new surroundings and looks around. In the corner there's a writing table, looking cool and comfortable. And there, leaning over some papers, is Hitler.

The Jew asks, in horror, 'Isn't this supposed to be hell?'

'Take it easy,' another Jew reassures him. 'He has to translate *Mein Kampf* into Hebrew.'

An old Jew in Berlin is surrounded by a group of raucous Nazis who knock him to the ground and ask him, derisively, 'Jew, who was responsible for the war?'

The old Jew is no fool. 'The Jews,' he replies, 'and the bicycle riders.'

'Why the bicycle riders?' asks the Nazis.

'Why the Jews?'

A couple of Australian tourists are wandering through Vienna, marvelling at the art nouveau architecture. They come upon a little old coffee shop and go inside for a break and a slice of cake. Sitting in the corner they see a bloke who looks uncannily like Goebbels. He's watching a bloke playing darts. He is a dead-ringer for Hitler.

Fascinated, the Australians order their cakes and coffees and sit at a nearby table. They watch the two men very, very carefully. The resemblances to Hitler and Goebbels are absolutely eerie. They look exactly the same as the fuhrer and his offsider looked in the early 1940s, over half a century ago. They try to eavesdrop on their conversation but don't understand German.

Finally one of the Australians goes over to the bloke playing darts, the one who looks uncannily like Hitler, and says, 'You look uncannily like Hitler.'

'That's because I am Hitler,' comes the snarled reply.

'And you, you look exactly like Goebbels.'

'And why wouldn't I look like Goebbels? I am Goebbels.'

The Australians are astonished. 'How could this be? I mean, you've both been dead for 50 years.'

The bloke who looks like Hitler says, 'We are the embodiment of the finest German science. We are clones, created from surviving pieces of tissue.'

'Tissue taken from us at the time of our death,' adds Goebbels.

'And what are you going to do?'

'We're going to start all over again. We are going to establish a Fourth Reich.'

'Are you going to do all the same things?'

'Almost exactly,' says Hitler. 'We will, for example, kill six million Jews.'

'And two tennis players,' adds Goebbels.

The Australians look at each other in horror and astonishment. And one of them asks, 'Who are the tennis players?'

Whereupon Hitler turns to Goebbels and says, triumphantly, 'I told you no one cared about the Jews.'

A salesman calls on a business with three partners. Cohen, Goldberg and Lipschits. He steps up to the information window and addresses a woman sitting on a stool.

'Good morning, my dear. I want to talk to Mr Cohen.'

'He's out of town.'

'I'll talk to Mr Goldberg.'

'He's away.'

'What about Mr Lipschits?'

'He's tied up.'

The salesman comes back in the morning.

'I want to talk to Mr Cohen.'

'He's out of town.'

'I'll talk to Mr Goldberg.'

'He's away.'

'What about Mr Lipschits?'

'He's tied up.'

The same sequence of events occurs five days in a row. The same questions, the same answers. 'I demand the truth!'

'Sir, every time Cohen and Goldberg leave town they tie up Lipschits.'

A Jewish guy's got a parrot. It talks fluently. He goes into a pub and bets everyone that the parrot can talk. Gets odds of 25 to one. Ready to clean up. The parrot won't talk. He has to pay out all the money. He goes home determined to kill the parrot. As he wraps his fingers around its neck, the parrot says, 'Hey, just think of the odds you'll get tomorrow night.'

How many Hassidics does it take to change a light globe?

The question is irrelevant. We Hassidic Jews never change anything.

Mrs Cohen was bragging to her friends about her son. 'Ladies,' she said, 'you don't know what it means to have a good son. My boy lives in a penthouse and he's built on three rooms with a kitchen specially for me. He takes me out to dinner every night. We go to the theatre three times a week. Last month he took me on a cruise of the South Pacific. He don't do nothing without talking to me first.

'And ladies,' added Mrs Cohen, 'my son goes to a psychiatrist five times a week. And who do you think he spends the whole time talking about? Me!'

Two Jews were lined up before a firing squad in Poland when the officer asked if they had any last requests.

One said he'd like a cigarette. When the Nazi came close enough, he spat in his face.

'Please, Moishe,' said his mate, 'don't make trouble.'

Two Americans, one Jew and one Chinaman were sitting on a park bench in New York reading their newspapers.

Suddenly the Jewish bloke jumped up and started beating the crap out of the Chinese man. As he lay on the ground he looked up and said, 'What you do that for?'

To which the Jewish bloke replied, 'Pearl Harbour!'

As he got up and dusted himself off, the Chinese bloke replied, 'But I Chinese, not Japanese.'

The Jewish bloke said, 'Chinese, Siamese, Japanese – they're all the same to me!'

They recommenced reading their newspapers. Suddenly the Chinese bloke jumped up and started to karate chop the Jewish man. As he looked up, very dazed, he asked, 'What did you do that for?'

The Chinese bloke replied, 'The Titanic.'

'But that was an iceberg.'

'Goldberg, Steinberg, iceberg – they're all the same to me!'

A young Effie goes to Hollywood and after three months phones his momma. 'I'm married, Momma.'

'No! Next you'll be telling me you've married a goy.'

'No, Momma.'

Then what's her name?'
'Goldberg, Momma.'
'Thank goodness. And her first name?'
'Whoopi, Momma.'

A couple of blokes were standing side by side in a public loo when the shorter of the two said, 'Are you Jewish?'

'Yes.'

'And do you come from around Elwood?'

'Yes.'

'And at your circumcision, were you cut by the cock-eyed Liebler?'

'Yes. How do you know all these things?'

'Because Liebler always cuts with a left bias, and you're pissing on my shoes.'

When the young couple returned from their honeymoon, the bride went straight home to mum and dad. She explained that her husband was not doing his marital duties. Concerned, the family consulted a rabbi who promised to talk to the young man.

'My boy, when you're in bed tonight, you must put the longest part of your body into the hairiest part of hers.'

He promised he would.

A few days later, the bride returned to her parents, still feeling unloved.

Once again the rabbi was called in and once again he spoke to the young man.

'But, Rabbi, I've been putting my nose into her armpit just like you told me to.'

A Scot, an Englishman and a Jew were eating together in Acland Street. As a waiter cleared away the coffee, he heard the Scot ask for the bill.

Next day the *Herald Sun* headline read JEWISH VENTRILOQUIST SHOT IN ST KILDA RESTAURANT.

To celebrate their 30th anniversary, Mrs Cohen takes her husband to Double Bay and points to a block of flats. 'It's ours, darling.'

'Ours? How?'

'Well, all these years I've been charging you $20 each time we made love. I saved all those dollars and bought this block of flats.'

'Oh, dearest, if only I'd known. I would have given you all my business.'

An American tourist arrived at Bondi Beach and approached an old bloke sitting by the water.

'Excuse me, I'm a stranger here. But is this a good time of the year for swimming?'

'Lukewarm,' said the bloke.

So the American dived in and was immediately afflicted by hypothermia.

'Christ, it's freezing! Why the hell did you tell me it was lukewarm?'

'Vell, it luke varm to me.'

'Now, let me get this straight, Ms Goldfarb. First the water turned to blood, then there were frogs, lice, flies and a murrain on all the cattle, followed by boils, hail, locusts, darkness all over the land and the death of the first born. Now, why do I get the feeling you're about to ask for the day off?'

It's a Sydney Symphony Orchestra concert at the Opera House. A subscription ticket holder is concentrating on a violin concerto when an old Jewish bloke sits beside him. 'The violinist is Jewish,' he says. After a few seconds he adds, 'Also the conductor. And the cellists. And the harpist. There is a marvellous solo from a flautist, also Jewish.'

'Oh, Jesus,' said the concert-goer in exasperation.

'Also Jewish!'

An Irishman returns to Belfast after an Australian holiday. His family ask for a report.

'Australians? The most hospitable people I've ever met. They'll share their house, their food, they share everything. It's those white bastards you have to watch.'

Cultural Cringe

A famous ophthalmologist performed a cataract operation on an old, greatly venerated Australian painter. To express his gratitude, the painter insisted on painting a huge mural across the front of the hospital.

When the ophthalmologist saw the great work – depicting a vast eyeball surrounded by lashes – he said, 'Thank Christ I decided not to be a gynaecologist.'

Two marble statues, one depicting a naked man, the other a naked woman, had been poised on their plinths in a park for many years. They were positioned so that they faced each other, and each was enchanted by the beauty of the other. But being statues precluded hanky-panky.

Whereupon an angel appeared and told them that because they'd stood there so steadfastly through an endless succession of hot summers and harsh winters, they'd be rewarded by half an hour of human life. This would allow them to do whatever they'd been wanting to do.

Brought to life, the statues clambered off their pedestals, looked at each other and said, 'Shall we?'

'Yes, let's.' And they disappeared into some bushes where passers-by might have heard a lot of rustling. After a while they emerged from the foliage all hot, flustered and happy. The angel observed that they'd only used a small part of their allotted time.

'Why not start all over again?'

The statues giggled and the marble man said to the woman, 'Yes, let's do it again. Only this time the other way round. I'll hold down the fucking pigeon and you can shit on it.'

Two old mates meet in the pub.

'G'day, Arthur,' said Fred. 'Haven't seen you for yonks. How's the family?'

'Fine,' said Arthur. 'We've all taken up music. I play the violin, my wife plays the triangle, one of the kids plays the flute and the other plays the saxophone. Come around one night and we'll play you some Mozart. Now, what about your mob?'

'Oh, pretty much the same,' said Fred. 'We're into martial arts. I've taken up judo, my wife does karate, and the kids do tae kwon do. Come round one night and we'll belt the shit out of you.'

'**Y**ou're not one of those fuckin' hypnotists, are you?' asked the doorman of the Leagues Club.

'No,' said the bloke. 'I'm a singer.'

'Okay,' said the doorman. 'You want to see the secretary. His office is the second door on the right.'

So the singer went in and fronted the club secretary.

'You're not going to tell me you're a fuckin' hypnotist,' said the secretary.

'No! I'm a singer.'

'Okay,' said the secretary. 'You can go and see the pianist and he'll arrange your music.'

Whilst he was rehearsing 'I Did It My Way', the pianist said, 'You don't do anything else in your act, do you? Fuckin' hypnotism, for example?'

'No,' said the bloke. 'I keep telling everybody that I'm a singer. That's it. Why all this bullshit about hypnotism?'

'Well, it's like this,' said the pianist. 'Last Saturday we had a hypnotist, and he was pretty bloody good. Got the entire audience in a trance. Hundreds of them.'

'What's wrong with that?'

'Well, halfway through the act he tripped over the microphone cable and went arse over tit down those little stairs. Got a blood nose and yelled "shit!". Well, the cleaners were at it all Sunday.'

A couple were sitting in an opera box above the stage when during Mahler's Fifth Symphony, the woman gave her boyfriend a hand job. He ejaculated vigorously, right into the orchestra pit hitting a violinist right in the middle of his bald head.

'Shit,' he said. 'I've been hit by a flying fuck.'

'And so you should be,' said the conductor. 'You've been playing like a cunt all night.'

The Newcastle Symphony Orchestra was holding a fundraising night, but unfortunately, Roger Woodward couldn't make it. So they hired an old local pianist who, 30 years before, had been a stand-in pianist for the Berlin Philharmonic.

Since moving to Newcastle he'd fallen on hard times and hard drink. He wasn't in the best of shape. But he was the best available. So he trundled out on stage in his stained tuxedo and lowered himself onto a wicker chair that he had insisted on bringing.

Unfortunately there was a split in his trousers, and a gasp of horror from the audience.

'Do you know your knackers are hanging through the old wicker chair?' hissed the first violinist.

'No,' the old bloke said, 'but if you hum the tune I'll soon pick up on the melody.'

In the wee hours of the morning a once-famous scriptwriter staggered towards his bed after yet another three-day drug and booze binge, but just before he lapsed into unconsciousness he heard . . . *Tap, tap, tap, tap.* It sounded like the typewriter in his study. Too bombed to do anything about it, he passed out.

A day later he woke, and as he stumbled past his study he saw, sitting on his desk by his typewriter, a pile of A4 paper. Bewildered, he took a closer look and found a script, 120 pages long with his name on it. He read it and marvelled at how fantastic it was. 'My God, I don't even remember writing this,' he muttered, before sending it to his agent. The film went on to become a great success. And so, overcome with delight, the writer went back to bingeing and boozing and womanising. Years passed and not another word was written. Then, one night, as he stumbled drunkenly towards his bed, he heard . . . *Tap, tap, tap, tap.* This time he forced himself to his study door and saw an elf perched on his chair, happily typing away. 'It was you, wasn't it? You wrote that last script,' he said.

'That's right,' said the elf, as he tap, tap, tapped away.

'Are you going to finish this one?' asked the excited scriptwriter.

'Maybe,' said the elf, 'maybe not.'

'What'll it take to make you finish?' the scriptwriter demanded. 'I know! Cocaine! I'll go out and buy you the best cocaine. I always find that helps me.'

'No, thank you,' said the elf, 'I don't do drugs.'

'Okay, I know! Booze! I'll buy you the best cognac and champagne money can buy.'

'No, thank you,' said the elf, typing away, 'I don't drink.'

'Women, then,' said the desperate writer. 'Surely a bevy of beautiful models will excite you enough to finish it.'

Tap, tap, tap. The elf continued writing. 'No, thank you. I'm happily married.'

'Well, what then?' exploded the scriptwriter. 'What do you want to finish the script? Surely there's something I can give you.'

Tap, tap, tap. Then the elf paused, looked at the scriptwriter, and said, 'Well, there's one thing.'

'Yes! Yes! What? Just name it!'

'Well, this time I'd like a co-writing credit.'

The scriptwriter looked down at the elf, his

nostrils flared, his eyes opened wide, and he
screamed, 'Oh, get fucked!'

A bloke takes his wife to the Opera House for the
first night of *Nambucco*. It is a very eccentric
production, combining all sorts of odd, unlikely
visual elements. The bloke is bored silly and, even
worse, needs a piss. So he extricates himself from the
row, apologising as he squeezes past scores of knees.
But out in the foyer he can't find the loo. He pushes
at this door and that and finally hears tinkling water.
Desperate, he rushes inside to find a fountain. It's too
much. He can't bear it. So he has a quick piss into
the ornate bowl. Finally he apologises his way back
to his seat, surprised by various slaps on the back
and sporadic bursts of applause.

'Have I missed much of the second act?' he
whispered to his wife.

'Missed it?' she says, indicating the stage where
the singers are bellowing around the fountain. 'You
were the star.'

A couple are trying to enjoy the movie but there's a
bloke sitting a few seats in front of them moaning
and groaning.

They call an usher. 'You obviously need medical help. Where are you from?'

'The balcony,' came the agonised reply.

An artist was commissioned to paint a mural to celebrate Governor Phillip's landing. He took the job on, on the understanding that no one was to see it until it was completed. When the time came for the unveiling – shock, horror. The wall was a mass of pictures illustrating, in most biological detail, all the positions from the Kama Sutra, and up in the top right-hand corner a fish with a halo. The first man to recover his breath cried out in rage.

'That's art!' declared the painter.

'But what has it go to do with Captain Phillip's landing?'

'Holy Mackerel, look at all them fucking Kooris!'

The daughter of a well-known Shakespearian scholar, after her first-year examination in English at university, took home the questions to her father. He looked at the exam paper and said, 'This first question is easy. It asks you to name the four great plays of Shakespeare. What did you write?'

'I wrote, "Three inches, Six inches, Nine inches and Twelve inches".'

'But that's nonsense. Shakespeare wrote no such plays.'

'But he did, Father. The terms I used are the new verbal shorthand used by students at universities these days. You see, three inches is the shorthand for *Much Ado About Nothing*. Six inches means *As You Like It*, Nine inches is *Midsummer Night's Dream* and Twelve inches is *The Taming of the Shrew*.'

A history teacher was testing the knowledge of his new class. 'Which British explorer discovered Australia? And in what year?' he asked. Row after row of silent, blank faces. Finally a little Japanese boy, the son of a Toyota executive, waved his hand.

'Please, sir,' he cried excitedly. Trouble was that this kid knew all the answers, irrespective of the subject, so the teacher turned desperately to the rest of the class. 'Surely one of you must know when Australia was discovered.'

No takers, only the Japanese kid.

'Please, sir, please, sir.' His little arm was flailing in the air. 'All right, tell us.'

'Please, sir, it was Captain James Cook. And the year was 1770.'

Infuriated by the other dunderheads, the teacher roared at them. 'Aren't you ashamed of yourselves? Look how it takes a visitor to our country to know the answer.'

He turned to the little Japanese boy. 'Thank you for showing these idiots their idiocy. You may go home at three o'clock but all the other kids will stay in and write an essay on . . . Captain Cook.' Whereupon a voice piped up from the rear of the classroom. 'Fucking Japs!'

'Who said that?' roared the teacher.

'Please, sir,' came the reply. 'Douglas Macarthur. In 1942.'

'**I** don't like to talk about the war,' said Helen Demidenko, 'because my grandfather died in a concentration camp. He fell out of a watch tower.'

When Burke and Wills set out on their great journey, they had an Afghan to drive the camels, a German to read the maps and they put a Chinaman in charge of supplies. On the dawn of the beginning of their great trek, the Afghan was in position, leading the long line of camels. The German, with his monocle polished, was sitting in his dray poring over the maps. But there was no sign of the Chinaman. Worse still, there was no sign of any supplies.

But they headed off anyway, convinced that he'd be coming along behind them.

But he never came. And the trip turned into a catastrophe. Finally, when Burke and Wills were almost dead from exposure and starvation, in the middle of nowhere, the Chinaman jumped out from behind a tree and said, 'Surplise! Surplise!'

Heard of the bloke who's half Japanese and half black?

Every year on December the seventh he attacks Pearl Bailey.

Two Iraqi generals were sitting sweating in a bunker in the middle of the desert, awaiting the full force of Desert Storm. And they passed the time by discussing their Russian weapons.

'Our Russian tanks are really good,' said one general. 'Lots of thick armour and big, loud, powerful guns.'

'Yes, the new tanks are very good. But I'm worried by the operating instructions.'

385

'Why?'

'Well, under the heading "Tactics", it says, "When attacked, retreat, and draw the enemy forces deep into your territory. Then await the snows of winter".'

Mark Anthony returned to Egypt after years of war with the Hittites and the Babylonians. 'Where's Cleopatra?' he demanded of the servant.

'My lord, she's in bed with hepatitis.'

Mark Anthony unsheathed his sword and yelled, 'I'll kill that Greek bastard!'

After the Gulf War, the Americans had to put out hundreds upon hundreds of burning oil wells, deliberately set ablaze by the retreating army of Saddam Hussein. Finally, only one was left, but it proved intractable. There was nothing they could do to put it out. And they tried everything.

They called for Red Adair, offering him two million dollars if he'd dash over and do the job. But Red was busy putting out an oil rig fire in Siberia.

'Why not Green Adair?' someone suggested.

'Who?'

'Green Adair. He's Irish. Works cheaper than Red.'

So they phoned him in Dublin and offered him one million dollars.

A few hours later the blokes from Caltex were astonished to see a giant helicopter hovering over them. They were even more astonished when, after it landed and the nose opened, a truck driven by Green Adair and his crew went charging at the fire. Instead of stopping as it neared the flames, it went right into the middle of them, and for a while they lost it from sight. Then they glimpsed Green Adair and his offsider leaping out, jumping up and down on the flames.

It took them the best part of an hour but they emerged badly singed but triumphant. Three cheers rang out across the desert.

'And what will you do with the million dollars?' asked the bloke from Caltex.

'The first thing?' said Green Adair. 'Get some brakes for that fucking truck.'

It was Anzac Day and an old digger climbed on the bus. He found himself opposite a Salvation Army officer. He stared blearily at the uniform and finally inquired, 'What's your regiment? I don't seem to recognise it.'

'I'm a soldier of the Lord,' said the Salvo. 'I go to Townsville to fight the devil, then to Brisbane to fight him and then down to Newcastle, Sydney and Melbourne.'

'Good on ya, mate,' said the digger. 'Keep on headin' the bastard south.'

Displaying a lot more enthusiasm than worldliness, the young education officer arranged to address a company of diggers just back from a search-and-destroy patrol in Vietnam. A gnarled old sergeant called the troops to order with, 'Righto, youse lot, quieten down. The lieutenant has come all the way from Saigon to give youse a talk, and the least youse can do is listen to him.'

He then turned to the education officer and asked quietly, 'What will you be speaking about, sir?'

Just above a whisper, the lieutenant replied, 'Well, sergeant, after what they've been through, I thought a little talk about some of the finer things of life might be appropriate. What if we have a little chat about Keats?'

'Yes, certainly, sir,' said the sergeant, as he turned to address the muttering, disgruntled troops. 'Quiet there in the ranks!' he began. Then, as the troops became silent, he continued. 'Now, listen, youse ignorant lot. The lieutenant is going to talk to youse about Keats. And you'd better shut up and listen, because half youse mob wouldn't know one end of a bloody keat from the other!'

It was Anzac Day and an old digger, obviously the worst for wear, was lolling back in the tram. A woman was shocked to notice that his fly was open and his penis was in full view. What to do? Should she just avert her eyes and pretend not to have noticed? No. It was Anzac Day, he'd fought for his country and she must do her duty. So she leant over, tapped him on the knee and said, 'Excuse me, sir, but do you know that your John Thomas is sticking out?'

He looked down, pondered for a second, and replied, 'Don't kid yourself, lady, it's only hanging out!'

'I shall return.' – General Douglas Macarthur

'We will fight them on the beaches.' – Winston Churchill

'Fuck, what was that?' – The mayor of Hiroshima

Ned Kelly was holding up the mail coach. He lined up the passengers and ordered his men to hang the women and fuck the men. A passenger corrects him, saying, 'Mr Kelly, you mean hang the men and fuck the women?'

Whereupon a man up the back of the coach cried out, 'Who'th robbing thith coach, you or Misther Kelly?'

An English economist, a don at Cambridge, had been visiting Australia to study the influence of Thatcherism on government policies. On his return, he addressed a local community group about what he'd seen in the colonies.

At question time, an audience member commented that while there'd been much emphasis on Australia's primary production and mining sector, there'd been absolutely no mention of cultural matters.

The questioner recognised that the speaker was an economist, but, nonetheless, felt he might have something to say about the state of the arts in Australia.

The economist said that despite its many and varied achievements, Australia remained a non-event in the artistic and cultural areas. 'Indeed,' he said, 'Australians are, in this regard, absolute barbarians.'

Whereupon a voice could be heard from the rear of the room. 'Pig's fucking arse we are!'

'King Arthur, I have raped and pillaged all the Saxons to the south.'

'You idiot, Lancelot. I told you to rape and pillage the Saxons to the north. I don't have any enemies in the south.'

'I'm afraid you do now.'

Australian Graffiti

Graffiti is for people who can't write books.

If you've got water on the knee, you're not aiming straight.

Why are waterbeds cutting down on adultery?
    Ever tried to crawl under one?

John Wayne is dead.
    The hell I am!

Bronwyn Bishop kick-starts jumbos.

Being a member of a union is like using a franger – you get a false sense of security while being screwed.

But for Venetian blinds it would be curtains for all of us.

Tutankhamen has changed his mind – he wants to be buried at sea.

Transcendental meditation is better than sitting around doing nothing.

Before the Howard government came to power we were on the edge of an economic precipice. Since then we've taken a great step forward.

A stitch in time would confuse Stephen Hawking.

Teenagers are God's punishment for having sex.

I'm pink therefore I'm spam.

Things may be bad but they're better than next year.

Cigarettes cause statistics.

Cancer cures smoking.

What do you say to a sociology student with a job?

A cheeseburger, a coke and fries.

End violence to women now.
    Yes, dear.

Sex is just one damp thing after another.

Ignore this sign.

Roses are reddish
    Violets are bluish
    If it wasn't for Jesus
    We'd all be Jewish.

Religion is man's attempt to communicate with the weather.

Is reincarnation making a comeback?

Due to Paul Keating's deficit, the light at the end of the tunnel will be turned off at weekends.

Reality is for people who can't cope with drugs.

Racism is a pigment of the imagination.

I'm bisexual. When I can't get it, I buy it.

Elvis is dead.
    Good career move.

Power corrupts – absolute power is even more fun.

Politically correct graffito:
    Ethnics out!

Help the cops – beat yourself up.

The best-laid plans of mice and men are lost in the files.

'A piano is a piano is a piano.' – Gertrude Steinway.

Just because you're paranoid doesn't mean they're not out to get you.

Aural sex gives eargasms.

Save money on obscene calls – reverse charges.

What did we do before we discovered nostalgia?

If you notice this notice you will notice that this notice is not worth noticing. So don't notice it.

Nervous breakdowns are hereditary. You get them from your kids.

Necrophilia means never having to say you're sorry.

Necrophilia is dead boring.

Beam me up, Scotty. There's no intelligent life down here.

Masturbation is the thinking-man's television.

The meek shall inherit the Earth, but not the mineral rights.

Marriage is a fine institution. But who wants to live in an institution?

I'd rather have a full bottle in front of me than a full frontal lobotomy.

Jesus is alive and well and signing copies of the Bible at readings.

Jesus saves – with St George.

The first three minutes of life are very dangerous.
    So are the last.

Jesus lives!
    Does this mean no holidays at Easter?

On the tits of a barmaid from Sale
  Were tattooed the prices of ale
  And on her behind
  For the sake of the blind
  Was the same information in braille.

Bo-peep did it for the insurance.

Keep incest in the family.

My inferiority complex isn't as good as yours.

Keep Australia green.
  Have sex with a frog.

This door will shortly appear in paperback.

God is dead.
    Oh, no I'm not!

'God is dead.' – Nietzsche.

'Nietzsche is dead.' – God.

I like sadism, necrophilia and bestiality. Am I
flogging a dead horse?

Archduke Franz Ferdinand found alive. First World
War a mistake.

Feudalism: your count votes.

Avoid the end of the year rush – fail your exams
now.

Don't drink and drive. You'll spill it.

Diarrhoea is hereditary. It runs in your jeans.

The decision is maybe and that's final.

All men are cremated equal.

I used to be conceited. Now I'm perfect.

We want new clichés.

Australians are living proof that Aborigines screw kangaroos.

405

Art is what you can get away with.

I couldn't care less about apathy.

Be alert. Your country needs lerts.

My wife's an angel.
    You're lucky. Mine's still alive.

Paparazzi with the Lot

A lion was drinking from a pool with its bum in the air when a chimpanzee passed by. Mistaking the gender of the big cat, the chimp crept up behind it to play hide the sausage.

The lion let out an agonised roar and the chimp rapidly departed. Infuriated, the lion chased it through the jungle. The chimp dashed into a safari camp, snatched a pith helmet, sat in a chair and pretended to read a copy of *The Times*.

The lion arrived in the clearing and asked, 'Have you seen a chimp around here?'

'You mean the chimp that rooted the lion down by the stream?'

'Christ,' said the lion, 'don't tell me it's in the papers already!'

Elvis Presley knock-knock joke:
Knock, knock.
Who's there?
Wurlitzer.
Wurlitzer who?
Wurlitzer one for the money, two for the show . . .

Prince Charles has to go to Glynbourne-on-Sea to judge the local flower show. It's a particularly distinguished affair and has been staged very successfully for 200 years, stopping only during the Boer War and the First and Second World Wars. He arrives beautifully dressed in his Jermyn Street suit, but is wearing a fox hat which looks somewhat out of place.

Finally the Anglican vicar of Glynbourne-on-Sea cannot contain his curiosity. He's asks him to explain how someone who looks as smart as a rat with a gold tooth can be so silly as to wear a fox hat.

The prince attempts an explanation. 'This morning Mother heard I was coming to Glynbourne-on-Sea and she said, "where the fuck's that?"'

The bloke couldn't believe his luck. There he was, shipwrecked with Elle Macpherson. But they realised they'd have to behave themselves because he was married and she was very famous. And it was only a matter of time until they'd be rescued. They agreed to stay on opposite sides of the island and to meet once a week to check on provisions.

But when they met a week later they yielded to their sexual appetites. Afterwards, they felt somewhat ashamed of themselves and decided to go their separate ways. They would scan the horizon for signs of ships and meet in a week's time.

A week later, they met on the same lonely beach. But this time the bloke had brought a change of clothing. 'Could you dress up as a man?' he asked Elle. 'I found these on the shore.'

Elle looked at him suspiciously. 'Are you telling me you're kinky?'

'No, not a bit.'

She reluctantly agreed and no sooner had she climbed into the clobber than he put his arm around her and said, 'G'day, mate. You'll never guess who I fucked last week!'

Her Majesty invited a distant cousin, Prince Ludwig, to stay at Buckingham Palace, only to discover that he couldn't keep his hands off the pageboys.

'Ludwig,' her Majesty said to the prince, 'you

must stop this. I've got enough trouble with the tabloids without this. We cannot have these goings on at Buckingham Palace.'

'Sorry, ma'am,' said the prince. 'I'll turn over a new leaf.'

But next day Ludwig saw a pageboy leaning out a palace window. He raced over, slammed the window down on the boy's neck to trap him and was just removing his trousers when the Queen walked in.

'Ludwig! And you said you were going to turn over a new leaf!'

'And I will, ma'am, I will. Just as soon as I get to the bottom of this page.'

Princess Di was asked to launch a ship at Newcastle dockyards. After busting the bottle of Bollinger, she expressed the desire to meet some of the men who'd built the proud vessel. 'And this, your Highness, is our Dave. Dave is one of the strongest blokes on the waterfront. Tell her Highness how much you can lift, Dave.'

Dave shuffled his feet, looked at the ground and said modestly, 'Aw, about a fuckin' ton.'

'Break it down!' whispered the shocked official.

'Well, about half a fuckin' ton.'

The late actress Tallulah Bankhead is leaving Harrods wearing her new full-length sable coat. As she's about to climb into her limousine, a beggar woman approaches her, saying, 'Please, Miss Bankhead, help me. I haven't eaten in three days.'

Ms Bankhead smiles understandingly and says, 'Well, my dear, you must *force* yourself!'

In happier days the Queen and Lady Di went on a tour of Northern Ireland. They left their hotel and went for a ride in the Rolls Royce, but took a wrong turn in Belfast and got hijacked by the IRA. The leader, Paddy, said to Di, 'Give us all those diamonds Prince Charles has given you.'

And Di said, 'I'm sorry, I didn't bring any of my jewels with me.'

Whereupon the IRA searched the car and Lady Di but couldn't find any diamonds.

They then turned to her Majesty and said, 'All right, give us the crown jewels.' But the Queen said, 'I'm sorry, but I didn't bring any of my crown jewels with me.'

Whereupon they searched the Queen and the car and couldn't find any crown jewels.

So Paddy said, 'Right, we'll just have to steal the car.' And they evicted the royals and drove off.

After they'd gone, the Queen turned to Lady Di

and said, 'Di, my dear, you were wearing your diamonds when we left the hotel. Where did you hide them?'

Diana said, 'As soon as I saw the IRA I quickly hid them in that little secret place only Prince Charles knows about. But, ma'am, you were wearing your crown jewels when we left the hotel. Where did you hide them?'

And the Queen said, 'As soon as I saw the IRA I hid them in that little secret place only Prince Philip knows about.'

Then Lady Di said, 'Jeez, we should have brought Princess Margaret. We could have saved the Rolls Royce.'

Kerry Packer was playing polo when he went arse over tit off the horse. And lay very, very still. The ambulance arrived, found he was dead, connected their defibrillator and gave him a few thousand volts. The tycoon stirred. Opening his eyes he said, 'You saved my life. What can I do for you?'

'Well, Mr Packer,' said the ambulance driver, 'I'm a keen golfer. You might like to buy me a couple of clubs.'

Packer went out and bought him Royal Melbourne and Huntingdale.

Lady Renouf was being chauffeured home when the Rolls Royce got a puncture. The car wobbled to a dignified halt and the chauffeur got out. There was a long delay. Lady Renouf wound down the window.

'Do you want a screw, driver?' she asked.

The chauffeur said, 'Might as well, Lady Renouf. 'I can't get this bloody hubcap off.'

The new Australian ambassador to the English court had opened his term with a splendid afternoon garden party. All the VIPs were there, including the Queen herself.

After the formalities were finished, the ambassador approached the Queen. After the requisite small talk, the ambassador enquired whether the lady would care for a drink.

'A sherry or a port, your Majesty?' he asked.

'Ah, sherry,' she sighed. 'Ambrosia, the nectar of the gods. The colour redolent of English autumn, the sylvan settings, the Turner landscapes. The fragrance enchanting, bouquet at its best, transporting me to heights of pleasure. The flavour so pleasing, it sets me awash with the joy of tasting truly.'

'And port, your Majesty?'

'Port? No, Mr Ambassador. For some unknown reason it always gives me an itchy twat!'

Bob and Blanche were on a second honeymoon in
the Sahara. Blanche had planned a moonlight ride on
a camel. The evening was balmy and they glided
across the silver sands. When they came to an oasis
they dismounted and Blanche produced a bottle of
Bollinger. They sat and toasted their future together.
Clutching their white robes, they remounted the
camel to return to their far-off tent. But the camel
refused to budge. After much walking around,
pleading, kicking, promising that no camel would be
deprived by the year 2000, Bob still hadn't managed
to budge the beast.

Blanche got down on her hands and knees to
examine the brute. With a snort and a lunge, the
huge animal got to its feet and pounded off into the
distance.

'Jeez, Blanche, what did you do?'

'Well, I saw this swelling between his legs,' said
Blanche, 'and I bit it.'

'Well, for God's sake, bite mine. I've got to
catch him,' said Bob.

What ends with -u-n-t and smells fishy?
Rex Hunt.

What's brown and runs around Ayers Rock?
A dingo doing a lap of honour.

What's a test tube baby's worst enemy?
A dingo with a straw.

What's the difference between driving a Volvo and putting your hand down the front of Bob Hawke's pants?
You feel a bigger dick driving a Volvo.

What's fat, blonde and lives in Florida?
Salman Rushdie.

What do you call Bob Hawke's balls?
Blanched hazelnuts.

What's fe-fi-fo, fe-fe-fi-fo?
Ita Buttrose's phone number.

How many Arthur Tunstalls does it take to change a light bulb?

None. He's from the Dark Ages.

Why did Martin Bryant stop at 35?

Because after that he knew he'd be shooting his relatives.

Arnold Schwarzenegger was tired of being battered and bruised in action sequences. Even though his double did the major stunts, there were still scenes to be shot in which Schwarzenegger could be clearly identified.

So he spent some of his vast fortune on developing a clone. And when it was delivered from the lab, it was absolutely remarkable. Every detail of Schwarzenegger's face and physique was perfectly replicated, down to the last mole. There was even a scar on the left elbow Arnie had got in his weightlifting days.

But there was one problem. The clone had an enormous penis. And it was given to huge, prolonged erections. As well, the clone got more and more ambitious and tried to push the original Arnie out of scenes. Finally, the two of them got to fighting. The LAPD got a phone call from Schwarzenegger asking them to come to his suite at the Beverly Hills Hotel. By the time they arrived, horrified crowds had gathered to watch Schwarzenegger and his naked clone struggling on the roof of the building. To make matters worse, the clone had a huge erection.

Finally, desperately, Schwarzenegger grabbed the clone by the penis and threw him off the building.

'Sorry, Mr Schwarzenegger,' said the LAPD, 'we're going to have to arrest you and charge you with Murder One.'

'Murder One? But it was in self-defence.'

'Nonetheless, it was you who made the obscene clone fall.'

A bloke is walking through Hyde Park in Sydney where he sees a couple of tickets for Channel Nine's *Midday Show* nailed to a tree. Terrific, he thinks as he rushes over to the tree, and steals the nails.

B rian Johns is desperate for ratings and so insists that the ABC have a quiz show to rival *Sale of the Century*. One segment has a contestant think of a four-letter word, spell it and put it in a sentence in order to win a prize, which, like all ABC prizes, is really boring. It's a book token you can redeem at an ABC Shop.

In the first episode, there's a contestant who answers every question, just about the brightest quiz contestant since Barry Jones. And they get to the four-letter-word segment.

'Okay, what's your word?'

'GARN. G-A-R-N,' says the contestant.

'Garn? What sort of word is that?' says Quentin Dempster, who's managed to land the quizmaster gig.

'GARN GET FUCKED!' shouts the contestant.

The switchboard is jammed with complaints, and Johns cancels the show.

Six months later they decide to give it one last chance. In the first episode there's a bearded bloke who looks uncannily like Barry Jones and who turns out to be as brilliant as his predecessor. He gets a perfect score, and, then, it's four-letter-word time.

'SMEE. Capital S, capital M, double E!!'

'What do you mean SMEE?' says Quentin.

Whereupon the bloke rips off his false beard and yells, 'SMEE AGAIN. GARN GET FUCKED!'

The Nine Network decided to bring back *New Faces*. Bert Newton was lured back to his old job, and, pretty soon, it was rating like a beauty. Nonetheless truly original, imaginative acts were few and far between. But then, one night, Bert introduced a woman who astonished the audience by simply dropping a mouth organ into her knickers. Whereupon they heard, somewhat muffled, a thoroughly professional rendition of 'Advance Australia Fair'.

After the program Bert decided to introduce her to Paul Dainty. He rang Paul up and said, 'Paul, I've got a great act. You'll be able to make a fortune out of her.'

'What does she do?'

'Just listen to this.'

And he handed the woman her mouth organ which she promptly dropped down the front of her knickers. He brought the phone close as she started to play, 'Australians all, let us rejoice'.

When the performance was over, Bert said, 'There, Paul. What do you think of that?'

Paul said, 'It just sounds like some cunt playing the mouth organ.'

Steven Spielberg dies and goes to heaven where he's met by St Peter. 'Stevie, baby. Great to see you. You're looking good. Now, have I got a project for you!'

'Are you crazy?' says Spielberg. 'I'm dead. I had a heart attack from over-work. I want heaven's version of Hawaii, and I want it now.'

'Come on, Steve, lighten up,' said St Peter. 'This is a dream deal. The script is by William Shakespeare.'

'I don't care,' says Spielberg. 'I want a holiday.'

'Just listen to the concept,' says St Peter. 'It's a musical, and the score is by — wait for it, you're going to love it — Beethoven!'

'Okay, it sounds terrific, but the answer's still no.'

'But, Steve, the sets are going to be by Michelangelo.'

St Peter's eyes glisten as Spielberg considers the deal. 'Okay, I'll do it.'

'Fantastic! Wonderful!' says St Peter, as he throws an arm around Spielberg's shoulders and walks him through the gates of heaven. 'Now, we only have one small problem. You see, God's dating this chick and she thinks she can sing . . .'

Given her religious proclivities, Blanche Hawke was very, very worried whether her late husband, Bob, would make it into heaven. So she made a telephone call.

'This is the Virgin Mary,' said the receptionist, 'can I help you?'

'Yes, has Mr Hawke arrived as yet?'

'No, he hasn't.'

A little later Blanche repeated the call.

'This is the Immaculate Mary, Mother of God. May I help you?'

Blanche called heaven the next day and the call was answered slightly differently. 'This is Mary, may I help you?'

She turned to her friends and said, 'Bob's in heaven.'

Some time before achieving fame as a cameraman for *Dances with Wolves*, Dean Semler was being presented to Queen Elizabeth in a line-up of notables at a Royal Command Performance. Not recognising him – as he works behind the camera rather than in front of it – Queen Elizabeth asked him what he did. 'I'm a photographer, ma'am,' he replied.

'Oh, how interesting!' she said. 'I had a brother-in-law who was a photographer!'

'Well, isn't that a coincidence!' he said. 'I had a brother-in-law who was a queen!'

Shortly after Evel Knievel's attempt to jump over the Grand Canyon on a rocket-powered motorbike, some tourists were gazing down at the great fissure, marvelling at its depth, width and emptiness. 'It's a mile wide, a mile deep and not a thing living in it,' said the guide.

'Hang on,' said one of the tourists, who was studying the bottom of the canyon with his binoculars. 'There's a dead donkey down there. And there seems to be someone stuck under it.'

The guide reported the sight to the park guards who journeyed to the bottom of the canyon and found a tragic sight. Beneath the dead donkey was a skeleton wearing a T-shirt reading 'PADDY KNIEVEL'

Sydney or the Bush!

A farmer was standing on the verandah farewelling a couple of visitors. When they were about 30 metres away he called out, 'Oo'roo.' The couple turned, waved and called, 'Oo'roo' back. A few yards further on, the farmer called, 'Oo'roo' again. And again the couple responded, waving and calling, 'Oo'roo'. A few yards further down the track the farmer called, 'Oo'roo' for the third time. And this time they turned giving a half-hearted wave and a less enthusiastic, 'Oo'roo'. Whereupon the farmer yelled out, 'For Christ's sake, will you shut up! That's the name of me bloody dog.'

Dad and Dave were hunting for wild pigs with their dogs when they heard some piglet squeals coming from beneath a fallen log. While Dad kept watch in case the parents came back, Dave squeezed right underneath the log into what turned out to be a large burrow. Whilst he was grabbing at the piglets, everything turned black. 'Dad, what's blocking the light?'

'Son, you'll find out if the sow's tail breaks.'

Dad won the lottery. Next day Snake Gully was full of people coming to congratulate him. Dave and Mabel drove over with the grandkids, and neighbours who hadn't spoken to him for years turned up for a beer.

After they'd all left, Dad and the missus sat at the kitchen table having a cuppa. She said, 'What do you think we should do now we've got all this money?'

Dad thought for a while. 'I reckon we might just keep farming till it's all gone.'

Dave took Mabel to Paris and while she was having an afternoon nap at the hotel, he wandered off to look at the Eiffel Tower. He stood staring up at it, full of wonderment and awe. There was nothing like it in Snake Gully.

After a few minutes a pretty young woman
came up to him and whispered, ''Ello, mon cher.
Would you like a bit?'

'Why? Are they pulling it down?'

It was Mabel's birthday and Dave asked her what
she'd like for a prezzo. She said, 'Dave, I'd like you
to get circumcised.' So he went into town and asked
the doctor.

'That'll cost you $500.'

'Too much,' said Dave, so he went across to the
vet's. They told him they'd do the job for $100.

'Too much,' said Dave.

So he went home and decided on do-it-
yourself. He sharpened his axe and went around to
where he beheaded chooks. And he whacked his
dick on a bloodstained stump. And then he lifted his
axe and went *whack*. 'Too much,' said Dave.

Early one morning the phone rings at Dave and
Mabel's in Snake Gully. 'Is that Snake Gully 127?' a
voice asks.

'No, it's Snake Gully 271,' says Dave, sleepily.

'Oh, sorry to disturb you. I must have the
wrong number.'

'No trubs,' says Dave, 'the phone was ringing anyway.'

Dad and Dave decided to diversify into chooks but were having teething troubles. They knew it was important to have high-quality roosters and felt that the old one they'd bought probably wasn't up to it. So they kept buying others, with unfortunate results.

Whenever they let a young rooster into the pen it would swagger up to the old rooster and say, 'All them hens are mine. And you can piss off.'

'I'll tell you what, I'll race you round the chook shed,' the old rooster would say, 'and if I win, I keep half the hens. If I lose, you can have the lot.'

'Okay,' the young rooster would say, 'and because of your age, I'll give you a head start.'

And off they'd go. The old rooster was racing for all he was worth, but the young rooster was catching up fast. Then Dave would come out with his shotgun and blast the young rooster.

'Dad, that's the third poofter rooster we've had in a row.'

Dad was charged with bestiality by the Snake Gully police. Dad visited his son whilst he was awaiting his court appearance in the cells.

'Tell me about it, son,'

'Well, Dad, Mabel wasn't talking to me. And I got really, really lonely. And I noticed our pet emu was bending over and I just couldn't resist it.'

'The pet emu?' said Dad incredulously. 'Wasn't that a bit difficult?'

'Oh, for the first 200 metres,' said Dave, 'then we got in step.'

Dave announced his intention of enlisting in the army. When Ma heard the news she asked Dad to speak to him. So he took his son out on the verandah and began to lecture him.

'Dave,' said Dad, 'you must beware the demon drink.'

'Don't worry, Dad,' said Dave, 'I've never touched the stuff. Never will.'

'And Dave,' said Dad, 'you must avoid gambling.'

'No worries, Dad. I've never bet in my life. Never will.'

Dad took a deep breath and continued. 'And son, I have to warn you about women. The temptations of the flesh!'

'No trubs, Dad,' said Dave, 'I'll never go out with women. I'm going to keep myself nice for Mabel.'

Dad walked into the kitchen. 'No need to worry, Ma. The army won't take him. He's a bloody half-wit.'

Dave and Mabel received an invitation to the Snake Gully Fancy Dress Ball. They were wondering what they could wear when Dave remembered that he'd slaughtered a cow a couple of weeks earlier and had hung the skin over the fence to cure. So they decided they'd go as a cow, with Dave playing the front half and Mabel the back.

The ball was a great success and Dave and Mabel won the prize for the most original cossie. It was well after midnight when they took their leave and, as it was a fine moonlit night, they decided to take a short cut home across the paddock. Off they went, still dressed as a cow, with Dave in front and Mabel behind. Halfway across the paddock they were startled to hear a loud snorting and a stamping of hooves.

'Christ,' called out Mabel. 'It's the bull! What'll we do?'

'You better brace yourself, Mabel,' said Dave. 'I'm gonna start chewin' grass.'

In the good old days, before wool prices crashed, a cocky went to London to order another Rolls Royce. He went to see the dealers in Berkley Square and turned down the first two or three models. It seemed they just weren't good enough.

Finally, they unveiled the latest, greatest Rolls Royce priced at £250,000.

'Yeah, that'll do. But I want one of them press-button glass windows between the front and back seats.'

'Of course, sir,' said the salesman. 'But do you mind me asking you something? Sliding glass windows like that aren't very popular these days. They're regarded as old fashioned, even a bit elitist. And we didn't think Australians went in for that sort of thing.'

'Then none of you buggers have ever had the back of your neck licked by a sheep on the way to market.'

Two cobbers had been humping their blueys out back o' Bourke for months. One morning, through the heat haze, they see something big and black and very dead. As they approach they also realise that it's in an advanced stage of decomposition. A few hours later, trudging on in silence, one bloke says to the other, 'Did you see that dead ox?'

Come evening, when the campfire was blazing,

the other replied, 'That wasn't no ox, that was a 'orse.' Then he rolled himself up in the blanket and went to sleep.

Next morning the first bloke had decamped. He'd disappeared, leaving only a scrap of paper under a stone where his swag had been. On it he'd scribbled the following words: *There's too much bloody argument in this camp.*

The old bushie decided to visit the big smoke, but he had never travelled by train, so he didn't know what to do.

'Just go up to the ticket window,' his mates told him. 'They'll put you right.'

So the old bushie got a lift into town, found the railway station and joined the queue at the ticket window. The young woman in front gave some money to the booking clerk, saying, 'Alice Springs, single.'

When the bushie's turn came, he plonked a $50 note down and said, 'Mick O'Brien, married with two kids.'

'Tough? Where I come from, tough? Christ, the ground's so stony we have to blast the seed in with shotguns. And harvest it with search warrants.'

It's late at night in the middle of the bush. A bloke in an FJ hears a bang and feels the car swerve. Bugger it, a blow out. But it's okay, he's got a spare. But what he doesn't have is a jack. Bum, bum, bum.

Then, across the paddocks, he glimpses a light. Yes, it's from a farmhouse window. 'He'll be able to lend me a jack,' mutters the bloke, and sets off towards the farm.

He steps into some cow shit, tears his coat climbing through a barbed-wire fence, and has to kick at a couple of barking kelpies. And he's not sure what sort of welcome he's going to get. 'It's late. He's probably had a real bastard of a day. He's gone to bed early and is dead to the world. And I'm going to have to wake him up.'

As he got closer to the farmhouse he thought, 'He's now climbing out of bed. He's really cranky.'

When the farmer opened the door with a friendly smile, the bloke was already turning away. 'Get fucked, you miserable bastard. And stick your jack up your arse.'

A census official arrives in a small town in north Queensland. 'What's the population of the place?' he asks of the local undertaker.

'One thousand and sixteen.'

'Is it growing or declining?'

435

'Neither. It's always been one thousand and sixteen.'

'It can't always be the same. It's got to go up or down.'

'No,' said the undertaker, 'always one thousand and sixteen.'

'But aren't any babies ever born here?'

'Of course,' said the undertaker. 'Lots. And every time there's a baby, some young bloke has to leave town.'

A man lies dying of thirst in the middle of the Nullarbor when he sees a kangaroo approaching with a salesman on its back. The salesman dismounts and attempts to sell him a paisley tie. The man rasps, 'Christ, a bloke's dying of thirst and you want to sell him a bloody tie.'

The salesman remounts and goes bounding off on his kangaroo. The parched man drags himself along until he sees a restaurant shimmering in the distance. As he crawls closer he is delighted to see hoardings advertising all types of cold drinks. He crawls to the door. 'Please let me in to buy something to drink.'

'Sorry,' says the doorman. 'No one's admitted without a tie.'

A bloke was looking around the goldfields at Bendigo and found an open mineshaft that seemed to go down and down and down forever. He pulled a coin out of his pocket and dropped it down the hole. And though he listened very carefully he didn't hear it touch the bottom. So he threw a large rock that was lying close by. Once again, he didn't hear it hit the bottom.

He then spied a railway sleeper so he dragged it towards the hole and dropped it down. As he did this, a billy goat came thundering up behind him and threw itself down the hole. 'Shit!' he said. 'I wonder why the goat did that?'

Whereupon an old man appeared on the scene and said, 'Excuse me, have you seen a goat anywhere around here?'

And he said, 'Funny you should say that. A dirty great goat just came charging up behind me and threw itself down the mineshaft.'

'Oh,' said the old man, 'it couldn't have been my goat. I had it tethered to a railway sleeper.'

'Is that the train for Hay pulling out?' the young jackeroo yelled as he dashed to the barrier at Central Station.

'Either that,' said the guard, 'or the station's backing up.'

A couple of swaggies were making camp one night, under a coolibah tree near a billabong. While one rolled a smoke, the other went down to fill the billy. 'There's a chap down there,' he said on his return.

    'Gettin' fish, is he?'

    'Nope.'

    'Gettin' rabbits then?'

    'Nope.'

    'What's he gettin'?'

    'Drowned.'

An old swaggie was trapped on the wrong side of a flooded river and, after a few weeks, ran out of food. He tried to stuff a jumbuck in his tuckerbag but the ground was so slippery he couldn't catch one. So he had to kill his dog – a faithful pooch that had been his only companion for almost ten years. And after he'd eaten all the meat, he sat staring sadly into his campfire. And he noticed how the flames were lighting bits of the dog's skeleton. And he said, 'My old dog would have liked them bones.'

A rugged old bushwhacker in a pub is scoffing at tales of present-day hardship and telling how things were really tough in his day. He caps every story with,

'You blokes, you talk about 'ard times.' At last he comes to the time when he was out in the middle of the Gibson Desert, all his water gone and left with only a handful of flour which he could make into a damper if only he had water. So he squats, holding the flour in his cupped hands between his legs so that he can piss on it. But before he can piss, he farts and blows all the flour away. 'You blokes, you talk about 'ard times.'

A Tasmanian discovered a flock on the roadside outside Launceston and stopped for a chat with the drover. 'Where are you from?'

'Up Coonabarabran way,' drawled the drover.

'Christ, how did you get your flock across Bass Strait?'

'Aw, I didn't come *that* way.'

While driving around the backblocks, an English tourist ran over a rooster and killed it. Being an honest chap he stopped and knocked on the farm door. 'I'm afraid I've killed your cock, madam, but I'd very much like to replace him.'

'Whatever you want,' said the farmer's wife. 'Go around the side there and you'll find the hens in the back.'

A bloke knocked on the door of a farm and offered to do some fencing.

'How much fence do you reckon you can put up in a day?' asked the farmer.

'Aw, about a mile.'

'Not enough. I've got a local fella who puts up so much fence in one day that it takes him two days to walk back.'

A bloke was tramping through the wheatbelt during the Depression looking for work. He called into a farm and asked the cocky if he had any jobs. The farmer said, 'Done any ploughing?'

'On a small scale,' the bloke replied.

'Have you done any furrowing?'

'On a small scale,' the bloke said.

'What about sowing? Have you done any?'

'On a small scale,' came the reply.

The cocky was becoming jack of this and said, 'Listen, mate, is there anything you've done on a big scale?'

'Yeah, I fucked a pig on a weighbridge once.'

There was a country dance and the young jackeroo invited the farmer's wife to waltz. After a couple of circuits of the floor she whispered in his ear, 'Come outside.'

Feeling a bit scared, he declined. Only to feel her holding him tighter. 'Come outside,' she said again.

Finally, fearfully, he agreed. Outside it was pitch dark so he pulled the torch from his pocket. 'Did you have that torch in your pocket while we were waltzing?' said the farmer's wife. 'Yeah,' said the jackeroo.

'Well, let's go back to the dance.'

A farmhand from out the back o' Bourke rode into Sydney on his camel to live it up and spend his big pay cheque. He'd really tried one on this day, and had ridden across the Harbour Bridge and decided to have just one last drink in North Sydney before sleeping it off. When he staggered out of the pub, he couldn't find his camel where he'd left it, so weaved into the police station to report its theft.

Officer: 'Now, sir, that you've given us your name and address and reported the theft of your camel, we'll take down a few details and a description of your camel for our records please. Did the camel have one hump or two?'

Farmhand (after some consideration): 'Aw, I think it had one . . . no, two humps. Ah, Jeez . . . no, one. I'm a bit hazy about that.'

Officer (restraining his irritation): 'Well then, sir, could you please tell us the colour of the camel?'

'Aw, sort of black. No, more brownish-black. Then again, perhaps greyish-beige. Ah, Jeez, hard to describe the colour exactly, officer.'

'Well then, sir, what about its height – how many hands was it?'

'Oooh,' said the farmhand, lifting his arms and squinting his eyes in concentration, 'about up to here. Then again,' lowering his arms, 'more about this high. Bit hard to tell ya, officer.'

'Well then, sir, I suppose it'd be impossible for you to be able to tell us the sex of this camel?' the officer asked.

'No, no, officer. It's female.'

'Look, sir. How can you be so sure? You couldn't tell us how many humps your camel had, you couldn't tell us the colour it was or even give us a fair idea of how high it stood. How come you're so sure of its sex?'

'Oh, that's easy, officer,' said the farmhand proudly. 'As I rode over the bridge this mornin', I heard some blokes call out from a passing car, "Look at the silly cunt on that camel!".'

There was a single bloke who won the lottery and bought himself a huge property in the Northern

Territory. He'd just settled in and was relaxing one evening on his porch, sipping a cup of tea and watching the sun going down. He saw a speck of dust on the horizon, which grew and grew. It materialised into another bloke on horseback.

'G'day! Welcome to the district!' said the bloke on the horse.

'G'day!' said the new owner, 'and thanks.'

'There's a bit of a party at my place Saturday night. Wanna come?'

'What'll it be like?'

'Oh, you know. Plenty of grog, plenty of tucker, plenty of rootin' and plenty of fightin'.'

'Sounds all right. Will I need to dress up?'

'Nah. It's just the two of us.'

F our Sydneyites were lost out back o' Bourke. They'd been driving around for hours on dirt roads and not getting anywhere. They came to an old codger leaning on a gate. 'Excuse me,' said the driver of the car, 'which road can we take to get back to Sydney?'

The bloke said nothing in reply.

'Listen, mate,' said the driver, 'should we go straight ahead?'

'I dunno.'

'Well, should I go left?'

'Dunno.'

'Or right?'

'Dunno.'

'You don't know much, do you?' said the driver.

'No,' said the codger, 'but I'm not bloody lost.'

A young bloke from outback Queensland, who'd never been away from his small country town, found himself the holder of the winning ticket in a raffle, first prize being a return trip to London with lots of spending money.

Within days he found himself in London. He was in a wonderful room in an upstairs flat in Chelsea with the best-looking sheila he had ever seen. Things had gone exceedingly well for him. She was naked on a four-poster king-size bed waiting for him. He stripped.

To her amazement, he didn't come directly to her but began to throw the furniture out of the French doors onto the road below. When he'd finished, tens of thousands of pounds worth of fine antiques had vanished out the doors. He turned to her at last.

'What did you do that for?' she whimpered.

'Well, I've never fucked a woman before. But if it's anything like a kangaroo, I'm gonna need all the room I can get!'

Out near Uluru the flies were dreadful. A tourist spotted an old bloke there. 'How do you find the flies here, mate?'

'You don't have to,' he replied, 'they find you.'

'But don't you want to do something for them?'

'No, I let 'em fend for themselves.'

'But don't you shoo them?'

'No, I let 'em run round barefoot.'

'But I don't like all these flies here, mate.'

'Well, let us know the ones you do like and I'll hunt the rest.'

'But seriously, do you know the progeny of a single fly can number thousands?'

'Strewth,' said the old-timer, 'what would the progeny of a married one be?'

Things were crook in the bush and the farm, like the sheep, was on its last legs. One day a bloke knocked at the door and announced that he worked for an oil company and was seeking permission to sink an exploratory hole. Yes, there'd be a few bob in it, even if they didn't find anything.

The farmer agreed, and a huge rig was dragged in and drilling began. But after they'd past the 500 m mark without a trace of oil, the company gave up and moved out. Whereupon the farmer decided to use some of the money he'd made from the oil company to build himself a little dunny right over the 500 m shaft. Why waste a good hole?

A year later the farmer decided that he was sick of hard seasons and put the place up for sale. The first to inspect were a city couple with dreams of being hobby farmers. While the wife looked over the house, the husband asked if he could use the dunny. The farmer showed him to the new building and the city bloke stepped inside.

Time passed and he didn't return. Worried, the farmer and the wife pushed the door open and found the husband collapsed on the dunny seat. Very dead.

'Did your husband have a heart condition?'

'No, no,' sobbed the wife. 'He was very fit and healthy.'

'Did he do anything . . . odd, when he was on the loo?'

'Well, he did have this silly habit of holding his breath until he heard the splash.'

At a family farm way out in the bush a farmer was down behind the chook shed repairing some wire as night approached.

'Tea's ready, love,' called the wife from the back door. 'You'd better come in now!'

'Not yet,' came the distant reply.

An hour later she called out, 'You'll miss the news on the telly, love. You'd better come in now.'

'Not yet!'

Another hour passed. 'I'm going to bed! Now will you come in?'

'Not yet!'

The wife called into the darkness. 'It's dark, it's late, it's getting cold. Give me three good reasons why you won't come in.'

'I'll give you four. One, I'm not hungry. Two, I don't feel like watching the telly. Three, I'm not sleepy. And four, I can't get my foot out of this bloody dingo trap.'

An old cocky has lost his best cow. He checks the neighbours' paddocks, takes a trip into the local pound and alerts the local constabulary just in case it's been nicked.

Finally he asks the rector if he would make an announcement during the Sunday service. As is the outback custom, a wedding had been arranged in conjunction with the service so the cocky had to sit right up the back.

Being a bit deaf he finds it hard to hear what the rector is saying, and fails to realise that, in fact, he is uniting a Reg Dow and a Mary Jones in holy matrimony. At this point the cocky mumbles to

447

himself, 'Ah, here it comes now,' the appeal for information about his red cow.

He waits politely until, at the end, the priest concludes, 'Therefore, if anyone knows any reason why these two persons should not be joined in matrimony, he should now declare it.' Whereupon the cocky sings out, 'Don't forget to tell 'em she's got one blind tit and all the hair scratched off her belly.'

In a shearing shed back o' Bourke a new arrival asked, 'What do you do for sex around here?'

'Well, on Friday nights we fuck the cook for $33.'

'Why so much?'

'Well, the cocky's manager doesn't approve, so we slip him 20 bucks and the cook doesn't like it. So we pay $2 each for four blokes to hold him down.'

After a long drought it had begun to rain. And it rained for days and days. The river had swollen, broken its banks, and the whole district was flooded.

Not to be outdone by the weather, a travelling salesman rowed a boat across to the homestead, where a farmer, his wife and children were sitting on the galvo roof.

'Pretty bad, eh?' called the salesman, clambering

up into the gutter. As he sat chatting he noticed a battered old Akubra moving round and round in circles on the floodwater.

'Do you see that?' asked the salesman.

'Oh, that,' said the farmer. 'That's Grandpa. Last week he said that come hell or high water, he was going to mow the lawn today.'

A female bureaucrat from the Department of Agriculture was addressing a meeting of farmers on the subject of animal pest control. 'It is no longer permissible to kill dingoes,' she said, 'but male dingoes can be legally trapped, castrated and released.'

An exasperated cattle farmer jumped to his feet and said, 'Will someone tell this bloody woman that the dingoes are eating my calves, not rooting them.'

A bloke who had a cattle stud in Queensland was telling a friend from the city that he could weigh bulls without using scales. 'It's easy. An ancient skill handed down in my family for generations. I tell their weight by just feeling their testicles.'

'Bull,' said the bloke from the city. 'I don't believe a word of it.'

So the farmer went over to one of his bulls, felt its balls and announced, 'Fifteen hundred kilos.'

They pulled the bull onto the scales and it was exactly 1500 kilos. 'Christ, that's amazing! Can anybody else do it?'

'Well, as a matter of fact, the wife can. She's better at it than me.'

'Okay, here's a hundred bucks that says she can't find me a 2000 kilo bull just by feeling its balls.'

Whereupon the farmer told his son to fetch Mum.

He came back without her. 'Sorry, Dad, Mum's busy.'

'Busy? What's more important than winning $100?'

'I dunno,' said the boy, 'but I think she's weighing the milkman.'

A young jackeroo picked up the new governess from the railway station. Driving her back to the property they passed a bull fucking a cow. 'How do they know when it's the right time to do that?' inquired the governor.

'Sense of smell,' said the jackeroo.

Then they saw a stallion mounting a mare and a ram attending a flock of ewes.

'How do they know when it's the right time to do that?'

'Sense of smell.'

When they reached the homestead the jackeroo unloaded the young woman's luggage from the horse and cart and plonked it on the verandah. 'See you around,' he said.

'Yes,' said the governess, 'come over when your cold gets better.'

There was an agricultural show in a country town and the spruikers were going hammer and tong. The Jimmy Sharman Boxing Troupe was the big drawcard and all the young blokes were listening to Sharman bellowing through his megaphone. 'Who's gonna have a go? No, not with one of the boxers. We've got matches for all of them. I want someone to wrestle my wrestler. The Masked Monster from Murrurundi. Is anyone game to wrestle the Masked Monster?'

No takers. No surprise – the Masked Monster was built like a brick dunny.

'How about you, young fella?' Sharman said to a young stockman. 'Five bucks if you have a go, and ten bucks if you win.'

'I don't know nuthin' about no wrestlin',' said the kid. 'Only wrestlin' I've done is throwin' the big poddies at brandin' time.' But after much urging he agreed to take on the Masked Monster from Murrurundi.

'You'd better take your belt off,' said Sharman, pointing to a belt with a knife pouch.

451

'Nah. If I take me belt off, me daks'll fall down.'

'Okay then. Leave it on,' said Sharman.

And the two of them began wrestling, sending up a huge cloud of dust. Suddenly there was an agonised scream and the stockman emerged from the cloud. He looked at his watch. 'Not bad,' he muttered. 'Threw him, earmarked him and castrated him in eight seconds.'

A Collins Street cocky bought a farm in the Western District, just down the road from Malcolm Fraser's Nareen. He paid through the nose for it, mainly because of the really great tree growing by the homestead. A huge old gum said to be around 500 years old. He was really proud of the tree and showed photographs of it to all his mates in Melbourne. He even got Arthur Boyd to do a painting of it.

But his mates refused to believe the tree was 500 years old. So he phoned the farm manager to get more details. He said he'd find out what he could.

A couple of days later he called his boss. 'That tree by the homestead, it's exactly 553 years old.'

'Five hundred and fifty-three,' said the grazier proudly. 'And how can you be so sure?'

'No probs,' said the manager. 'We just chainsawed the bastard down and counted the rings.'

It was on the black soil plains of Queensland during the wet. The cocky was riding his horse very, very carefully through the mud when he spotted a familiar Akubra. Reaching out with his stock whip he lifted it up. And there, beneath it, was his bullocky, up to his ears in mate.

'Christ,' said the cocky, 'you're really in it.'

'I'm okay,' said the bullocky, 'but the team's in pretty deep.'

The squatter hired a new hand and sent him out to the back paddock to dig 20 post holes. At the end of the day he drove out in the four-wheel drive to inspect the work and found the hand lying under a tree smoking a cigarette.

'Hey, I told you to dig 20 holes and there are only 18.'

'Well, boss,' said the new hand, taking another drag on the fag, 'I dug 20. Some bastard must have pinched a couple.'

Two young blokes are backpacking their way around outback Queensland and get caught in the floods. So they ask for help at a nearby cattle station. The owner, a widowed lady, welcomes them as if they are her own sons and gives them a good, hearty meal. But she thinks it's inappropriate that they sleep in the house. The hay barn, however, will be perfectly comfortable.

The pair leave the next day and, after having traipsed around much of Australia, separate.

Years later, meeting in Brisbane, they go off to a local pub and start reminiscing.

'Remember the floods, and the hay barn?'

'Of course I do.'

'We always used to be truthful to each other, didn't we?'

'I hope we still are.'

'Okay, when I was asleep, did you creep in and kip down with the widow?'

'Yeah, I did.'

'And did you give her my name and address instead of yours?'

'Yeah, I did. Sorry, mate.'

'Don't be. Two years back she died and left me the whole 100 000 acres.'

A couple of boundary riders from the north-west came down to Perth. After years of hard yakka they felt like a bit of fun. But after a couple of weeks of boozing, their money ran out. So they applied for jobs with a local council where they were told to see the foreman in his office at the works yard.

The first boundary rider went into the office to be interviewed. The foreman said, 'If I was to poke you in the eye with my finger, what would you be?'

He replied, 'Half blind.'

'And if I was to poke you in both eyes?'

'Totally blind.'

'Fine. You can start on Monday. And when you go out, send your mate in.'

Outside, the boundary rider said to his mate, 'Look, you only get asked two questions. The answers are easy. Half blind, and totally blind.'

Feeling confident, the second boundary rider sat opposite the foreman. 'If I cut your left ear off, what would you be?'

'Half blind,' said the boundary rider with a broad grin.

The foreman looked at him incredulously. 'And if I cut both your ears off?'

'Totally blind.'

'How the hell do you make that out?'

'Well, me hat would fall over me eyes.'

A young bloke had been working on a sheep station for a few months when he felt an insistent stirring in the loins. So he spoke to an old hand. 'What's a fella do if he wants a fuck around here?'

The old hand told him where to find the prettiest wethers. But the young bloke didn't think much of that.

A few months later, however, he changed his mind. But he couldn't get the sheep to cooperate. So he went back to the old bloke, who was well into his seventies, for help.

The old bloke grabbed the best-looking ewe and, despite his age, undid his fly buttons and got stuck into it.

The young bloke was very impressed and couldn't wait for his turn. But he had a question. 'Before you started rooting the wether, you looked all around the place. Why?'

'Well,' said the old bloke, 'I've been keeping company with an emu.'

At Nar Nar Goon, they grow very, very big pumpkins. So big that they carve them out and use them for weekenders. One bloke was hacking away at a giant pumpkin when he dropped his axe down the hole. So he threw down a knotted rope and began, very carefully, to lower himself down into the gloom. After a while his eyes adjusted to the darkness and he saw a faint light. It turned out to be an old-timer holding a hurricane lamp. 'Have you seen my axe?' he asked.

'No,' said the codger. 'Have you seen a team of horses?'

'The drought up here is so bad that the council's had to close two lanes of the swimming pool.'

The drought seemed to be getting worse and worse. There was no feed on the properties and bugger all on the long paddock.

The drought got worse. A sympathetic tourist asked a farmer, 'Do you think it'll rain?'

'Hope so,' said the farmer, peering sadly at the sky. 'Not so much for my own sake as for the boys'. I've seen it rain.'

How do you get rid of a boomerang?
Throw it down a one-way street.

Why do they bury cockies only three feet deep?
So that they can still put their hands out.

A couple of battlers from the bush, who'd been through everything together, finally won millions in the lottery. They celebrated with a beer in the local pub and agreed that a few million dollars wouldn't change things. Except for the flash cars they'd always wanted.

Leaving the pub somewhat unsteadily, they went straight to a showroom where they astonished the salesman by buying two Rolls Royces. One each.

One codger produced his cheque book and reached for his pen. The other said, 'No, no, mate. Fair go. You paid for the beers.'

A yuppie parks his Porsche outside a country pub and wanders in for a beer. A local farmer is sitting at the bar and the yuppie inquires after his health.

'Not . . . too . . . bad,' comes the slow, measured response.

'You from around here?' asks the yuppie.

'Yeah . . . got a place . . . down the . . . road a bit.'

'Excuse me saying this,' said the yuppie, 'but you speak very, very slowly.'

'Do yer . . . reckon? Around . . . here . . . I'm . . . regarded . . . as a . . . bit of a . . . sparkling . . . conversationalist. My brother . . . Arthur . . . speaks . . . really . . . slowly. And . . . my sister . . . speaks . . .

slower . . . than him. So when . . . a bloke . . . put the
. . . hard . . . word . . . on her . . . and . . . before she
could . . . say she . . . wasn't . . . that kind . . . of a . . .
girl . . . she bloody-well . . . was.'

The barman at the bush pub was one of the toughest
guys you've ever seen, muscles, tattoos, unshaven,
sweaty and pulling beers in a black singlet. The
shearer couldn't take his eyes off him. 'What the hell
d'yer think yer staring at?' said the barman
eventually.

'I just can't get over the likeness. It's a truly
remarkable resemblance,' said the shearer. 'You're a
dead-ringer for my wife. In fact, if it wasn't for the
moustache . . .'

'I haven't got a moustache,' interrupted the
barman.

'No, but my wife has!'

A pommy tourist arrives in Australia, hires a car and
drives into the outback. He looks out the window
and is deeply shocked to see a bloke bonking a
kangaroo.

Hoping to steady his nerves, he stops at the
next pub and orders a Pimms. No sooner has he

raised it to his lips than he notices a one-legged bloke masturbating at the other end of the bar.

He turns to the barman. 'What's the matter with you people? Are all you Australians depraved? I've been here a few hours and I've already seen one guy having intercourse with a kangaroo and another masturbating in public.'

'Fair go, mate,' says the barman, 'you can't expect a bloke with one leg to catch a kangaroo!'

An intrepid Englishman, a teacher by profession, booked himself a cycling holiday in outback Queensland during the big wet. It was 90 degree heat and 100 per cent humidity. Inevitably he became lost; his maps were all soggy; he had to push his bike along dirt roads with the wheels up to the rims in mud. Despite his pith helmet and stiff upper lip, he was soaked to the skin and unhappy. Being hot, he was thirsty; not sweating, he needed to relieve his bladder; being a self-perceived English gentleman, he was averse to going behind or even in front of the nearest tree.

He was feeling exhausted and anxious when, through the teeming rain, he saw a fingerpost. When he came to it, he removed his glasses, carefully wiped them on his damp handkerchief, replaced them, and, before they were misted, managed to read the sign – TIP. Believing it to be some form of civilisation, he followed the road, and to his relief came upon a country hotel.

After hitching his bike to the horse-rail, he staggered through the door marked BAR. It was a stark room with a wooden floor and a few dilapidated tables, at one of which sat four men in heavy-duty clothes. Each was wearing a bush hat with corks suspended from the brim. They were drinking from straight ten-ounce glasses. Dripping his way to the bar, he asked the barman, who stared at him rather suspiciously, for a beer. As it was served he whispered, 'Do you have a loo?'

The barman stared even more intently, but made no response.

'The loo? The John? The toilet? Oh, for God's sake, the lavatory – please?'

The barman pointed silently to a dark door at the far end of the room. Thankful, our hero nursed his bladder to the door and opened it to the pouring rain and a paddock. There, on the left, was a pile of shit about 40 foot high, dripping and leaning thixotropically. On the right was another pile, this one only ten foot high, also dripping but looking much more stable.

'Thank God someone had the sense to start a new pile,' he muttered, as he braved the rain to the smaller pile.

He was in the middle of relieving himself when

he was stopped mid-stream by a bullet thudding into the pile next to his ear. Desperately trying to get back into his trousers and turn at the same time, he saw one of the corked-hatted men standing in the doorway with a smoking .22 in his hand. The man removed his cigarette from his mouth and said, 'Get outta the Ladies', yer pommie bastard!'

An Australian was on the piss in Earl's Court where, despite his crude behaviour, he found himself being eyed warmly by the barmaid. She confessed that she was partial to Aussies and invited him back to her flat. It turned out to be about 20 flights up a narrow, rickety staircase. First she gave him a few extra beers – she had some cans of Fosters in the fridge – then heated him a meat pie in the oven and doused it in Rosella tomato sauce. Finally she said there were other indoor pastimes they could enjoy. Would he like to come into the next room? The Aussie clambered enthusiastically to his feet. 'Christ, how did you get a pool table up here?'

The scene is a urinal at the back of a pub. An Aussie and a pom enter for a pee. The Aussie finishes and heads straight back for the bar. The pom finishes, washes his hands and, as he re-enters the bar, complains in a loud voice, 'Don't they teach you colonials to wash your hands?'

To which the Aussie replies, 'Nah, mate, they teach us not to piss on them.'

A bus full of tourists arrived in Kakadu. Everyone piled off, except for one old bloke. 'Don't you want to see the Aboriginal carving?'

'No thanks,' he said. 'I've lived on a farm all my life and I've seen plenty of cows calving. So I don't suppose it'd be much different.'

Grab Bag

Phonetic Dictionary

Ad Hoc:	Cooking with wine
Adder:	Tally clerk
Adenoid:	Irritated by adverts
Alimony:	Arab coins
Alpaca:	Kerry's brother
Anemone:	Foe
Antelope:	Absconding insect
Aphrodisiac:	Trapeze artists from Zaire
Arable:	Islamic
Armada:	Which art in heaven
Badinage:	Memory, six, teeth
Barbecue:	Awaiting haircut
Blackguard:	Negro sentry
Bulletin:	Loaded
Canteloupe:	Chaperoned
Capsize:	Seven and three-quarters

Carrion:	Continue
Castanet:	Go fishing
Castrate:	Theatre review
Chinchilla:	Aftershave
Condescending:	Greek Paratrooper
Copulate:	Tardy policeman
Counter-culture:	Retailing
Curlicue:	Friendly dog
Cyclamate:	Tandem
Divest:	Princess's garment
Dragster:	Transvestite
Emulate:	Dead bird
Equilibrium:	Sedative for horses
Equivocal:	Duet
Farthing:	Distant object
Felonious:	Monk
Flatulent:	Borrowed apartment
Fodder:	Male parent
Foolhardy:	Stan Laurel
Forensic:	Ill migrants
Foreplay:	Bridge
Foresight:	Saga
Forfeit:	Quadruped
Frigate!:	Angry exclamation
Frontispiece:	Penis
Gangplank:	Political platform
Gangrene:	IRA hitsquad
Grateful:	Enough firewood
Gunwale:	Harpoon

Handicap: Useful hat
Homophone: Gay hotline
Huguenot: Large tangle
Ideal: You shuffle
Infantry: Seedling
Injury: Empanelled
Innuendo: Italian suppository
Inquire: Member of chorus
Intercourse: Sorbet
Internee: Cartilage
Jargon: Lost container
Jaywalker: Whisky
Juniper: Hebrew child
Lactose: Ungulate
Lieutenant: Vacant apartment
Littoral: Precise
Lobotomy: Sagging arse
Macabre: Scottish tree
Malefactor: Sperm
Manifold: Origami
Masturbator: Accomplished fisherman
Matelot: Promiscuous
Moorish: Habit-forming
Musket: Sweet wine
Napkin: Short sleep
Nobility: Thirsty swagman
Nomad: Sane
Notice: Melted
Opine: Irish tree

Palindrome:	Friend at airport
Palliasse:	Friendly donkey
Paradox:	Two hounds
Pasturage:	Older
Picnicker:	Select underwear
Pique:	Mountain top
Polygon:	Dead parrot
Propaganda:	True goose
Racketeer:	Tennis player
Ramparts:	Sheep's balls
Ruminant:	Hungry insect
Rumour:	Boarder
Sari:	So am I, very!
Scatology:	Jazz speak
Scintillate:	Nocturnal orgy
Semen:	Sailors
Signet:	Young swan
Silicon:	Dumb trick
Slapstick:	Teacher's cane
Sorghum:	Pyorrhea
Support:	Imbibe fortified wine
Surcingle:	Unmarried baronet
Sycamore:	Chronically ill
Syntax:	Fred Nile's ambition
Tartar:	Goodbye
Thinking:	Slender monarch
Truculent:	Borrowed lorry
Undertake:	Bury
Vicarious:	Clergyman's debts

Wedlock: Chastity belt
Yataghan: Once more

A bloke arrives at Australia Square and asks where
he can find Harry Siedler's office.

'Top floor. But the lift's on the blink, so you'll
have to use the stairs.'

Just as the bloke was beginning his long trudge,
the guard calls out. 'And if you see the gorilla on the
way up, for Christ's sake don't touch him!'

The gorilla? the bloke thought to himself. Don't
touch the gorilla?

Up and up he climbs. Up and up and up. And
somewhere near the 39th floor he finds himself
confronted by a dirty great gorilla – with its back to
him.

Despite the warning of the guard, he can't resist
reaching out and touching the gorilla on the
shoulder.

The gigantic creature spins around, the bloke
screams and starts running downstairs, with the
gorilla close behind him. Down the stairs they go –
down, down, down. In and out of doors, along
corridors. Finally the bloke can't go on. He collapses
on the floor, sobbing helplessly. And the gorilla
looms over him, touches him on the shoulder and
says, 'You're it!'

There was a horse sale in Scone. They'd knocked down a few yearlings from Segenhoe and a few polo ponies from Kerry Packer's place at Ellerston. They rounded the auction off with a few cheap horses for cattle work and, finally, there was only one left. A broken-down hack that nobody wanted. Whereupon a timid-looking bloke in a suit – he might have been a local accountant – bid $100. And the horse was knocked down to him. He then asked for help to get the horse home. So one of the kids who'd been helping at the sale loaded the horse on to a float and took it through the town to a neat, fussy little house on the outskirts. But there was no paddock. No stable. Not even a big garden.

'Just do what I ask,' said the little bloke, 'and I'll give you $50.'

'Okay, mate.'

'In here,' said the little bloke, opening the front door.

With considerable difficulty, the kid got the horse into the hall.

'Now, up there,' said the little bloke, pointing to a flight of stairs.

Finally they got the horse upstairs.

'In here.'

'The bathroom?'

'Yes, stand him in the bath.'

This took considerable time. At last the horse was standing in the bath.

'Now shoot him.'

'Shoot him?'

'Fifty dollars. Shoot him.'

Later, downstairs, the bloke gave the kid the $50.

'Look here, Mister. Before I leave, what's going on?'

'Well, my brother is coming to stay. He's a know-all. Every time I open my mouth he butts in and says, "I know, I know". He always knows. And I'm determined to get my own back. After dinner he'll go up to the bathroom for a piss. Then he'll come down shouting, "There's a dead horse in your bath!" And I'll say, "I know, I know".'

A sailor, an ostrich and a cat walked into a pub. They climbed on to one, two, three bar stools. The ostrich shouted a round. The sailor shouted a round. But the cat simply looked the other way when it was his shout.

'Why doesn't the cat buy a round?' asked the barman.

'It's a long, sad story,' said the sailor. 'I was alone on a desert island when a bottle came bobbing through the surf. When I opened it, a genie appeared and he granted me one wish. And all I asked for was a long-legged bird with a tight pussy.'

A fellow walked into a shoe shop one day wanting to buy a pair of shoes. A lady served him and asked what size he was.

'Size five', was the reply.

'Oh!' said the lady. 'You look like a size ten to me.' But the customer insisted on a size five. So the lady got them and the guy tried to squeeze into them without much luck, so he asked for a shoe horn and after another 15 minutes, finally got them on and said, 'No, too big. I'll take a size four.'

So the lady came back with a size four, and the guy tried for 20 minutes with no luck. He asked for a crowbar and after another 15 minutes finally got them on and said thanks, then paid for them and walked out in obvious pain.

Two weeks later the shop lady saw this guy walking down the street. He was almost doubled over in pain, and as he shuffled his feet you could see the agony on his face. She stopped him and asked why he insisted on wearing these shoes.

'Well,' he said, 'last month my mother and father died in a tragic accident. A week after that I had the winning numbers in the lottery but forgot to register them. Then my wife ran off with another man, and my daughter announced she's pregnant and her brother is the father. The taxman is hassling me, a weird religious sect has moved in next door and the council has just put my rates up. The only joy I get in life these days is when I go home and take these bloody shoes off!!!'

A young bloke applies for a job in a menswear shop in a country town.

'Listen, son,' said the manager, 'we've had a drought here for the last ten years and the local abattoir's closed down. So times are tough. I could only afford to hire you if you're a really, really good salesman.'

'Ooh, but I am, I am!'

'Okay, I'll give you a go. I'm going out to lunch and by the time I get back I want you to have sold these pink hotpants. They're identical to the ones that that Don Dunstan bloke wore to Parliament in the early '70s and I've never been able to sell them. You flog those and you're hired.'

When the owner returned from lunch he found that the pink hotpants had, in fact, disappeared from stock. But the young salesman was in bad shape, his trousers ripped and his face was covered in scratches.

'What happened?'

'Well, I sold the hotpants. The bloke was really pleased with them. But his seeing-eye dog gave me buggery.'

Little Red Riding Hood was skipping through the forest on her way to Grandma's house when out jumped the Big Bad Wolf.

'I'm going to eat you all up,' he snarled.

'What's the matter?' said Little Red Riding Hood. 'Doesn't anybody fuck any more?'

A bloke started talking to Captain Hook in a bar and said, 'Gee, you've been in the wars. What happened to your leg?'

'Well,' said Captain Hook, 'I got into this battle, see, with Peter Pan, and the cannon goes off and the ball cuts my leg clean off. And I had to get this wooden one put on.'

'How about the hook? What happened to your hand?'

'Well, see, I got into this fight with Peter Pan, this big sword fight and – *swish!* – the blade takes off my whole hand and I had to have this hook put on.'

'And the patch on your eye? What happened there?'

'Well, I'm out on the boat and I look up to the sky and this seagull craps right into it. Lost the whole eye.'

'Hang on,' said the bloke, 'you can't lose an eye because a seagull craps in it.'

'You can,' says Captain Hook, 'if you've only had your hook for one day!'

Once upon a time, there was a very handsome young prince, and he was as good and kind as he was handsome. One day when he was out hunting unicorns, he came across a very old lady sitting crying on the banks of a creek, as if her heart would break. Getting off his charger, he asked her what ailed her. She said she had to cross the creek to get back home. There was too much water in the creek; it was very cold and muddy, and she couldn't find a bridge. He told her to dry her tears and he would carry her across. This would be very difficult, given that she weighed a great deal and smelt something awful.

On putting her gently down on the other side, the old woman suddenly turned into a fairy godmother (not a princess). She told him that she had heard how good looking he was, and that this was exceeded by his great care and kindness for others. She would now grant him anything he wished.

Looking at his magnificent stallion, the prince said he would like to have the genitals of his horse. She said his wish was granted, and vanished into thin air.

Back at the court the prince had a wonderful time, besieged by all the ladies. News of this reached the king's ear, so he decided to go in search of the fairy godmother. Next day he was out hunting and came across the old woman sitting on the banks of the creek. He again carried her across the creek and once again she changed into a fairy godmother. She told the king that she would grant him anything he wanted. Excitedly the king asked for the genitals of his horse, and she told him his wish was granted. However, the king had been riding a mare that day. So, of course, the king and the prince lived happily ever after!

A UFO lands in the Rundle Mall just as a garbage truck comes along. Spotting the UFO, the driver tries to do a wheelie and one of the bins falls off and rolls across to where the extraterrestrial is standing. It doesn't hesitate for a second. The extraterrestrial picks up the bin and runs after the speeding truck.

'Madam! Madam!' he calls. 'You've dropped your handbag!'

Having waddled to the bus stop in a very tight mini skirt, the young woman was finding it hard to board the high step. She reached round, loosened the zip but still couldn't get her leg up. So she reached behind and unzipped it a little further. But she still couldn't quite make it.

Whereupon she was suddenly lifted onto the bus by a pair of hands on her bum. She turned around, determined to slap the bloke's face. 'How dare you!'

'I thought you wouldn't mind,' he said, 'not after you opened my fly twice.'

A battered Volkswagen was stopped at the traffic lights. A luxurious stretch limo slowed to a halt beside it. The bloke in the VW opened his window and banged on the window of the limo. The chauffeur touched a button and the window slid silkily down.

'Got a TV in there?' asked the bloke in the VW.

'Of course,' said the limo driver, 'and a phone and a fax, a cocktail cabinet, and a CD player.'

'Yeah,' said the VW driver, 'I've got all them too. Have you got a spa, but?'

'No,' said the limo driver.

'Well, I've got a spa in here,' said the bloke in the VW.

The lights changed and the limo driver roared off, leaving the VW floundering.

Next day the limo driver went to Stretch Limos Pty Ltd and had a spa fitted. Not just a spa, but a double spa.

A few weeks later he saw the VW again, parked by the side of the road. The chauffeur pulled up, got out and approached the old car. Its windows were all steamed up, so he had to bang on the roof to attract attention.

The window of the VW came down an inch or so, rather shakily.

'It's me,' said the chauffeur. 'I just wanted you to know that I've got a spa in my limo. A double spa.'

The bloke in the VW looked really angry. 'Shit!' he snarled. 'You got me out of the shower just to tell me that?'

Mr and Mrs Merchant Banker returned to their mansion to find that they'd been robbed – in a big, very systematic way. Obviously the naughties had backed a removal truck into the driveway leading to the triple garage and loaded up the lot. The Bang and Olufsen tellies and hi-fi sets had gone, the Brett Whiteleys, the microwave oven, the Miele appliances and the Braun rechargeable razor. They'd taken the leather lounge suite, the Armani clothes, the antique Persian rugs and the autographed photo of the Merchant Banker with President Reagan. The only thing left was, astonishingly, the very, very expensive Nikon camera and a couple of toothbrushes.

Not to worry. Everything was insured. And the couple joked about the kindness of the robbers in at least leaving them their toothbrushes. Oh, and the Nikon.

A few weeks later they completed the roll in the

camera and sent it off for processing. It came back showing a couple of blokes in balaclavas bending over with toothbrushes shoved up their arses – the toothbrushes Mr and Mrs Merchant Banker had been using ever since the robbery.

It was the Melbourne Motor Show at the Exhibition Buildings and one of the centrepieces was a gleaming Rolls Royce. Beside it stood a salesman, wearing a white tie, a dinner jacket and striped trousers.

A little old lady toddled up to him and said in a tiny voice, 'Please, sir, could you tell me where the loo is?'

Whereupon the salesman took the old lady by the arm, walked her to the loo, put a coin in the slot for her and then used his silk handkerchief to wipe her backside.

'Oh,' she said, 'thank you so much. You've been so kind.'

'Not at all,' said the salesman. 'Yours was the only genuine inquiry I've had all day.'

A laconic cow cocky was sitting over a beer listening to his mate who had just returned from working in the outback.

'. . . then I rolled the car bloody miles from nowhere. When I came to, I was trapped, couldn't move. Do you know that I was stuck in there for two days! Not a truck, not a car, nothin' came along that bloody road.'

'Yeah,' the cocky drawled, 'I'd believe that.'

'And then, blow me down, but two cars came along within five minutes!'

'Oh yeah?'

'Yeah, was I bloody glad to see them – the Johnstons and the Balls.'

'Yeah?'

'Yeah.'

The cow cocky thought for a moment. 'Hope you were dragged out by the Johnstons.'

Some years ago this old Tumbarumba drover gets a telegram to say his daughter in Wagga Wagga has just given birth to his first grandson. He decided he must pay her a visit, so gets out his old pushbike and sets off. The bike hasn't been used in years and the front wheel squeaks with each revolution. 'Only one thing to fix that,' he says to himself. 'Gotta get meself some goanna oil.'

So he props his bike against a gumtree, ambles off into the bush and comes back ten minutes later dragging a four-foot goanna by the tail, which he cuts off. And, with a motion similar to wringing out a wet towel, squeezes the oil out of the goanna's tail into the hub of his front wheel.

Back in the saddle, the bike fairly takes off down the slight slope. What a difference! But now the slope gets steeper and the bike really rockets, with the old feller hanging on for his life. They come to a bend halfway down the hill, he loses control, leaves the road and wakes up in Wagga Hospital with a fractured pelvis, two dislocated shoulders and three broken ribs. Upon his release three weeks later, having seen his daughter and grandson, he begins the long walk back in search of his bike.

When he reaches the spot, he can't see the bike anywhere . . . until he pushes back the brim of his Akubra to scratch his head. He looks up and there, way up in the tree, hanging from a branch, is the old bike. And would you believe it – that flamin' front wheel's still going around!

The Ku Klux Klan guy drives into a service station in Kalgoorlie and orders $20 worth of petrol. The attendant says, 'Shall I check under the hood?'

The travelling salesman's car broke down and he stumbled over a paddock to the farmhouse. He explained his predicament and asked if he could stay the night. 'Of course,' said the farmer, 'but I must warn you that I don't have daughters. I'm a bachelor and you'll have to share my bed.'

'Bugger it,' said the salesman, 'I'm in the wrong joke.'

Did you hear what happened when the fuses blew at the contortionists' club?

It was so dark you couldn't see your bum in front of your face.

What's the difference between an angry audience and a mad cow?

One boos madly and the other moos badly.

Knock, knock.
Who's there?
Ken.
Ken who?
Ken I come in?

Knock, knock.
>Who's there?
>A little old lady.
>A little old lady who?
>I didn't know you could yodel.

Knock, knock.
>Who's there?
>Ammonia.
>Ammonia who?
>Ammonia a little boy who can't reach the doorbell.

What has four wheels, five doors and hangs around French cathedrals?
>The hatch-back of Notre Dame.

An amateur archaeologist rings up the National Museum and tells them that he's unearthed a 4000-year-old mummy that died of a heart attack.

>Whilst impressed with the find, the museum people doubted that the mummy had had a coronary. But they decided to conduct a post mortem.

485

'You were absolutely right,' they reported to the archaeologist. 'The mummy did die of a heart attack. But how did you know when you hadn't unwrapped the bandages?'

'Well, when I dug him up he was holding a bit of papyrus in his hand. And when I deciphered the hieroglyphs it said, "Ten thousand shekels on Goliath".'

The Accident Appreciation Squad was grilling a young woman who'd been involved in a collision. 'What gear were you in?'

'What gear? This simple, black chiffon number from Sportsgirl.'

A judge in petty sessions was having trouble with the witness's name. 'You say your name is Peach?' he said. 'Well, how do you spell it?'

'P-i-e-t-z-c-h-e, your Worship,' replied the man.

'Tell me then,' said the judge. 'How would you spell "apricot"?'

Fetherstonhaugh, the young subaltern posted to a dangerous area of India, asks the experienced colonel for his chosen safety priorities. Says the colonel,

'Watch out for the dreaded wishband snake . . .
protect your men at all costs. When you see its long,
banded body slithering through the undergrowth, go
fearlessly forward, run your hand quickly up from
the tail area, and *snap*! Break its neck.'

A month later the colonel visits the outpost and
calls on Fetherstonhaugh. The subaltern is in a
sickbed, swathed from head to toe in bandages. 'My
God! What happened?' asks the colonel.

'Sir,' chokes out Fetherstonhaugh, 'Do you recall
telling me to beware of the dreaded wishband snake?'

'Yes,' replies the colonel.

'And advising me to tackle it by running my
hand quickly up its long, banded body?'

'Of course, my boy.'

'Sir, have you ever shoved your thumb up a
tiger's bum?'

A bloke was sitting in front of Young & Jackson's,
his head in bandages and crutches on his lap. One
arm was in a sling and the other held his hat.

'You poor fellow,' said a matron, dropping a few
coins in the hat. 'But things could be worse. After all,
you could be blind.'

'That's right, lady. When I was blind I kept
getting foreign coins.'

Vietnam. A wounded GI arrives in an Australian field hospital. He looks up at the Aussie nurse and faintly inquires, 'Did I come here to die?'

'No, love, yer came here yesterdie,' she said reassuringly.

A flash bloke from the coast drove his Mercedes sports out to a little mud pub at Bedourie. He then started boring the locals with facts – zero to 100 in five seconds, a top speed of 300 km/h, worth $300 000.

'Well, mate, we've got a bloke here who can top that.'

Bets are placed. 'Call Jim,' they shout, and the race is on. Flash Jack is off like the clappers – first gear, second gear – when he hears a thumping on his car door.

'Oi, can't you go any faster?' shouts Jim.

'Of course I bloody well can.' And the Merc tears away.

Third gear, through fourth to fifth and the Merc hits 300 km/h. Suddenly he hears a hell of a thump on the car door and Jim, like bloody Superman, screams past – off into the blooming scrub, smashing small trees en route.

That sundown, Jim, ripped to bits, his T-shirt gone, ears, nose and lips split, hobbles quietly into the mud pub at Bedourie. 'Good on ya, mate,' the blokes in the bar chorus. 'But you're a bit scratched, eh, cobber?'

'Strike me fuckin' dead. How would you feel if you got a blow-out in your left sandshoe doing 350 kilometres?'

'**I**'m telling you, mate, that Murray cod I caught last week was six foot long.'

'Well, where is it then?'

'Oh, it broke the line and got away.'

'Well, I fished that same stretch of river last week and was casting near where that old paddle-steamer sank. And I hooked the old lantern. And when I pulled it up, it was still burning.'

'Fair go. You don't expect a bloke to believe that.'

'Well, chop three feet off your Murray cod and I'll blow out the candle.'

An old codger with a bald head and a wooden leg wanted to go to the fancy-dress party at the twilight home but was too mean to spend much on a costume. He went to a couple of fancy-dress shops but wouldn't pay the $20 for even the cheapest costume. There was, finally, only one shop.

'I haven't got much money,' he told the manager. 'What have you got for $5?'

The manager looked at the old codger, focused on his bald head then had a decco at his wooden leg. Finally he reached under the counter and produced a tin of treacle. 'That'll be five bucks.'

'That's not a fancy-dress outfit,' protested the codger. 'That's just a cheap tin of treacle.'

'Look, it's the best I can do for five bucks. Pour the treacle over your bald head, stick your wooden leg up your arse and go as a toffee apple.'

An old farmer turned 90. The local cops sent him a letter saying that he'd have to hand in his driver's licence. That is, unless he could pass a short written test and a medical, as well as demonstrate his driving skill to the local sergeant.

Well, he passed the medical with flying colours and got all the answers right in the written test. So he started driving the sergeant around the town in his Land Cruiser. And to the sergeant's surprise, he did very well indeed. Outside the station the sergeant said, 'Oh, by the way, can you make a U-turn?' The farmer sat quietly for a moment and then, with a sly, sidelong glance at the copper said, 'Nah, but I can sure make their eyes water!'

An old loony went to the post office to send a telegram. The postmaster read out the telegram as he counted up the words. It was 'Foozle, foozle, foozle, foozle, foozle, foozle'.

'Do you really want to send this?' he asked the loony. 'It doesn't make sense.'

'Yes,' said the loony, 'that's what I want to send.'

'Oh well,' answered the postmaster, entering into the spirit of the thing, 'but for the same money you could put in three more foozles.'

'No,' said the loony firmly, 'that would be silly!'

A drunk climbed on board the number 48 tram and spoke to the bloke sitting opposite. 'Hey, what's your name then?'

'Paul,' said the man, intensely embarrassed by becoming the focus of attention of the other passengers.

The drunk was silent for a few moments, then asked, 'Say, did those Thessalonians ever write back to you?'

Reality is for people who can't handle computers.

Too many cooks make the phone book heavy.

Two missionaries in Papua New Guinea were captured by a group of tribesmen wearing lots of bird of paradise feathers and those interesting little cone things on their dicks.

They were tied to a tree and were approached by the chief who spoke pretty good English. 'You have two choices. You can either choose death or oogabooga.'

The first missionary decided that death didn't sound too good so he'd take a punt on oogabooga.

On hearing this, the tribesmen became very excited and yelled 'oogabooga, oogabooga' a lot. Then they took the cone devices off their dicks and pack-raped the missionary.

The chief now approached the second missionary. 'I am a good Christian and, rather than suffering the shame of your heathen practice, I shall practice martyrdom. Give me death.'

'Fine,' said the chief, 'death by oogabooga!'

A salesman from Harvey World Travel had just won a sales competition. The prize was a trip for two to Bali. But he was sick and tired of travel and his idea of a holiday was to stay at home. He was sitting at his desk feeling sorry for himself when he saw an old man and an old woman looking through the window of the shop. Their noses were pressed against the glass and their eyes were focused on photographs of . . . Bali.

He made up his mind in an instant. Rushing outside, he dragged them into his office and said, 'I know that on your pension you couldn't hope to afford a holiday, let alone one in Bali. Well, you're going to have one. And I won't take no for an answer.'

He asked his secretary to present them with the two flight tickets and details of the hotel bookings in Denpasar. They left the shop astonished.

Some months later he saw the little old lady in the street. 'And how did you like Bali?' he asked her.

'Oh, everything was wonderful. The flight was marvellous and the room was lovely and the beach was beautiful. I don't know how to thank you. But one thing has puzzled me. Who was that old bloke I had to share the room with?'

A Qantas jet was about to leave Mascot for Singapore, en route to London. The passengers were all on board, then the pilot appeared. He was wearing a pair of very dark glasses and carrying a white stick. To general astonishment, he tapped his way up the aisle to the flight deck.

'Christ,' a woman whispered to her husband, 'the pilot's blind.'

'Crap,' he said.

'But he is blind. The dark glasses! The white stick! You must go and speak to him, see what's going on.'

So the husband went to the flight deck and spoke to the pilot. 'Excuse me, but are you really blind?'

'Yes, I am.'

'But how can you possibly fly the plane if you're blind?'

'It's easy. Look at the instrument panel. You'll see that everything's in braille – the controls, the dials, the levers.'

'But, for Christ's sake, you can't see! How do you know when you pull back on the joystick?'

'That's easy. Do you see the Hilton Hotel at the end of the runway?'

'Of course.'

'Well,' said the pilot, 'I start the engines, roar down the runway and when I hear everyone screaming "Shit!" *then* I pull back on the joystick.'

The *Sydney Morning Herald's* travel writer was touring America and he decided to visit one of the newly opened casinos on the Indian reservation. It was a Mohawk casino, and sitting in the lobby was a marvellous old bloke with a feathered headdress. 'That's Big Chief Forget-Me-Not,' said the manager. 'Because this is Indian territory, he's allowed free use of the hotel for the rest of his life.'

'Why is he known as Big Chief Forget-Me-Not?' asked the writer.

'Because of his memory. Although he's almost a hundred he can remember every detail of his life.'

The travel writer decided to test the chief's memory. 'Okay, what did you have for breakfast on your 18th birthday?'

'Eggs,' came the reply.

The travel writer checked out the next day and happened to return to the hotel after another four weeks. There, in the foyer, was the old Indian chief. 'How?' said the Australian.

'Scrambled,' said the chief.

Index

PENGUIN – THE BEST AUSTRALIAN READING

The Penguin Book of Australian Jokes   collected by Phillip Adams and Patrice Newell

Jokes are a bit like electro-convulsive therapy. Laughter does to the brain what a good sneeze does to the nasal passages. If you read this entire volume in one sitting, it will be the equivalent of ten years in psychoanalysis. You will encounter bigotry, sexism, ageism, blondeism and homophobia.

So enter these pages at your peril, knowing that every time you split your sides you're having a laugh at someone else's expense . . .

The Penguin Book of Jokes from Cyberspace   collected by Phillip Adams and Patrice Newell

When the printing press was invented, it promised literature. People read comics.

When cinema was invented, it promised culture for the masses. We got *Rambo*.

When TV was invented, it promised education. We got *Melrose Place*.

The Internet promised unprecedented access to information across the globe and an end to national barriers. What we got was 30 million netheads – nerds, rock stars and your average punters – swapping politically incorrect jokes. Hundreds of which, we're unashamed to say, are contained within these pages.

The Penguin Book of Australian Slang   Lenie 'Midge' Johansen

The Penguin Book of Australian Slang scales the heights – and depths – of the Australian language. For twenty years Lenie Johansen has been tuning into and recording what Australians really say on the streets, in the pubs and to their family and mates. In this remarkable collection of classic and current colloquialisms she displays for readers all the inventiveness with words and the love of colourful expressions that have made Oz English unique.

Frequently rude, always direct and never, ever, politically correct, this is the Australian language as it has never been collected before.

PENGUIN – THE BEST AUSTRALIAN READING

The Penguin Book of 1000 Quiz Questions   Ron Goldman

The Penguin Book of 1000 Quiz Questions has something for everyone. Divided into nine categories, the easy-to-follow format can be used in a variety of ways. It provides all of us with the chance to test our own skills and improve our general knowledge, to become a specialist in a particular subject or just impress friends and family. These new questions can give that board game in the cupboard a new lease of life and are ideal for the Quizmaster on trivia fundraising nights. Ron Goldman gives some great tips on how to run such an occasion successfully.

Compiled and authenticated by a question writer and adjudicator of TV's *Sale of the Century, Ford Superquiz* and *Crossfire, The Penguin Book of 1000 Quiz Questions* is guaranteed to challenge, entertain and enlighten.